BARBADOS & ST. LUCIA

2nd Edition

Fodor's Travel Publications   New York, Toronto, London, Sydney, Auckland
www.fodors.com

Be a Fodor's Correspondent

Your opinion matters. It matters to us. It matters to your fellow Fodor's travelers, too. And we'd like to hear it. In fact, we *need* to hear it. When you share your experiences and opinions, you become an active member of the Fodor's community. Here's how you can help improve Fodor's for all of us.

Tell us when we're right. We rely on local writers to give you an insider's perspective. But our writers and staff editors also depend on you. Your positive feedback is a vote to renew our recommendations for the next edition.

Tell us when we're wrong. We update most of our guides every year. But things change. If any of our descriptions are inaccurate or inadequate, we'll incorporate your changes in the next edition and will correct factual errors at fodors.com *immediately*.

Tell us what to include. You probably have had fantastic travel experiences that aren't yet in Fodor's. Why not share them with a community of like-minded travelers? Share your discoveries and experiences with everyone directly at fodors.com. Your input may lead us to add a new listing or a higher recommendation.

Give us your opinion instantly at our feedback center at www.fodors.com/feedback. You may also e-mail editors@fodors.com with the subject line "Barbados & St. Lucia Editor." Or send your nominations, comments, and complaints by mail to Barbados & St. Lucia Editor, Fodor's, 1745 Broadway, New York, NY 10019.

Happy Traveling!

Tim Jarrell, Publisher

FODOR'S IN FOCUS BARBADOS & ST. LUCIA

Editor: Douglas Stallings, *series editor*

Editorial Contributor: Jane E. Zarem

Production Editor: Jennifer DePrima
Maps & Illustrations: David Lindroth and Mark Stroud *cartographers*; Bob Blake and Rebecca Baer, *map editors*; William Wu, *information graphics*
Design: Fabrizio La Rocca, *creative director*; Guido Caroti, *art director*, Nora Rosansky, *designer*; Melanie Marin, *senior picture editor*
Cover Photo: (The Pitons, St. Lucia) Robert Harding Images/Masterfile
Production Manager: Amanda Bullock

SPECIAL SALES

This book is available for special discounts for bulk purchases for sales promotions or premiums. Special editions, including personalized covers, excerpts of existing books, and corporate imprints, can be created in large quantities for special needs. For more information, write to Special Markets/Premium Sales, 1745 Broadway, MD 6-2, New York, NY 10019, or e-mail specialmarkets@randomhouse.com.

AN IMPORTANT TIP & AN INVITATION

Although all prices, opening times, and other details in this book are based on information supplied to us at press time, changes occur all the time in the travel world, and Fodor's cannot accept responsibility for facts that become outdated or for inadvertent errors or omissions. **So always confirm information when it matters,** especially if you're making a detour to visit a specific place. Your experiences—positive and negative—matter to us. If we have missed or misstated something, **please write to us.** We follow up on all suggestions. Contact the Barbados & St. Lucia editor at editors@fodors.com or c/o Fodor's at 1745 Broadway, New York, NY 10019.

PRINTED IN CHINA
10 9 8 7 6 5 4 3 2 1

CONTENTS

Be a Fodor's Correspondent.....3

About This Book 6

**1 EXPERIENCE BARBADOS
AND ST. LUCIA. 9**

What's Where 10

Barbados Planner 12

St. Lucia Planner. 14

Top Experiences 16

When to Go. 20

Great Itineraries 21

Weddings and Honeymoons. . . .22

2 BARBADOS 25

Exploring Barbados. 28

Where to Eat. 49

Where to Stay 63

Beaches. 100

Sports and Activities. 104

Nightlife. 113

Shopping 116

3 ST. LUCIA 121

Exploring St. Lucia. 124

Where to Eat. 149

Where to Stay 159

Beaches. 189

Sports and Activities. 193

Nightlife and the Arts. 201

Shopping 203

**TRAVEL SMART BARBADOS
AND ST. LUCIA. 209**

INDEX 227

ABOUT OUR WRITER 236

MAPS

Barbados. 28

Bridgetown 32

Southern Barbados. 35

Central Barbados 41

Northern Barbados. 47

St. Lawrence Gap 52

Holetown and Vicinity. 58

St. Lucia. 125

Vigie to Point du Cap 130

Castries 132

Soufriere and the South 141

Rodney Bay 151

ABOUT THIS BOOK

Our Ratings

We wouldn't recommend a place that wasn't worth your time, but sometimes a place is so experiential that superlatives don't do it justice: you just have to be there to know. These sights, properties, and experiences get our highest rating, **Fodor's Choice**, indicated by orange stars throughout this book. Black stars highlight sights and properties we deem **Highly Recommended**, places that our writers, editors, and readers praise again and again for consistency and excellence.

Credit Cards

Want to pay with plastic? **AE, D, DC, MC, V** after restaurant and hotel listings indicate whether American Express, Discover, Diners Club, MasterCard, and Visa are accepted.

Restaurants

Unless we state otherwise, restaurants are open for lunch and dinner daily. We mention dress only when there's a specific requirement and reservations only when they're essential or not accepted—it's always best to book ahead.

Hotels

Unless we tell you otherwise, you can assume that the hotels have private bath, phone, TV, and air-conditioning. We always list facilities but not whether you'll be charged an extra fee to use them, so when pricing accommodations, find out what's included.

Many Listings
★	Fodor's Choice
★	Highly recommended
⊠	Physical address
✛	Directions
⌂	Mailing address
☎	Telephone
📠	Fax
⊕	On the Web
✉	E-mail
☞	Admission fee
☉	Open/closed times
Ⓜ	Metro stations
▭	Credit cards

Hotels & Restaurants
🏨	Hotel
🛏	Number of rooms
⚖	Facilities
⑩	Meal plans
✕	Restaurant
☖	Reservations
⤡	Smoking
🆈	BYOB
✕🏨	Hotel with restaurant that warrants a visit

Outdoors
🏌	Golf
⛺	Camping

Other
☾	Family-friendly
⇨	See also
⊠	Branch address
☞	Take note

Experience
Barbados
and St. Lucia

WHAT'S WHERE

Caribbean

1 **Barbados**. Broad vistas, sweeping seascapes, craggy cliffs, and acre upon acre of sugarcane make up the island's varied landscape. A long, successful history of tourism has been forged from the warm, Bajan hospitality, welcoming hotels and resorts, sophisticated dining, lively nightspots, and, of course, magnificent sunny beaches.

2 **St. Lucia**. One of the most green and beautiful islands in the Caribbean is, arguably, the most romantic. The scenic south and central regions are mountainous and lush, with dense rain forest, endless banana plantations, and fascinating historic sites. Along the west coast, some of the region's most picturesque and interesting resorts are interspersed with dozens of delightful inns, appealing to families as well as lovers and adventurers.

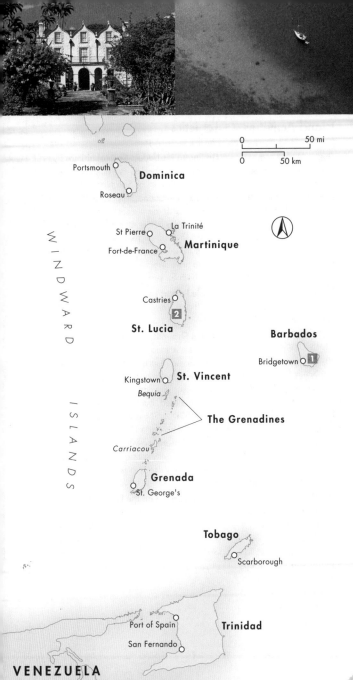

50 mi

50 km

Portsmouth

Dominica

Roseau

W I N D W A R D

St Pierre

La Trinité

Fort-de-France

Martinique

Castries

2

St. Lucia

Barbados

Bridgetown

1

Kingstown

St. Vincent

Bequia

The Grenadines

I S L A N D S

Carriacou

Grenada

St. George's

Tobago

Scarborough

Trinidad

Port of Spain

San Fernando

VENEZUELA

BARBADOS PLANNER

Island Activities	Logistics
There's always something to do in Barbados, and that's the appeal to most visitors. The soft, white-sand **beaches** await your arrival whether you choose to stay in the millionaire's row of resorts on the west coast or the more affordable south coast. Exceptional **golf** courses lure a lot of players to the island, but the private courses—at Royal Westmoreland and Sandy Lane—aren't for anyone with a light wallet. The island's **restaurant scene** is impressive; you can choose from street-party barbecue to international cuisine that rivals the finest dining on the planet. Getting out on the water is the favored activity, whether that's on a **snorkeling** day sail, in a **mini-sub**, on a **deep-sea fishing** boat, or on a **surfboard** at Bathsheba Soup Bowl.	**Getting to Barbados:** Several airlines fly nonstop to Barbados, or you may have to connect in Miami or San Juan. Grantley Adams International Airport (BGI) is in Christ Church Parish on the south coast about 15 minutes from hotels situated along the south coast, 45 minutes from the west coast, and about 30 minutes from Bridgetown. There is also now direct ferry service to Barbados from both St. Lucia and St. Vincent. **Hassle Factor:** Low because of many nonstop flights from airports around the United States. **On the Ground:** Ground transportation is available immediately outside the customs area. Some resorts arrange ground transfers if you make arrangements in advance. Otherwise, you can get a taxi. Airport taxis aren't metered, but fares are regulated (about $30 to Speightstown, $20–$22 to west-coast hotels, $10–$13 to south-coast hotels). Be sure, however, to establish the fare before getting into the cab and confirm whether the price quoted is in U.S. or Barbadian dollars. **Getting Around on the Island:** If you are staying in an isolated area, you may want or need to rent a car, but bus service is good, especially around the St. Lawrence Gap. Taxis may suffice for those travelers staying in busy resort areas.

Where to Stay

Whether you stay on the tony west coast or on the action-packed south coast, you'll have access to great beaches, but the east coast doesn't have easy access to good swimming beaches. Prices in Barbados can be twice as high in-season as during the quieter months. Most hotels include no meals in their rates, but some include breakfast and many offer a meal plan. Some require you to purchase the meal plan in the high season; a few offer all-inclusive packages.

Resorts: Great resorts run the gamut—from unpretentious to knock-your-socks-off—of size, intimacy, amenities, and price. Many are well suited to families.

Villas and Condos: Families and long-term visitors may choose from a variety of condos (from busy time-share resorts to more sedate holiday complexes). Villas and villa complexes range from luxurious to simple.

Small Inns: A few small, cozy inns may be found in the east and southeast regions.

Hotel and Restaurant Costs

Restaurant prices are for a main course at dinner, and include any taxes or service charges. Hotel prices are per night for a double room in high season, excluding taxes, service charges, and meal plans.

Tips for Travelers

The minimum legal drinking age in Barbados is 16.

Electricity in Barbados is 110 volts, just like in the United States. No converters or transformers are needed for U.S. appliances.

A 10% service charge is sometimes added to restaurant bills; otherwise, tip 10%–15%. Most hotels add some kind of service charge.

The Barbados dollars is pegged to the U.S. dollar at a rate of approximately Bds$1.98 to US$1. U.S. currency is accepted almost everywhere on the island, so many travelers never change their money into local currency. ATMs are widely available but dispense local currency only.

What It Costs in U.S. Dollars

	¢	$	$$	$$$	$$$$
Restaurants	under $8	$8–$12	$12–$20	$20–$30	over $30
Hotels*	under $80	$80–$150	$150–$250	$250–$350	over $350
Hotels**	under $125	$125–$250	$250–$350	$350–$450	over $450

* Indicates hotels on the European Plan (EP—with no meals), Continental Plan (CP—with a Continental breakfast), or Breakfast Plan (BP—with full breakfast).
** Indicates hotels on the Modified American Plan (MAP—with breakfast and dinner), Full American Plan (FAP—including all meals but no drinks), or All-Inclusive (AI—with all meals, drinks, and most activities).

ST. LUCIA PLANNER

Island Activities	Logistics
The island's **beaches** are decent, but you won't find many long stretches of fine white sand since St. Lucia is a volcanic island; Reduit Beach, in the north, is considered the island's best.	**Getting to St. Lucia:** St. Lucia's primary gateway is Hewanorra International Airport (UVF) in Vieux Fort, on the island's southern tip; all large planes land at Hewanorra, which is somewhat more convenient to resorts in the Soufrière area. Some airlines fly into George F. L. Charles Airport (SLU) in Castries, which is also referred to as Vigie Airport and is more convenient to resorts in the north; it may be worth the hassle to change to a smaller plane in San Juan if you are staying in the Rodney Bay or Marigot Bay areas. The drive between Hewanorra and resorts in the north takes 90 minutes; the trip between Hewanorra and Soufrière takes about 30 minutes.

St. Lucia has excellent **diving** along its southwest coast near Soufrière. One upscale resort, Anse Chastanet, specializes in diving from its base near the Pitons.

Deep-sea **fishing** is also good. A **day sail** is one of the best ways to see a good bit of the island and a good way to travel from Castries to Soufrière, or vice versa.

However, St. Lucia's crown jewel is its well-preserved **rain forest**, which can best be explored on a guided hike.

Climbing one of the twin **Pitons** is a rewarding—if arduous—experience and can be done without any special mountain- or rock-climbing experience (though that never hurts). You must hire a guide, however.

Hassle Factor: Medium to high, because of the long drive from Hewanorra International Airport.

On the Ground: Taxis are available at both airports if transfers are not included in your travel package, but it's an expensive ride to the north from Hewanorra (at least $75); the transfer time is about 90 minutes. For resorts in the Soufrière area, the transfer time from Hewanorra is about 60 minutes and costs about $55. A helicopter is available to the Rodney Bay area resorts from Hewanorra; it's a costly ($145 per person) but convenient option, cutting the transfer time to about 10 minutes.

Getting Around: A car is more of a necessity if you are staying at a small inn or hotel away from the beach. If you're staying at an all-inclusive beach resort, taxis are a better bet.

Where to Stay

St. Lucia's resorts and small inns are nearly all tucked into lush, secluded coves, unspoiled beaches, or forested hillsides in three locations along the calm Caribbean (western) coast. The most developed area is in and around Rodney Bay and around Marigot Bay. A few resorts are in the south.

Big Beach Resorts: Most people choose to stay in one of St. Lucia's many beach resorts, the majority of which are upscale and fairly pricey. Several are all-inclusive, including three Sandals resorts, two Almond resorts, and two Sunswept resorts (The Body Holiday at LeSPORT and Rendezvous).

Small Inns: If you want something more intimate and perhaps less expensive, a locally owned inn or small hotel is a good option, but it may not be directly on the beach.

Villas: Luxury villa communities and independent private villas are a good alternative for families. Many of these are in the north in or near Cap Estate.

Hotel and Restaurant Costs

Restaurant prices are for a main course at dinner and do not include 8% tax or the customary 10% service charge. Hotel prices are per night for a double room in high season, excluding 8% tax and meal plans (except at all-inclusives).

Tips for Travelers

The minimum legal drinking age in St. Lucia is 18.

Electricity in St. Lucia is 220 volts, 50 cycles, as in the United Kingdom. U.S. appliances will require a plug adaptor (square, three-pin) and may require a transformer.

A 10% service charge is usually added to restaurant bills; otherwise, tip 10%–15%.

The Eastern Caribbean dollar is pegged to the U.S. dollar at a rate of approximately EC$2.67 to US$1. U.S. currency is accepted almost everywhere on the island, but it's helpful to have local currency to shop in smaller markets and to use on local buses.

What It Costs in U.S. Dollars

	¢	$	$$	$$$	$$$$
Restaurants	under $8	$8–$12	$12–$20	$20–$30	over $30
Hotels*	under $80	$80–$150	$150–$250	$250–$350	over $350
Hotels**	under $125	$125–$250	$250–$350	$350–$450	over $450

* Indicates hotels on the European Plan (EP—with no meals), Continental Plan (CP—with a Continental breakfast), or Breakfast Plan (BP—with full breakfast). ** Indicates hotels on the Modified American Plan (MAP—with breakfast and dinner), Full American Plan (FAP—including all meals but no drinks), or All-Inclusive (AI—with all meals, drinks, and most activities).

TOP
EXPERIENCES

Dine in Period Style at Sunbury Plantation House and Museum, Barbados

(A) Period furnishings and a complete, loving restoration after a major fire in 1995 have created a picture-postcard vision of plantation life in the 18th and 19th centuries. A very special, albeit expensive ($100 per person) five-course dinner served in the house's period dining room at a long mahogany table is held two nights a week during the high season.

Tour Diamond Botanical Gardens, St. Lucia

(B) This private botanical garden is still owned and operated by a descendant of the original Devaux brothers, who were deeded the land for their vast estate by King Louis XIV in 1713. It's claimed that Empress Joséphine bathed in the sulfurous waters when she was a girl (and long before she met M. Bonaparte); for an extra fee, you can also take a soak. Hire one of the private guides outside the gates to get the full story, and if you are looking for a souvenir, check out the pieces offered by the woodcarver who is usually stationed in the parking lot.

Spelunk in Style through Harrison's Cave, Barbados

(C) Major renovations have greatly improved the visitor experience at this extensive and interesting cave system that winds its way through the limestone underneath Barbados. There's even a 40-foot waterfall. This is one of the island's most popular sights, so try to plan around the cruise-ship crowds.

Taste Some Barbados Rum at the Source

(D) Several Barbados rum distilleries offer tours, but Mount Gay Rum (distilled since 1703) is the world's oldest surviving rum company. A tour of the historic rum distillery (a larger newer, modern plant is in the north of the island) includes a tasting, of course, and the opportunity to take home a bottle or two.

Take a Picture of the Amazing Pitons, St. Lucia

(E) These twin peaks—which have become a symbol of St. Lucia—rise precipitously from the cobalt-blue Caribbean Sea just south of Soufrière. You can either stay in the Jalousie Plantation resort that stretches between them, climb them (with a certified guide), or just stop to take in the views to get your shot. But this UNESCO World Heritage Site is a don't-miss attraction on the island.

Sail into Marigot Bay, St. Lucia

The island's most beautiful harbor—a secluded bay within a bay—has been a movie location, a popular anchorage for yachts, and now a destination for landlubbers, too. The bay is lined with lovely resorts and villas and even has a small sandy beach. It offers a quiet getaway for the day or a week.

Take a Hike in the Barbados Flower Forest, Barbados

More than 100 species of tropical flora line the pathways of this 50-acre reserve in central Barbados. From the paths, you can get a view of Mt. Hillaby (1,100 feet), the highest point on Barbados.

TOP EXPERIENCES

It's a low-key way to relax and recharge when you get tired of the beach.

Play a Round at Sandy Lane, Barbados

(F) On an island with several spectacular courses, this resort has three of the best. Golfers who are not guests at Sandy Lane can play on the Old Nine or the 18-hole Country Club Course. (The famous Green Monkey Course is reserved for resort guests or club members only.) Fees are high, but so is the quality of play.

Buy a Piece of Barbados

(G) If you're looking for a genuine local souvenir to take home, consider a piece of the blue or green pottery from Earthworks Pottery. This family-owned business has been producing beautiful hand-made ceramics that are both decorative and usable since 1983.

Party with the Locals at the Oistins Fish Fry, Barbados

(H) One of the Caribbean's best street parties takes place in this south-coast fishing village every Friday night. The food is good and inexpensive (about $10 gets you a huge plate of grilled chicken or fish). There's plenty to drink as well as music to dance to.

Dine at Dasheene, St. Lucia

(I) If you have the opportunity to dine at the Ladera Resort's wonderful Dasheene restaurant, take advantage of it. Not only is the food good, but the view—looking straight out between the fabulous Pitons—is magical. It's a casual and quiet lunch spot that gets more festive at night and is especially nice at sunset.

Take It Out to Sea, St. Lucia

(J) The best way to get your first glimpse of the Pitons is on a sailing excursion or boat trip along the island's amazingly beautiful west coast. The sea route is also the best way to get from Rodney Bay or Vigie Cove down to Soufriére. Most of the daylong sailing excursions include some time on land to see the sights in the southern part of the island.

Dance in the Street at the Gros Islet Jump-Up, St. Lucia

It seems that Fridays bring people out to the streets all over the Caribbean. This popular street party near Rodney Bay brings together both islanders and tourists to enjoy cheap barbecue, dance to the latest reggaeton, or just relax and "lime." Don't be surprised if you see a spontaneous dance-off by local youth.

Dive in at Anse Chastanet, St. Lucia

Anse Chastanet, which is just around the bend from the Pitons and has a coral-lined wall right off shore that drops from 20 to more than 140 feet, is the island's best beach-entry dive site. But there are many more opportunities for great diving, either around the Pitons or elsewhere on the west shore of the island.

WHEN TO GO

The Caribbean high season is traditionally from December 15 through April 15—when northern weather is at its worst. During this season you're guaranteed that all hotels and restaurants will be open and busy. It's also the most fashionable, the most expensive, and the most popular time to visit. British tourists in particular come to both Barbados and St. Lucia for two or three weeks during the high season. If you wait until mid-May or June, prices may be 20%–50% less, and this is particularly true of Barbados; however, some hotels close, particularly later in summer and early fall. The period from mid-August through late November is typically the least busy time in both Barbados and St. Lucia.

Climate

The Caribbean climate is fairly constant. Summer, however, can bring somewhat higher temperatures and more humidity because the trade winds slow. The Atlantic hurricane season begins on June 1 and stretches all the way through November 30. While heavy rains can happen anytime throughout the year, it's during this six-month period when tropical fronts are most likely. Major hurricanes are a relatively rare occurrence in Barbados because the island is 100 mi farther east than the rest of the Lesser Antilles chain (giving hurricanes less chance to gain in strength from the warm Caribbean waters).

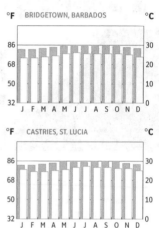

GREAT ITINERARIES

Barbados from Bottom to Top. You can't come to Barbados and not visit Harrison's Cave. The underground tram will thrill the whole family. Afterward, visit Flower Forest and Orchid World, two beautiful gardens that also have snack bars where lunch is available. Stop at Gun Hill Signal Station on the way home.

A Day in Barbados's Wild Wild East. From Speightstown, you'll head east to Farley Hill and the Barbados Wildlife Reserve before continuing on to St. Nicholas Abbey (a lovely greathouse that's worth a stop). Cherry Tree Hill, a panoramic view of the whole Atlantic coast, is a definite photo op. The ride along the coastal road is particularly scenic. Stop for a Bajan buffet lunch at one of the cliff-side inns before heading back through the center of the island. From south-coast hotels, do the trip in reverse.

A Day in St. Lucia's South. Although most of the island's resorts are in the north, some of the most interesting sights are in the south. Take a sailing trip down the west coast and admire the views of the Pitons and you come into Soufriére Harbor. Take the tour and have lunch at Fond Doux Estate, tour Diamond Botanical Garden, and take a quick side trip to see sulfurous La Soufrière Drive-In Volcano.

A Day in St. Lucia's Rain Forest. One of the island's best natural attractions is a vast forest. There are two ways to enjoy it—from above or below. Kids may prefer a thrilling zip-line trip through the forest canopy, while adults may prefer the more sedate Aerial Tram that takes a slow, two-hour tour through the forest; both of these attractions are in the Castries Waterworks Rain Forest east of Rodney Bay. Those looking for a more down-to-earth experience may want to take a guided hike in the Edmund Forest Reserve in the central part of the island, but this is a more strenuous trip that requires you to hire a guide from the Forest & Lands Department.

A Day of Shopping and Sightseeing in Castries, St. Lucia. St. Lucia's capital may be traffic-clogged, but it has one of the most extensive souvenir markets you'll find. There are rows upon rows of vendors just next to the island's regular market, which sells spices, vanilla, and locally bottled sauces at bargain prices. There's also a large duty-free mall at the cruise pier. Little of historic Castries remains, but if you get tired of shopping, the best remaining buildings line Derek Walcott Square.

WEDDINGS AND HONEYMOONS

There's no question that Barbados and St. Lucia (especially the latter) rank among the Caribbean's foremost honeymoon destinations. The picturesque beaches, turquoise water, swaying palm trees, balmy tropical breezes, and perpetual summer sunshine put people in the mood for love. St. Lucia may be the most popular wedding and honeymoon destination in the Caribbean, but at resorts on both islands you'll find wedding planners who can help you put together your perfect special day.

The Big Day

Choosing the Perfect Place. When choosing a location, remember that you really have two choices to make: the ceremony location and where to have the reception, if you're having one. For the former, there are beaches, bluffs overlooking beaches, gardens, private residences, resort lawns, and, of course, places of worship. As for the reception, there are these same choices, as well as restaurants. If you decide to go outdoors, remember the seasons—yes, the Caribbean has seasons. If you're planning a wedding outdoors, be sure you have a backup plan in case it rains. Also, if you're planning an outdoor wedding at sunset—which is very popular—be sure you match the time of your ceremony to the time the sun sets at that time of year

Finding a Wedding Planner. If you're planning to invite more than a minister and your loved one to your wedding ceremony, seriously consider an on-island wedding planner who can help select a location, help design the floral scheme and recommend a florist as well as a photographer, help plan the menu, and suggest any local traditions to incorporate into your ceremony. Alternatively, most resorts have their own wedding planners on-site, so you will have someone right at the resort to coordinate everything. The Sandals resorts on St. Lucia offer free weddings.

Legal Requirements. There are minimal residency requirements on both Barbados and St. Lucia, and no blood tests or shots are required in either island. In Barbados, you must appear in person to obtain a wedding license, but the formalities can often be completed in less than half an hour at the Ministry of Home Affairs in Bridgetown; the costs are less than $100. In St. Lucia, you can either get married after being on the island for three days (for $125), or you can obtain a "special" license anytime after arrival—even the same day you land—for $200. There is about $40 in additional fees on top of

the license cost. On both islands, you must provide valid passports for identification and an original spousal death certificate or divorce decree if you were previously married. On Barbados, an official marriage officer (or magistrate or minister) must perform the actual ceremony.

Wedding Attire. In the Caribbean, basically anything goes, from long, formal dresses with trains to white bikinis. Floral sundresses are fine, too. Men can wear tuxedos or a simple pair of solid-color slacks with a nice white linen shirt. If you want formal dress and tuxedo, it's usually better to bring your formal attire with you.

Photographs. Deciding whether to use the photographer supplied by your resort or an independent photographer is an important choice. Resorts that host a lot of weddings usually have their own photographers, but you can also find independent, professional island-based photographers, and an independent wedding planner will know the best in the area. Look at the portfolio (many photographers now have Web sites), and decide whether this person can give you the kind of memories you are looking for. If you're satisfied with the photographer that your resort uses, then make sure you see proofs and order prints before you leave the island.

The Honeymoon

Do you want champagne and strawberries delivered to your room each morning? A maze of a swimming pool in which to float? A five-star restaurant in which to dine? Then a resort is the way to go, and both Barbados and St. Lucia have options in different price ranges (though Barbados resorts are more luxurious and expensive, especially during high season). Whether you want a luxurious experience or a more modest one, you'll certainly find someplace romantic to which you can escape. You can usually stay on at the resort where your wedding was held. On the other hand, maybe you want your own private home in which to romp naked—or maybe you want your own kitchen in which to whip up a gourmet meal for your loved one. In that case, a private vacation-rental home or condo is the answer.

Barbados

WORD OF MOUTH

"We discovered Barbados a few years ago, have been there twice, and dream about our next trip as we enjoy the island so much."

—Knowing

By Jane E. Zarem

WITHOUT QUESTION, BARBADOS IS THE most "British" island in the Caribbean. In contrast to the turbulent colonial past experienced by neighboring islands, which included repeated conflicts between France and Britain over dominance and control, British rule in Barbados carried on uninterrupted for 340 years—from the first established British settlement in 1627 until independence was granted in 1966. That's not to say, of course, that there weren't significant struggles in Barbados, as elsewhere in the Caribbean, between the British landowners and their African-born slaves and other indentured servants.

With that unfortunate period of slavery relegated to the history books, the British influence on Barbados can still be felt today in local manners, attitudes, customs, and politics—tempered by the characteristically warm nature of the Bajan people. ("Bajan," pronounced *bay*-jun, derives phonetically from the British pronunciation of "Barbadian.") In keeping with British traditions, many Bajans worship at the Anglican church; afternoon tea is a ritual; cricket is the national pastime (a passion, most admit); dressing for dinner is a firmly entrenched tradition; and patrons at some bars are as likely to order a Pimm's Cup or a shandy as a rum and Coke. And yet, Barbados is hardly stuffy—this is still the Caribbean, after all.

The long-standing British involvement is only one of the unique attributes that distinguishes Barbados from its island neighbors. Geographically, Barbados is a break in the Lesser Antilles archipelago, the chain of islands that stretches in a graceful arc from the Virgin Islands to Trinidad. Isolated in the Atlantic Ocean, Barbados is 100 mi (160 km) due east of St. Lucia, its nearest neighbor. And geologically, while most of the Lesser Antilles are the peaks of a volcanic mountain range, Barbados is the top of a single, relatively flat protuberance of coral and limestone—the source of building blocks for many a plantation manor. (Many of those historic greathouses, in fact, have been carefully restored. Some are open to visitors.)

Bridgetown, both the capital city and the commercial center, is on the southwest coast of pear-shape Barbados. Most of the 280,000 Bajans live and work in and around Bridgetown, elsewhere in St. Michael Parish, or along the idyllic west coast or busy south coast. Others reside in tiny villages that dot the interior landscape. Broad sandy beaches, craggy cliffs, and picturesque coves make up the

BARBADOS TOP REASONS TO GO

■ Great resorts run the gamut—from unpretentious to knock-your-socks-off—in terms of size, intimacy, amenities, and price. Choose one on the lively south coast or on the ritzy west coast.

■ Golfers can play on some of the best championship courses in the Caribbean—including a public course on the south coast with very reasonable green fees.

■ Great food includes everything from street-party barbecue to international cuisine that rivals the finest dining found anywhere in the world.

■ With a wide assortment of land and water sports, sightseeing options, historic sites, cultural festivities, and nightlife, there's always plenty to do and see in Barbados.

■ Bajans are friendly, welcoming, helpful, and hospitable. You'll like them; they'll like you.

coastline, while the interior features forested hills and gullies and acre upon acre of sugarcane.

Tourist facilities are concentrated on the west coast in the St. James and St. Peter parishes (appropriately dubbed the Platinum Coast) and on the south coast in Christ Church Parish. Traveling along the west coast to historic Holetown, the site of the first British settlement, and continuing to the northern city of Speightstown, you can find posh beachfront resorts, luxurious private villas, and fine restaurants enveloped by lush gardens and tropical foliage. The trendier, more commercial south coast offers more competitively priced hotels and beach resorts, and its St. Lawrence Gap area is jam-packed with shops, restaurants, and nightlife. The relatively wide-open spaces along the southeast coast are proving ripe for development, and some wonderful inns and hotels already take advantage of the intoxicatingly beautiful ocean vistas. For their own holidays, though, Bajans escape to the rugged east coast, where the Atlantic surf pounds the dramatic shoreline with unrelenting force.

All in all, Barbados is a sophisticated tropical island with rich history, lodgings to suit every taste and pocketbook, and plenty to pique your interest both day and night—whether you're British or not!

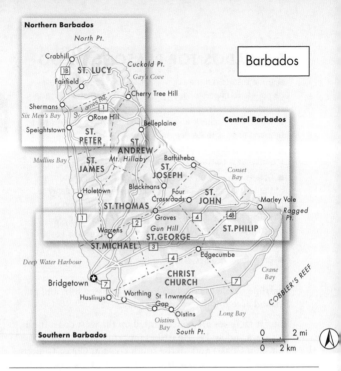

Barbados

EXPLORING BARBADOS

The terrain changes dramatically from any one of the island's 11 parishes to the next, and so does the pace. Bridgetown, the capital, is a rather sophisticated city. West-coast resorts and private estates ooze luxury, whereas the small villages and vast sugar plantations found throughout central Barbados reflect the island's rich history. The relentless Atlantic surf shaped the cliffs of the dramatic east coast, and the northeast is called Scotland because of its hilly landscape. Along the lively south coast, the daytime hustle and bustle produce a palpable energy that continues well into the night at countless restaurants, dance clubs, and nightspots.

ABOUT THE HOTELS

Prices in Barbados can be twice as high in peak season (December 15–April 15) as during the quieter months. Most hotels do not include meals in their rates, but some will offer breakfast or a meal plan. Others require you to purchase a meal plan during high season, and a few offer all-inclusive packages.

Families and long-term visitors can choose from a wide variety of villas and condos—everything from an individual luxury villa overlooking the sea or nestled in the hillside to busy villa complexes with resort-style amenities. A few small, cozy inns are found along the east, southeast, and northwest coasts. They can be ultraluxurious, fairly simple, or something in between.

Assume that all hotels operate on the European Plan (**EP**—with no meals) unless we specify that they use the Continental Plan (**CP**—with a Continental breakfast), Breakfast Plan (**BP**—with full breakfast), or the Modified American Plan (**MAP**—with breakfast and dinner). Other hotels may offer the Full American Plan (**FAP**—including all meals but no drinks) or may be All-Inclusive (**AI**—with all meals, drinks, and most activities.)

ABOUT THE RESTAURANTS

First-class restaurants and hotel dining rooms serve sophisticated cuisine—often prepared by chefs with international experience—which can rival that served in the world's best restaurants. Most menus include seafood, prepared every way imaginable. Expect dorado (also known as mahimahi or dolphin—the fish, not the mammal), kingfish, marlin, snapper, and flying fish, which is so popular that it has officially become a national symbol. Shellfish also abounds, as do steak, pork, and local black-belly lamb.

Local specialty dishes include *buljol* (a cold salad of pickled codfish, tomatoes, onions, sweet peppers, and celery) and *conkies* (cornmeal, coconut, pumpkin, raisins, sweet potatoes, and spices, wrapped in a banana leaf and steamed). *Cou-cou,* often served with steamed flying fish, is a mixture of cornmeal and okra, usually topped with a spicy creole sauce made from tomatoes, onions, and sweet peppers. Bajan-style pepper pot is a hearty stew of oxtail, beef chunks, and "any other meat" in a rich, spicy gravy that's simmered overnight.

For lunch, restaurants often offer a traditional Bajan buffet of fried fish, baked chicken, salads, macaroni pie (macaroni and cheese), and a selection of steamed or stewed local roots and vegetables. Be cautious with the West Indian condiments—like the sun, they're hotter than you think. Typical Bajan drinks, besides Banks Beer and Mount Gay Rum, are *falernum* (a liqueur concocted of rum, sugar, lime juice, and almond essence) and *mauby* (a nonalcoholic drink made by boiling bitter bark and spices, straining the mixture, and sweetening it). You're also sure to enjoy a lime squash or the fresh fruit or rum punch.

The dress code for dinner in Barbados is conservative, casually elegant, and, on occasion, formal—a jacket and tie for gentlemen and a cocktail dress for ladies in the fanciest restaurants and hotel dining rooms during the winter holiday season. Jeans, shorts, and T-shirts (either sleeveless or with slogans) are always frowned upon at dinner. Beach attire is appropriate only at the beach. And any form of camouflage—even a baby's T-shirt—may not be worn anywhere in Barbados and will be confiscated by the police.

WHAT IT COSTS IN U.S. DOLLARS					
	¢	$	$$	$$$	$$$$
Restaurants	under $8	$8–$12	$12–$20	$20–$30	over $30
Hotels*	under $80	$80–$150	$150–$250	$250–$350	over $350
Hotels**	under $125	$125–$250	$250–$350	$350–$450	over $450

*EP, BP, CP **AI, FAP, MAP
Restaurant prices are for a main course, excluding the customary 10% service charge. Hotel prices are for two people in a double room in high season, excluding the 7½% VAT, customary 10% service charge, and meal plans (except at all-inclusive hotels).

SAFETY

Crime isn't a major problem in Barbados, but take normal precautions. Lock your room, and don't leave valuables—particularly passports, tickets, and wallets—in plain sight or unattended on the beach. Use your hotel safe. For personal safety, avoid walking on the beach or on unlighted streets at night. Lock your rental car, and don't pick up hitchhikers. Using or trafficking in illegal drugs is strictly prohibited in Barbados. Any offense is punishable by a hefty fine, imprisonment, or both.

TIMING

Barbados is busiest in the high season, which extends from December 15 through April 15. Off-season hotel rates can be half what they are during this busy period. During the high season, too, a few hotels may require you to buy some kind of meal plan, which is not usually required in the low season. As noted in the listings, some hotels close in September and October, the slowest months of the off-

A steelpan band plays at the Cropover Festival

season, for annual renovations. Some restaurants may close for brief periods within that time frame, as well.

In mid-January the **Barbados Jazz Festival** is a weeklong event jammed with performances by international artists, jazz legends, and local talent.

In February the weeklong **Holetown Festival** is held at the fairgrounds to commemorate the date in 1627 when the first European settlers arrived in Barbados.

Gospelfest occurs in May and hosts performances by gospel headliners from around the world.

Dating from the 19th century, **Crop Over,** a monthlong festival similar to Carnival that begins in July and ends on **Kadooment Day** (a national holiday), marks the end of the sugarcane harvest.

BRIDGETOWN

This bustling capital city is a major duty-free port with a compact shopping area. The principal thoroughfare is Broad Street, which leads west from National Heroes Square.

Sights in Bridgetown are plotted on the Bridgetown map.

← TO
BRIDGETOWN
PORT

Bridgetown

Restaurants

Waterfront Cafe, **1**

Wispers on
the Bay, **2**

Kensington New Rd.

Baxters Rd.

Lightfoot La.

Whitepark Rd.

Walton St.

Waldron St.

Pin Fold

Coleridge St.

Magazine La.

Nidhe Israel
Synagogue

Roebuck St.

Crumpton St.

Que
Pa

Mason Hall St.

Reed St.

Milk Market

James St.

High St.

Spry St.

Church St.

St. Michael's Cathed

Lakes Folly

Suttle St.

Swan St.

St. Michael's Row

Cheapside

Lower Broad St.

St. George St.

Broad St.

McGregor St.

Parliament
Buildings

St. Michael's St.

Bridge St.

Princess Alice Hwy.

National Heroes
Square

TO
HWY. 6

Wharf St.

◆The Careenage

Constitution R.

Fairchild St.

Careenage

Pierhead La.

Bay St.

Wellington St.

TO
HWY. 7

0   1/8 mile

0   200 meters

Caribbean Sea

KEY

❶ Restaurants

WHAT TO SEE

The Careenage. Bridgetown's natural harbor and gathering place is where, in the early days, schooners were careened (turned on their sides) to be scraped of barnacles and repainted. Today the Careenage serves as a marina for pleasure yachts and excursion boats. A boardwalk skirts the north side of the Careenage; on the south side, a lovely esplanade has pathways and benches for pedestrians and a statue of Errol Barrow, the first prime minister of Barbados. The Chamberlain Bridge and the Charles Duncan O'Neal Bridge cross the Careenage.

National Heroes Square. Across Broad Street from the Parliament Buildings and bordered by High and Trafalgar streets, this triangular plaza marks the center of town. Its monument to Lord Horatio Nelson (who was in Barbados only briefly in 1777 as a 19-year-old navy lieutenant) predates Nelson's Column in London's Trafalgar Square by 36 years. Also here are a war memorial and a fountain that commemorates the advent of running water on Barbados in 1865.

Errol Barrow, National Hero

Errol Barrow (1920–87), trained in Britain as a lawyer and economist, led his native Barbados to independence in 1966 and became the island nation's first prime minister. During his initial tenure, which lasted through 1976, Barrow expanded the tourist industry, reduced the island's dependence on sugar, introduced national health insurance and social security, and extended free education to the community college level.

Barrow was reelected prime minister in 1986 but collapsed and died at his home a year later. He is honored as a national hero and the "Father of Independence," and his birthday—January 21—is celebrated as a national holiday. On that day in 2007, a 9-foot-tall statue of Errol Barrow was erected on the esplanade along the Careenage, picturesquely sited between the city's two bridges and facing Parliament.

Nidhe Israel Synagogue. Providing for the spiritual needs of one of the oldest Jewish congregations in the western hemisphere, this synagogue was formed by Jews who left Brazil in the 1620s and introduced sugarcane to Barbados. The adjoining cemetery has tombstones dating from the 1630s. The original house of worship, built in 1654, was destroyed in an 1831 hurricane, rebuilt in 1833, and restored with the assistance of the Barbados National Trust in 1987. Friday-night services are held during the winter months, but the building is open to the public year-round. Shorts are not acceptable during services but may be worn at other times. ✉ *Synagogue La., St. Michael* ☎ *246/426–5792* 🎫 *Donation requested* ⏰ *Weekdays 9–4.*

Parliament Buildings. Overlooking National Heroes Square in the center of town, these Victorian buildings were constructed around 1870 to house the British Commonwealth's third-oldest parliament. A series of stained-glass windows depicts British monarchs from James I to Victoria. ✉ *Broad St., St. Michael* ☎ *246/427–2019* 🎫 *Donations welcome* ⏰ *Tours weekdays at 11 and 2, when parliament isn't in session.*

Queen's Park. Northeast of Bridgetown, Queen's Park contains one of the island's two immense baobab trees. Brought to Barbados from Guinea, West Africa, around 1738, this tree has a girth of more than 51 feet. Queen's Park Art Gallery, managed by the National Culture Foundation, is the island's largest gallery; exhibits change monthly.

Queen's Park House, the historic home of the British troop commander, has been converted into a theater, with an exhibition room on the lower floor and a restaurant. ⌧ *Constitution Rd., St. Michael* ☎ *246/427–2345 gallery* ⌫ *Free* ⊙ *Daily 9–5.*

St. Michael's Cathedral. Although no one has proved it, George Washington, on his only trip outside the United States, is said to have worshipped here in 1751. The original structure was nearly a century old by then. Destroyed twice by hurricanes, it was rebuilt in 1784 and again in 1831. ⌧ *Spry St. east of National Heroes Sq., St. Michael.*

RENTING A CAR. If you're staying on the remote southeast or east coasts, you may want to rent a car for your entire stay. In more populated areas, where taxis and public transportation are readily available, you might rent a car or minimoke (a tiny, open-sided beach buggy) for a day or two of exploring on your own. Rates start at about $55 per day during the high season.

SOUTHERN BARBADOS

Christ Church Parish, which is far busier and more developed than the west coast, is chockablock with condos, high- and low-rise hotels, and beach parks. It is also the location of St. Lawrence Gap, with its many places to eat, drink, shop, and party. As you move southeast, the broad, flat terrain comprises acre upon acre of cane fields, interrupted only by an occasional oil rig and a few tiny villages. Along the byways are colorful chattel houses, which were the traditional homes of tenant farmers. Historically, these typically Barbadian, ever-expandable small buildings were built to be dismantled and moved as required.

Sights in Southern Barbados are plotted on the Southern Barbados map.

WHAT TO SEE

🕭 **Barbados Concorde Experience.** Opened to the public in April 2007, the Concorde Experience revolves around the British Airways Concorde G-BOAE (Alpha Echo, for short) that for many years flew between London and Barbados and has now made its permanent home here. Besides boarding the sleek supersonic aircraft itself, you'll learn about how the technology was developed and how this plane differed from other jets. You may or may not have been able to fly the Concorde when it was still plying the Atlantic, but

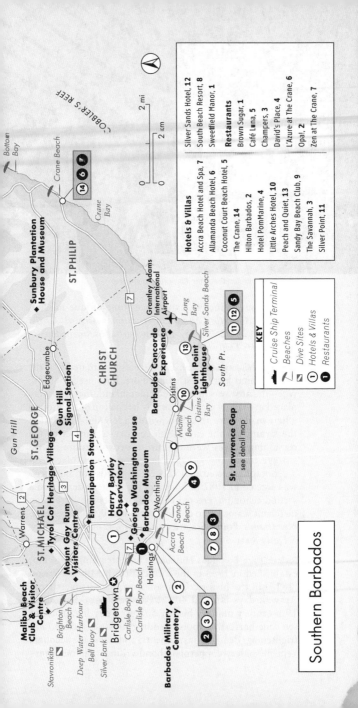

Southern Barbados

COBBLER'S REEF

Bottom Bay

Crane Beach

Crane Bay

ST.PHILIP

Sunbury Plantation House and Museum

Edgecumbe

Gun Hill Signal Station

Gun Hill

ST.GEORGE

CHRIST CHURCH

Barbados Concorde Experience

Grantley Adams International Airport

Long Bay

Silver Sands Beach

South Point Lighthouse

South Pt.

Oistins
Oistins Bay

Miami Beach

St. Lawrence Gap
see detail map

Worthing

George Washington House

Barbados Museum

Harry Bayley Observatory

Emancipation Statue

Tyrol Cot Heritage Village

Warrens

ST.MICHAEL

Mount Gay Rum Visitors Centre

Bridgetown

Carlisle Bay

Carlisle Bay Beach

Hastings

Accra Beach

Sandy Beach

Barbados Military Cemetery

Malibu Beach Club & Visitor Centre

Brighton Beach

Deep Water Harbour

Bell Buoy

Silver Bank

Stavronikita

KEY

⚓ Cruise Ship Terminal
Beaches
Dive Sites
① Hotels & Villas
❶ Restaurants

2 mi
2 km

Hotels & Villas

Accra Beach Hotel and Spa, **7**
Allamanda Beach Hotel, **6**
Coconut Court Beach Hotel, **5**
The Crane, **14**
Hilton Barbados, **2**
Hotel PomMarine, **4**
Little Arches Hotel, **10**
Peach and Quiet, **13**
Sandy Bay Beach Club, **9**
The Savannah, **3**
Silver Point, **11**
Silver Sands Hotel, **12**
South Beach Resort, **8**
Sweetfield Manor, **1**

Restaurants

Brown Sugar, **1**
Café Luna, **5**
Champers, **3**
David's Place, **4**
l'Azure at The Crane, **6**
Opal, **2**
Zen at The Crane, **7**

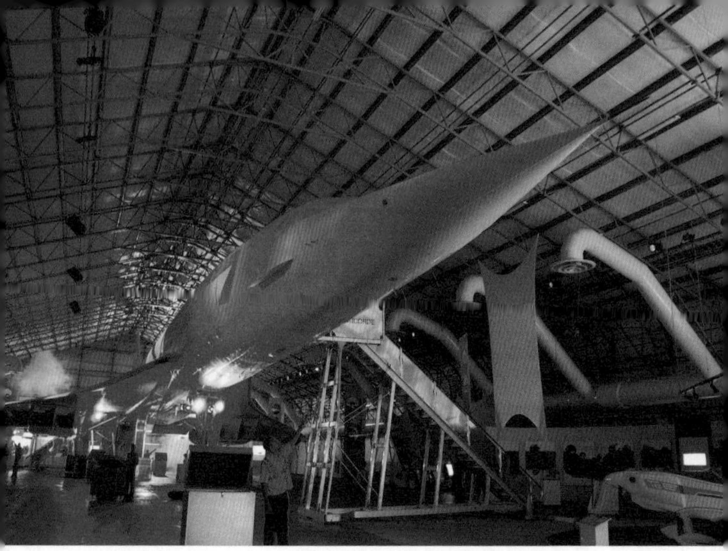

A supersonic Concorde on display at the Concorde Experience

this is your chance to experience some unique modern history. ✉ *Grantley Adams International Airport, Christ Church* ☎ *246/253–6257* 🌐 *www.barbadosconcorde.com* 🎫 *$17.50* ⏲ *Daily 9–5.*

Barbados Military Cemetery. The cemetery is situated near the shore behind historic St. Ann's Fort. First used in 1780, when the area was pretty much marshland, the dead were placed in shallow graves or simply left on top of the ground where many were absorbed, within a few short days, into the swamp. In the early 20th century, a number of the remaining graves were dug up to provide room for oil storage tanks; the salvaged headstones were placed on a cenotaph, erected in 1920–24. A "Cross of Sacrifice" was erected in 1982 to honor all the military dead, and a second cenotaph, erected in 2003, honors the Barbadian merchant seamen who died in World War II. ✉ *Graves End, Needham's Point, St. Michael* ☎ *245/426–0982* 🎫 *Free* ⏲ *Daily 8* AM*–4* PM.

★ Fodor's Choice **Barbados Museum.** This intriguing museum, established in 1933 in the former British Military Prison (1815) in the historic Garrison area, has artifacts from Arawak days (around 400 BC) and galleries that depict 19th-century military history and everyday life. You can see cane-harvesting tools, wedding dresses, ancient (and frightening) dentistry instruments, and slave sale accounts kept in spidery copperplate handwriting. The museum's

Harewood Gallery showcases the island's flora and fauna; its Cunard Gallery has a permanent collection of 20th-century Barbadian and Caribbean paintings and engravings; and its Connell Gallery features European decorative arts. Additional galleries include one with exhibits targeted to children. The Shilstone Memorial Library houses rare West Indian documentation—archival documents, genealogical records, photos, books, and maps—dating back to the 17th century. The museum also has a gift shop and a café. ☒ *Hwy. 7, Garrison Savannah, St. Michael* ☎ *246/427–0201 or 246/436–1956* ⊕ *www.barbmuse.org.bb* ☜ *$7.50* ☺ *Mon.– Sat. 9–5, Sun. 2–6.*

Emancipation Statue. This powerful statue of a slave—whose raised hands, with broken chains hanging from each wrist, evoke both contempt and victory—is commonly referred to as the Bussa Statue. Bussa was the man who, in 1816, led the first slave rebellion on Barbados. The work of Barbadian sculptor Karl Brodhagen was erected in 1985 to commemorate the emancipation of the slaves in 1834. ☒ *St. Barnabas Roundabout, intersection of ABC Hwy. and Hwy. 5, Haggatt Hall, St. Michael.*

★ **George Washington House.** George Washington slept here! This carefully restored and refurbished 18th-century plantation house in Bush Hill was the only place where the future first president of the United States actually slept outside North America. Teenage George and his older half-brother Lawrence, who was suffering from tuberculosis and seeking treatment on the island, rented this house overlooking Carlisle Bay for two months in 1751. Opened to the public in December 2006, the lower floor of the house and the kitchen have period furnishings; the upper floor is a museum with both permanent and temporary exhibits that display artifacts of 18th-century Barbadian life. The site includes an original 1719 windmill and bathhouse, along with a stable added to the property in the 1800s—and, of course, a gift shop and small café. Guided tours begin with an informative, 15-minute film appropriately called *George Washington in Barbados.* ☒ *Bush Hill, Garrison, St. Michael* ☎ *246/228–5461* ⊕ *www.georgewashingtonbarbados.org* ☜ *$12.50* ☺ *Mon.–Sat. 9–4:30.*

☾ **Harry Bayley Observatory.** The Barbados Astronomical Society headquarters since 1963, the observatory has a Celestron 14-inch reflector telescope—the only one in the eastern Caribbean. Visitors can view the moon, stars, planets, and astronomical objects that may not be visible from North America or Europe. ✉ *Off Hwy. 6, Clapham, St. Michael* ☎ *246/426–1317 or 246/422–2394* ✉ *$5* ⊘ *Fri. 8:30 PM–11:30 PM.*

Ragged Point. The easternmost point of Barbados is the location of East Coast Light, one of four strategically placed lighthouses on the island. While civilization in the form of new homes is encroaching on this once remote location, the view of the entire Atlantic coastline of Barbados is still spectacular—and the cool ocean breeze is beautifully refreshing on a hot, sunny day. ✉ *Marley Vale, St. Philip.*

South Point Light. This is the oldest of four lighthouses on Barbados. Assembled on the island in 1852, after being shown at London's Great Exhibition the previous year, the landmark lighthouse is located just east of Miami Beach and marks the southernmost point of land on Barbados. The 89-foot tower, with its distinguishing red and white horizontal stripes, is closed to the public, but visitors may freely walk about the site, take photos, and enjoy the view. ✉ *Atlantic Shores, Christ Church.*

★ **Fodor's Choice Sunbury Plantation House and Museum.** Lovingly rebuilt after a 1995 fire destroyed everything but the thick flint-and-stone walls, Sunbury offers an elegant glimpse of the 18th and 19th centuries on a Barbadian sugar estate. Period furniture, old prints, and a collection of horse-drawn carriages lend an air of authenticity. A buffet luncheon is served daily in the courtyard for $30 per person. A five-course candlelight dinner is served ($100 per person, reservations required) two nights a week at the 200-year-old mahogany dining table in the Sunbury dining room. ✉ *Off Hwy. 5, Six Cross Roads, St. Philip* ☎ *246/423–6270* ⊕ *www.barbadosgreathouse.com* ✉ *$7.50* ⊘ *Daily 9:30–4:30.*

☾ **Tyrol Cot Heritage Village.** This coral-stone cottage just south of Bridgetown was constructed in 1854 and is preserved as an example of period architecture. In 1929 it became the home of Sir Grantley Adams, the first premier of Barbados and the namesake of its international airport. Part of the Barbados National Trust, the cottage is now filled with antiques and memorabilia that belonged to the late Sir Grantley and Lady Adams. It's also the centerpiece of an outdoor "living museum," where artisans and craftsmen have their workshops in a cluster of traditional chattel houses. Workshops are open, crafts are for sale, and

Sunbury Plantation House

refreshments are available at the "rum shop" primarily during the winter season and when cruise ships are in port. ⊠ *Rte. 2, Codrington Hill, St. Michael* ☎ *246/424–2074 or 246/436–9033* 🖃 *$6* ⊘ *Weekdays 8–4.*

CENTRAL BARBADOS

On the west coast, in St. James Parish, Holetown marks the center of the Platinum Coast—so called for the vast number of luxurious resorts and mansions that face the sea. Holetown is also where British captain John Powell landed in 1625 to claim the island for King James. On the east coast, the crashing Atlantic surf has eroded the shoreline, forming steep cliffs and prehistoric rocks that look like giant mushrooms. Bathsheba and Cattlewash are favorite seacoast destinations for locals on weekends and holidays. In the interior, narrow roads weave through tiny villages and along and between the ridges. The landscape is covered with tropical vegetation and is riddled with fascinating caves and gullies.

Sights in Central Barbados are plotted on the Central Barbados map.

WHAT TO SEE

CUBAN MONUMENT. On October 6, 1976, Cubana Airlines Flight 455, a DC-8 aircraft en route to Cuba from Barbados, was brought down by a terrorist bombing attack, killing all 73 people on board. The aircraft crashed into the sea off Paynes Bay on the west coast of Barbados. Four anti-Castro Cuban exiles were arrested for the crime. Two were sentenced to 20-year prison terms; one was acquitted; the fourth was held for 8 years awaiting sentencing and later fled. A pyramid-shape granite monument dedicated to the victims was installed along Highway 1 at the approximate location where the wreckage was brought ashore; it was unveiled during a 1998 visit by Cuban president Fidel Castro.

★ Fodor'sChoice **Andromeda Botanic Gardens.** Beautiful and unusual plant specimens from around the world are cultivated in 6 acres of gardens nestled among streams, ponds, and rocky outcroppings overlooking the sea above the Bathsheba coastline. The gardens were created in 1954 with flowering plants collected by the late horticulturist Iris Bannochie. They're now administered by the Barbados National Trust. The Hibiscus Café serves snacks and drinks. ⊠ *Bathsheba, St. Joseph* ☎ *246/433–9384* ☎ *$10* ⊙ *Daily 9–5.*

Banks Brewery Visitor Centre. Since 1961, Banks has been the home brew of Barbados, and it's a very good brew at that. After a short audiovisual presentation in the "Brewseum," which is in the Old Brewhouse, see the original copper brewing kettles that have since been replaced by modern stainless-steel vats. Watch the computerized brewing, bottling, and crating process (10,000 bottles per day) as it occurs in the New Brewhouse and Bottling Hall, then visit the adjacent Beer Garden for a sample or two. The souvenir shop sells Banks logo gear. The tour lasts a half hour; reservations are required. ⊠ *Wildey, St. Michael* ☎ *246/228–6486* ⊕ *www.banksbeer.com* ☎ *$8; $18 including round-trip transportation* ⊙ *Weekdays 10, noon, and 2.*

Barclays Park. Straddling the Ermy Bourne Highway on the east coast, just north of Bathsheba, this public park was donated by Barclays Bank (now First Caribbean International Bank). Pack a picnic lunch and enjoy the gorgeous ocean view.

Central Barbados

Hotels & Villas
New Edgewater Hotel, **1**
Round House Inn, **2**
Sea-U Guest House, **3**

Restaurants
Bonito Beach Bar and Restaurant **3**
Cliffside at New Edgewater, **1**
Naniki Restaurant, **4**
Round House, **2**

KEY
🏖 Beaches
🤿 Dive Sites
① Hotels & Villas
❶ Restaurants

Ragged Pt.
Bottom Bay
Crane Beach
Marley Vale
Codrington Theological College
Conset Bay
ST. PHILIP
Bathsheba/Cattlewash Beach
Andromeda Botanic Gardens
Bathsheba
Barclays Park Beach
Belleplaine
Chalky Mount
Barclays Park
ST. ANDREW
ST. JOSEPH
Flower Forest
Mt. Hillaby
Blackmans
Four Crossroads
ST. JOHN
Orchid World
Sunbury Plantation House & Museum
4B
Edgecumbe
Gun Hill
ST. GEORGE
Gun Hill Signal Station
4
CHRIST CHURCH
6
Harrison's Cave
Welchman Hall Gully
Sir Frank Hutson Sugar Museum
ST. THOMAS
Groves
Warrens
ST. PETER
ST. JAMES
Mullins Beach
Mullins Bay
Folkestone Marine Park & Visitor Centre
Dottins Reef
Paynes Bay
Holetown & Vicinity see detail map
Mount Gay Visitor Centre
ST. MICHAEL
2
Warrens
Banks Brewery Visitor Centre
3
Malibu Beach Club and Visitor Centre
Stavronikita
Brighton Beach
Deep Water Harbour

2 mi
2 km

Holetown Landing

On May 14, 1625, British Captain John Powell anchored his ship off the west coast of Barbados and claimed the island on behalf of King James I. He named his landfall Jamestown. Nearly two years later, on February 17, 1627, Captain Henry Powell landed in Jamestown with a party of 80 settlers and 10 slaves. They used a small channel, or "hole," near the settlement to offload and clean ships, so Jamestown soon became known as Holetown. Today Holetown is a vibrant town with shopping centers, restaurants, nightspots, and, of course, hotels and resorts. It is also the site of the annual Holetown Festival—a week of parades, crafts, music, and partying—held in mid-February each year to commemorate the first settlement. The celebration begins at the Holetown Monument in the center of town.

Chalky Mount. This tiny east-coast village is perched high in the clay-yielding hills that have supplied local potters for 300 years. A number of working potteries are open daily to visitors. You can watch as artisans create bowls, vases, candleholders, and decorative objects—which are, of course, for sale.

Codrington Theological College. An impressive stand of royal palms lines the road leading to the coral-stone buildings and serene grounds of Codrington College, an Anglican seminary opened in 1745 on a cliff overlooking Conset Bay. You're welcome to tour the buildings and walk the nature trails. Keep in mind, though, that beachwear is not appropriate here. ⊠ *Sargeant St., Conset Bay, St. John* ☎ *246/423–1140* ⊕ *www.codrington.org* ⊠ *$2.50* ⊗ *Daily 10–4.*

★ **Fodor's Choice Flower Forest.** It's a treat to meander among fragrant flowering bushes, canna and ginger lilies, puffball trees, and more than 100 other species of tropical flora in a cool, tranquil forest of flowers and other plants. A 0.5-mi-long (1-km-long) path winds through the 50-acre grounds, a former sugar plantation; it takes about 30 to 45 minutes to follow the path, or you can wander freely for as long as you wish. Benches located throughout the forest give you a place to pause and reflect. There's also a snack bar, a gift shop, and a beautiful view of Mt. Hillaby, at 1,100 feet the highest point of land on Barbados. ⊠ *Hwy. 2, Richmond Plantation, St. Joseph* ☎ *246/433–8152* ⊠ *$10* ⊗ *Daily 9–5.*

○ **Folkestone Marine Park and Visitor Centre.** On land and off-
★ shore, the whole family will enjoy this park just north of
Holetown. The museum and aquarium illuminate some
of the island's marine life; and for some firsthand viewing,
there's an underwater snorkeling trail around Dottins Reef
(glass-bottom boats are available for nonswimmers). A
barge sunk in shallow water is home to myriad fish, making it a popular dive site. ⊠ *Church Point, Holetown, St.
James* ☎ *246/422–2314* ☎ *Free* ☉ *Park daily 9–5, museum
weekdays 9–5.*

★ Fodor's Choice **Gun Hill Signal Station.** The 360-degree view from
○ Gun Hill, 700 feet above sea level, gave this location strategic importance to the 18th-century British army. Using
lanterns and semaphore, soldiers based here could com-
municate with their counterparts at the Garrison on the
south coast and at Grenade Hill in the north. Time moved
slowly in 1868, and Captain Henry Wilkinson whiled
away his off-duty hours by carving a huge lion from a
single rock—which is on the hillside just below the tower.
Come for a short history lesson but mainly for the view;
it's so gorgeous, military invalids were once sent here to
convalesce. ⊠ *Gun Hill, St. George* ☎ *246/429–1358* ☎ *$5*
☉ *Weekdays 9–5.*

★ Fodor's Choice **Harrison's Cave.** This limestone cavern, complete
○ with stalactites, stalagmites, subterranean streams, and a
40-foot waterfall, is a rare find in the Caribbean—and one
of Barbados's most popular attractions. The cave reopened
in early 2010, following extensive renovations comprising
a new visitor center with interpretative displays, life-size
models and sculptures, a souvenir shop, improved restaurant facilities, and access for people with disabilities. The
one-hour tours are conducted via electric trams, which fill
up fast; reserve ahead of time. ⊠ *Hwy. 2, Welchman Hall,
St. Thomas* ☎ *246/438–6640* ⊕ *www.harrisonscave.com*
☎ *$20* ☉ *Wed.–Sun. 9–3:45 (last tour).*

Malibu Beach Club and Visitor Centre. Just north of Bridgetown,
the fun-loving Malibu Rum people encourage those taking
the distillery tour to make a day of it. The beach—which
has a variety of water-sports options—is adjacent to the
visitor center. Lunch and drinks are served at the beachside
grill. ⊠ *Black Rock, Brighton, St. Michael* ☎ *246/425–9393*
☎ *$10, $32.50 with lunch* ☉ *Weekdays 9–5.*

★ Fodor's Choice **Mount Gay Rum Visitors Centre.** On this popular
tour, you learn the colorful story behind the world's oldest

The famous lion at Gun Hill Signal Station

rum—made in Barbados since 1703. Although the distillery is in the far north, in St. Lucy Parish, tour guides explain the rum-making procedure. Both historic and modern equipment is on display, and rows and rows of barrels are stored in this location. The 45-minute tour runs hourly (last tour begins at 3:30) and concludes with a tasting and an opportunity to buy bottles of rum and gift items—and even have lunch or cocktails, depending on the time of day. ⊠ *Spring Garden Hwy., Brandons, St. Michael* ☎ *246/425–8757* ⊕ *www.mountgay.com* ☎ *$7, $40 with lunch, $30 with cocktails* ⊘ *Weekdays 9–5.*

Orchid World. Follow meandering pathways through tropical gardens filled with thousands of colorful orchids. You'll see Vandaceous orchids attached to fences or wire frames, Schomburgkia and Oncidiums stuck on mahogany trees, Aranda and Spathoglottis orchids growing in a grotto, and Ascocendas suspended from netting in shady enclosures. You'll find seasonal orchids, scented orchids, multicolor Vanda orchids, and more. Benches are well placed to stop for a little rest, admire the flowers, or simply take in the expansive view of the surrounding cane fields and distant hills of Sweet Vale. Snacks, cold beverages, and other refreshments are served in the café. ⊠ *Hwy. 3B, Groves, St. George* ☎ *246/433–0306* ☎ *$10* ⊘ *Daily 9–5.*

Sir Frank Hutson Sugar Museum. The Sugar Museum is located in an old boiling house in the yard of the Portvale Sugar

Factory, one of two sugar refineries in operation in Barbados. The museum has a collection of original machinery, old photographs, and other implements used to refine sugar and make molasses. A video presentation explains the production process from cutting the cane to sweetening your coffee and, of course, making rum. During the grinding season (February through May), you can also tour the modern factory to see how sugar is produced today. ⊠ *Hwy. 2A, Rock Hall, St. Thomas* ☎ *246/432–0100* ⊴ *$4; $7.50 includes factory tour* ☉ *Mon.–Sat. 9–5.*

Welchman Hall Gully. This 1.5-mi-long (2-km-long) natural gully is really a collapsed limestone cavern, once part of the same underground network as Harrison's Cave. The Barbados National Trust protects the peace and quiet here, making it a beautiful place to hike past acres of labeled flowers and stands of trees. You can see and hear some interesting birds—and, with luck, a native green monkey. The tour is self-guided (although a guide can be arranged with 24 hours' notice) and takes about 30 to 45 minutes; last tour begins at 4 PM. ⊠ *Welchman Hall, St. Thomas* ☎ *246/438–6671* ⊕ *www.welchmanhallgullybarbados.com* ⊴ *$9* ☉ *Daily 9–4:30.*

NORTHERN BARBADOS

Speightstown, the north's commercial center and once a thriving port city, now relies on quaint local shops and informal restaurants. Many of Speightstown's 19th-century buildings, with typical overhanging balconies, have been or are being restored. The island's northernmost reaches, St. Peter and St. Lucy parishes, have a varied topography and are lovely to explore. Between the tiny fishing towns along the northwestern coast and the sweeping views out over the Atlantic to the east are forest and farm, moor and mountain. Most guides include a loop through this area on a daylong island tour—it's a beautiful drive.

Sights in Northern Barbados are plotted on the Northern Barbados map.

WHAT TO SEE

Ⓒ **Animal Flower Cave.** Small sea anemones, or sea worms (resembling flowers when they open their tiny tentacles), live in small pools in this cave at the island's very northern tip. The view of breaking waves from inside the cave is magnificent. ⊠ *North Point, St. Lucy* ☎ *246/439–8797* ⊴ *$7.50* ☉ *Daily 9–4.*

Where de Rum Come From

For more than 300 years, a daily "tot" of rum (2 ounces) was duly administered to each sailor in the British Navy—as a health ration. At times, rum also played a less appetizing—but equally important—role. When Admiral Horatio Nelson died in 1805 aboard a ship during the Battle of Trafalgar, his body was preserved in a cask of his favorite rum until he could be properly buried.

Few Caribbean islands are without a locally made rum, but Barbados is truly "where de rum come from." Mount Gay, the world's oldest rum distillery, has continuously operated on Barbados since 1703, according to the original deed for the Mount Gay Estate, which itemized two stone windmills, a boiling house, seven copper pots, and a still house. The presence of rum-making equipment on the plantation at the time suggests that the previous owners were actually producing rum in Barbados long before 1703.

Today much of the island's interior is still planted with sugarcane—where the rum really does come from—and several greathouses, situated on historic sugar plantations, have been restored with period furniture and are open to the public.

To really understand rum, however, you need to delve a little deeper than the bottom of a glass of rum punch. Mount Gay offers an interesting 45-minute tour of its Bridgetown plant, followed by a tasting. You'll learn about the rum-making process from cane to cocktail, hear more rum-inspired anecdotes, and have an opportunity to buy bottles of its famous Eclipse or Extra Old rum at duty-free prices. Bottoms up!

Ⓒ **Barbados Wildlife Reserve.** The reserve is the habitat of her-
★ ons, innumerable land turtles, screeching peacocks, shy deer, elusive green monkeys, brilliantly colored parrots (in a large walk-in aviary), a snake, and a caiman. Except for the snake and the caiman, the animals run or fly freely— so step carefully and keep your hands to yourself. Late afternoon is your best chance to catch a glimpse of a green monkey. ✉ *Farley Hill, St. Peter* ☎ *246/422–8826* 💰 *$11.50* ☉ *Daily 10–5.*

Farley Hill. At this national park in northern St. Peter, across the road from the Barbados Wildlife Reserve, the imposing ruins of a plantation greathouse are surrounded by gardens and lawns, along with an avenue of towering royal palms and gigantic mahogany, whitewood, and casuarina

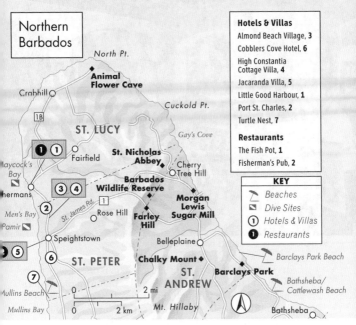

trees. Partially rebuilt for the filming of *Island in the Sun*, the classic 1957 film starring Harry Belafonte and Dorothy Dandridge, the structure was later destroyed by fire. Behind the estate, there's a sweeping view of the region called Scotland for its rugged landscape. ⊠ *Farley Hill, St. Peter* ☎ *246/422–3555* ⊠ *$2 per car, pedestrians free* ☉ *Daily 8:30–6.*

☼ **Morgan Lewis Sugar Mill.** Built in 1727, the mill was operational until 1945. Today it's the only remaining windmill in Barbados with its wheelhouse and sails intact. No longer used to grind sugarcane, except for occasional demonstrations, it was donated to the Barbados National Trust in 1962 and eventually restored to its original working specifications in 1998 by millwrights from the United Kingdom. The surrounding acres are now used for dairy farming. ⊠ *Cherry Tree Hill, St. Andrew* ☎ *246/422–7429* ⊠ *$5* ☉ *Weekdays 9–5.*

★ **Fodor's Choice St. Nicholas Abbey.** There's no religious connection here at all. The island's oldest greathouse (circa 1650) was named after the original British owner's hometown, St. Nicholas Parish near Bristol, and Bath Abbey nearby.

St. Nicholas Abbey, the island's oldest surviving plantation home

Its stone-and-wood architecture makes it one of only three original Jacobean-style houses still standing in the western hemisphere. It has Dutch gables, finials of coral stone, and beautiful grounds that include an old sugar mill. The first floor, fully furnished with period furniture and portraits of family members, is open to the public. Fascinating home movies, shot by a previous owner's father, record Bajan life in the 1930s. ⊠ *Cherry Tree Hill, St. Peter* ☎ *246/422–5357* ⊕ *www.stnicholasabbey.com* ⊠ *$15* ⊗ *Sun.–Fri. 10–3:30.*

CHERRY TREE HILL. The cherry trees for which this spot was named have long since disappeared, but the view from Cherry Tree Hill, just east of St. Nicholas Abbey, is still one of the most spectacular in Barbados. Although only about 850 feet above sea level, it is one of the highest points on the island and affords a broad view of the rugged east coast and the entire Scotland District— so named because its rolling hills resemble the moors of Scotland. Today, when approaching from the west, you drive through a majestic stand of mature, leafy mahogany trees.

Sugar: How Sweet It Is . . .

Sugarcane was introduced to Barbados in the 1630s. Considered "white gold" by the original plantation owners, sugar production relied on forced labor (African slaves) and indentured servants (white civilians who wanted to emigrate overseas, kidnapped individuals, and convicted criminals dubbed "Red Legs," presumably because of the chafing marks that the chains made on their white legs). Slavery was abolished in 1834, yet records show that Barbados still had 491 active sugar plantations in 1846, along with 506 operating windmills. And until 1969, when the mechanical harvester was introduced in Barbados, cane was cut by manual labor. Nowadays, few people want the backbreaking job of cutting cane, so nearly all cane grown anywhere is cut mechanically. Today in Barbados, some 1,500 small farms (about 200 acres each) produce about 60,000 tons of sugar annually, but only one operating windmill remains and just two companies refine sugar. Unfortunately, small farms and hilly terrain make mechanization inefficient. So while sugar remains an important agricultural product in Barbados, its value to the local economy has declined relative to tourism and other business interests.

WHERE TO EAT

The largest concentration of restaurants on the west coast is in Holetown, particularly on 1st and 2nd streets, where you'll find everything from poached fish to pizza, barbecue to bistro, curry to stir-fry. Many more excellent restaurants are scattered along Highway 1 south of Holetown—including some of the finest ones on the island. A handful of others are in Speightstown, in the far northwest. And don't dismiss the hotel restaurants, many of which are quite fabulous. On the south coast, the St. Lawrence Gap area is chockablock with popular restaurants—more than a dozen at last count. Seafood served at water's edge is a highlight, but you'll also find restaurants offering Mexican, Greek, Italian, Asian Fusion, and, of course, Bajan cuisine. Some of the local favorites, where businesspeople come for the daily Bajan buffet luncheon, are in or closer to Bridgetown. A few small inns perched on cliffs overlooking the east coast offer lunch—often a Bajan buffet—and beautiful ocean views to individuals and groups touring that rugged side of the island.

BRIDGETOWN

Bridgetown restaurant locations are plotted on the Bridgetown map.

$$$–$$$$ ✕ **Waterfront Cafe.** *Caribbean.* This friendly bistro alongside the Careenage is the perfect place to enjoy a drink, snack, or meal—and to people-watch. Locals and tourists alike gather for all-day alfresco dining on sandwiches, salads, fish, pasta, pepper pot stew, and tasty Bajan snacks such as buljol, fish cakes, or plantation pork (plantains stuffed with spicy minced pork). The panfried flying-fish sandwich is especially popular. In the evening you can gaze through the arched windows while savoring nouvelle Caribbean cuisine, enjoying cool trade winds, and listening to live jazz. There's a special Caribbean buffet and steel-pan music on Tuesday night from 7 to 9. ✉ *The Careenage, Bridgetown, St. Michael* ☎ *246/427–0093* ⊕ *www.waterfrontcafe.com.* bb ▭ *AE, DC, MC, V* ⊘ *Closed Sun.*

$$$$ ✕ **Wispers on the Bay.** *Eclectic.* Pass through the large wooden doors from the street and enter into a lush inner courtyard with gardens, walkways, small shops, a waterfall, and sitting areas. The restaurant itself is seaside, with wispy white curtains and crisp white tablecloths and seat covers. Dine outdoors on the breezy deck or inside in air-conditioned comfort. In terms of ambience, think Miami's South Beach transported to the Caribbean. At lunch, enjoy homemade soups, fresh salads, or a variety of entrées that might include pear-and-cheese tortellini, West Indian curried chicken, or steamed New Zealand mussels. Dinner menu choices range from charbroiled tuna or Angus tenderloin broiled to perfection to vanilla-scented salmon braised with lemon rice and herb-roasted rack of lamb. The catch of the day is served with steamed vegetables and pesto mashed potatoes and drizzled with pink grapefruit vinaigrette. Lunch is à la carte; the fixed-priced dinner menu ($96) includes an appetizer, entrée, and dessert. ✉ *Old Bayshore Complex, Bay St., Bridgetown, St. Michael* ☎ *246/826–5222* ⚎ *Reservations essential* ▭ *AE, MC, V* ⊘ *Closed Sun.*

SOUTHERN BARBADOS

Restaurant locations in southern Barbados are plotted on the Southern Barbados and St. Lawrence Gap maps.

$$–$$$ ✕ **Bellini's Restaurant.** *Italian.* Classic northern Italian cuisine is the specialty at Bellini's, on the main floor of the Little Bay Hotel. The atmosphere here is smart-casual. Toast the

Elegant Caribbean cuisine at Brown Sugar Restaurant

evening with a Bellini cocktail (ice-cold sparkling wine with a splash of fruit nectar) and start your meal with bruschetta, an individual gourmet pizza, or perhaps a homemade pasta dish with fresh herbs and a rich sauce. Move on to the signature garlic shrimp entrée or the popular chicken parmigiana—then top it all off with excellent tiramisu. We recommend making your reservations early; request a table on the Mediterranean-style verandah to enjoy one of the most appealing dining settings on the south coast. ✉ *Little Bay Hotel, St. Lawrence Gap, Dover, Christ Church* ☎ *246/435–7246* 🌐 *www.bellinisbarbados.com* *Reservations essential* ▭ *AE, D, MC, V* ⊗ *No lunch.*

★ **Fodor's Choice** ✕ **Brown Sugar.** *Caribbean.* Set back from the road in an old traditional home, the lattice-trimmed dining patios here are filled with ferns, flowers, and water features. Brown Sugar is a popular lunch spot for local businesspeople, who come for the nearly 30 delicious local and creole dishes spread out at the all-you-can-eat, four-course Bajan buffet. Here's your chance to try local specialties such as flying fish, cou-cou, buljol, *souse* (pickled pork, stewed for hours in broth), fish cakes, and pepper pot. In the evening, the à la carte menu has dishes such as fried flying fish, coconut shrimp, and plantain-crusted mahimahi; curried lamb, filet mignon, and broiled pepper chicken; and seafood or pesto pasta. Bring the kids—there's a special children's menu with fried chicken, fried flying-fish fingers, and pasta dishes. Save room for the warm pawpaw (papaya) pie or

$$$–$$$$

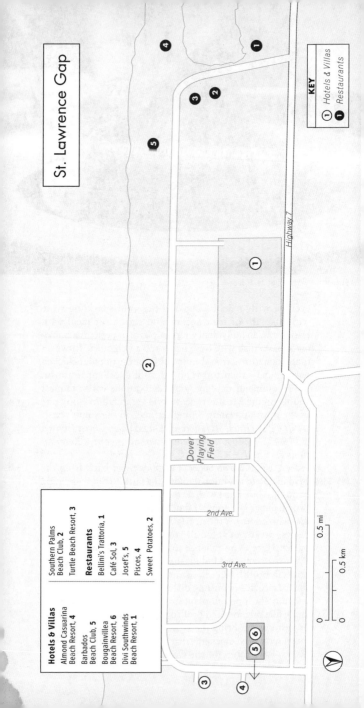

St. Lawrence Gap

Hotels & Villas
Almond Casuarina
Beach Resort, **4**
Barbados
Beach Club, **5**
Bougainvillea
Beach Resort, **6**
Divi Southwinds
Beach Resort, **1**

Southern Palms
Beach Club, **2**
Turtle Beach Resort, **3**

Restaurants
Bellini's Trattoria, **1**
Café Sol, **3**
Josef's, **5**
Pisces, **4**
Sweet Potatoes, **2**

Dover Playing Field

2nd Ave.

3rd Ave.

Highway 7

KEY
Ⓝ Hotels & Villas
❶ Restaurants

0   0.5 mi
0   0.5 km

Best Bets for Barbados Dining

With the many restaurants to choose from, how will you decide where to eat? Fodor's writers and editors have se lected their favorite restaurants in the Best Bets lists below. The Fodor's Choice properties represent the "best of the best." Find specific details about a restaurant in the full reviews.

Fodor's Choice: Brown Sugar, Champers, The Cliff, Daphne's, Fish Pot, Pisces, The Tides

Best Waterfront Setting: Café Luna, Champers, Cliffside at New Edgewater, Daphne's, David's Place, Fish Pot, L'Azure

at The Crane, Lone Star, Opal Black Pearl Seafood and Steakhouse, Pisces, The Tides, Round House Restaurant, Waterfront Cafe, Wispers on the Bay

Best for Families: Angry Annie's, Bellini's Restaurant, Brown Sugar, Café Sol

Most Romantic: The Cliff, Daphne's, Lone Star, The Mews, The Tides

Best for Local Bajan Cuisine: Bonito Beach Bar and Restaurant, Brown Sugar, Cliffside at New Edgewater, Fisherman's Pub, Naniki, Sweet Potatoes, Waterfront Cafe

Bajan rum pudding with rum sauce. ⊠ *Bay St., Aquatic Gap, St. Michael* ☎ *246/426–7684* ⊕ *www.brownsugarbarbados. com* ⊟ *AE, MC, V* ⊗ *No lunch Sat.*

$$$–$$$$ ✕ **Café Luna.** *Eclectic.* The sweeping view of pretty Enterprise (Miami) Beach from Café Luna, the alfresco dining deck on top of the Mediterranean-style Little Arches Hotel, is spectacular at lunchtime and magical in the moonlight. At lunch, sip on crisp white wine or a fruity cocktail while you await your freshly made salad, pasta, or sandwich. At dinner, owner and executive chef Mark de Gruchy prepares contemporary favorites from around the world, including fresh Scottish salmon grilled to perfection, oven-roasted New Zealand rack of lamb, fettuccine with fresh seafood, and local chicken breast with mango chutney. ⊠ *Little Arches Hotel, Enterprise Beach, Oistins, Christ Church* ☎ *246/428–6172* ⊕ *www.littlearches.com* ⌦ *Reservations essential* ⊟ *MC, V.*

$$–$$$ ✕ **Café Sol.** *Mexican.* Enjoy Tex-Mex nachos, tacos, burritos, and tostadas in this Mexican bar and grill in the heart of busy St. Lawrence Gap. Or choose a burger, honey-barbecue chicken, or flame-grilled steak from the gringo menu. Add helpings of Spanish rice and beans, a Corona, and plenty of jalapeño peppers, guacamole, and salsa to give everything a Mexican feel. Some people come just for the margaritas—15

fruity varieties rimmed with Bajan sugar instead of salt. Café Sol has two happy hours every night. ⊠ *St. Lawrence Gap, Christ Church* ☎ *246/426–7655* ⊕ *www.cafesolbarbados. com* ⊟ *AE, MC, V* ⊘ *No lunch Mon.*

★ **Fodor's**Choice ✕ **Champers.** *Eclectic.* Chiryl Newman's snazzy
$$$–$$$$ seaside restaurant and popular watering hole is situated in an old Bajan home on a quiet lane just off the main south-coast road in Rockley. Luncheon guests—about 75% local businesspeople—enjoy repasts such as char-grilled beet salad, Champers fish pie, grilled barracuda, or chicken-and-mushroom fettuccine in a creamy chardonnay sauce. Dinner guests swoon over dishes such as the roasted rack of lamb with spring vegetables and mint-infused jus, the sautéed sea scallops with stir-fried vegetables and noodles with red Thai curry sauce, and the Parmesan-crusted barracuda with whole-grain mustard sauce. But this isn't nouvelle cuisine. The portions are hearty and the food is well seasoned with Caribbean flavors, "just the way the locals like it," says Newman. The cliff-top setting overlooking Accra Beach offers diners a panoramic view of the sea and a relaxing atmosphere for daytime dining. At night, particularly at the bar, there's a definite buzz in the air. Nearly all the artwork gracing the walls is by Barbadian artists and may be purchased through the on-site gallery. ⊠ *Skeetes Hill, Rockley, Christ Church* ☎ *246/434–3464* ⊕ *www.champersbarbados.com* ⌂ *Reservations essential* ⊟ *AE, MC, V.*

$$$$ ✕ **David's Place.** *Caribbean.* Come here for sophisticated Bajan cuisine in a prime waterfront location on St. Lawrence Bay. Waves gently lap against the pilings of the open-air deck—a rhythmic accompaniment to the soft classical background music. Owner David Trotman personally keeps an eye on every detail. For starters, the pumpkin soup is divine, and the spicy fish cakes are classic. Specialties such as grilled flying fish, pepper pot stew, and creole shrimp all come with a selection of local vegetables and a choice of rice and peas, macaroni pie, or cou-cou—and delicious home-made cheddar-cheese bread. The menu always includes two or three vegetarian dishes as well, such as lemon-tossed linguine or vegetable crepes with a tomato-cream sauce. Dessert might be bread pudding, carrot cake with rum sauce, or coconut cream pie. Complement your meal with a glass of wine from the extensive list. ⊠ *St. Lawrence Main Rd., Worthing, Christ Church* ☎ *246/435–9755* ⊕ *www. davidsplacebarbados.com* ⌂ *Reservations essential* ⊟ *MC, V* ⊘ *Closed Mon. No lunch.*

$$$$ ×**Josef's Restaurant.** *Seafood.* The signature restaurant of Austrian restaurateur Josef Schwaiger, in a cliff-side Bajan dwelling surrounded by gardens, is one of the most upscale seaside dining spots on the south coast. Josef's cuisine fuses Asian culinary techniques and Caribbean flavors with fresh seafood. Dinner is prix fixe, with your choice of either a two-course ($65) or three-course ($75) option. Fruits of the sea—including seared yellowfin tuna with mango cilantro sauce or catch of the day with grilled vegetables and nutmeg creamed potatoes—are prominent, and the wine list is extensive. Try shredded duck with herbed hoisin pancakes as an innovative starter, or let the free-range chicken teriyaki with stir-fry noodles tingle your taste buds. Pasta dishes assuage the vegetarian palate. ⊠ *Waverly House, St. Lawrence Gap, Dover, Christ Church* ☎ *246/435–8245* ⊕ *www. josefsinbarbados.com* ⌕ *Reservations essential* ☰ *AE, MC, V* ⊗ *No lunch.*

$$$–$$$$ ×**L'Azure at The Crane.** *Seafood.* Perched on an oceanfront cliff, L'Azure is an informal luncheon spot by day that becomes elegant after dark. Enjoy seafood chowder or a light salad or sandwich while absorbing the breathtaking view. At dinner, candlelight and a soft guitar enhance a fabulous Caribbean lobster seasoned with herbs, lime juice, and garlic butter and served in its shell; if you're not in the mood for seafood, try the perfectly grilled filet mignon. Sunday is really special, with a Gospel Brunch at 10 AM and a Bajan Buffet at 12:30 PM. ⊠ *The Crane, Crane Bay, St. Philip* ☎ *246/423–6220* ⊕ *www.thecrane.com* ⌕ *Reservations essential* ☰ *AE, MC, V.*

$$$$ ×**OPA! Black Pearl Seafood and Steakhouse.** *Greek.* If you're in the mood for an authentic dinner of souvlaki, moussaka, or gyros—or simply a perfectly grilled steak or fresh catch of the day—this is the place for you. Sitting on the dining deck overlooking the sea, you'll begin to wonder if you're staring at the Caribbean or the Aegean. Never mind—sit back, sip your ouzo or chilled white wine, and nibble on a plate of *dolmades avgolemono* (stuffed grape leaves), spanakopita (spinach and feta cheese wrapped in buttery phyllo), or crispy calamari (tender rounds of squid) before choosing traditional Greek or just traditional. ⊠ *Shak Shak Complex, Main Rd., Hastings, Christ Church* ☎ *246/435–1234* ⊕ *www.blackpearlbarbados.com* ⌕ *Reservations essential* ☰ *AE, D, MC, V* ⊗ *No lunch weekends.*

★ **Fodor's** Choice ×**Pisces.** *Seafood.* For seafood lovers, this is
$$$–$$$$ nirvana. Prepared in every way—from charbroiled to gently sautéed—by chef-owner Larry Rogers, seafood specialties

may include conch strips in tempura, rich fish chowder, panfried fillets of flying fish with a toasted almond crust and a light mango-citrus sauce, and seared prawns in a fragrant curry sauce. Landlubbers in your party can select from the chicken, beef, and pasta dishes on the menu. Whatever you choose, the herbs that flavor it and the accompanying vegetables will have come from the chef's own garden. Save room for the homemade bread pudding, yogurt-lime cheesecake, or rum-raisin ice cream. Twinkling white lights reflect on the water as you dine. ⊠ *St. Lawrence Gap, Dover, Christ Church* ☎ *246/435–6564* ⊕ *www.piscesbarbados. com* ⚱ *Reservations essential* ⊟ *AE, MC, V* ⊙ *No lunch.*

$$–$$$ ✕ **Sweet Potatoes.** *Caribbean.* "Good Old Bajan Cooking" is the slogan at this popular restaurant in the Gap, and that's what you can expect. Of course, you'll want to start everything off with a chilled rum punch. Then whet your appetite with some favorite local appetizers such as bul-jol (marinated codfish seasoned with herbs and onions); sweet plantains stuffed with minced beef, pumpkin and spinach fritters; or deep-fried fish cakes. A selection of Bajan appetizers will make a good, filling lunch, as well. The dinner menu includes flying fish stuffed with local vegetables, grilled chicken breast in a Malibu rum sauce, catch of the day bathed in a creole sauce, and jerk pork. Rum cake, flambéed banana, and bread pudding with rum sauce are traditional desserts. ⊠ *St. Lawrence Gap, Dover, Christ Church* ☎ *246/420–7668* ⚱ *Reservations essential* ⊟ *AE, DC, MC, V.*

$$$ ✕ **Zen at The Crane.** *Asian.* Thai and Japanese specialties reign supreme in a magnificent setting overlooking Crane Beach. The centerpiece of the sophisticated, Asian-inspired decor is a 12-seat sushi bar, where chefs prepare exotic fare before your eyes. Try sizzling lobster kabayaki served in a cast-iron grill pan, teriyaki beef or chicken, tempura prawns, stir-fried meats and vegetables in oyster sauce, or a deluxe bento box. An extensive menu of Thai appetizers, soups, noodles, fried rice, and chef's specials and main courses from the wok are noted as being spicy, spicier, and spiciest. Choose to dine in the tatami room for a traditional Japanese dining experience. ⊠ *The Crane, Crane Bay, St. Philip* ☎ *246/423–6220* ⊕ *www.thecrane.com* ⚱ *Reservations essential* ⊟ *AE, MC, V* ⊙ *Closed Tues.*

EAST COAST

Restaurant locations on the east coast are plotted on the Central Barbados map.

$$ ✕ **Bonito Beach Bar and Restaurant.** *Caribbean.* The Bonito's wholesome West Indian home cooking has soothed the hunger pangs of many folks who find themselves on the east coast at lunchtime. The view of the Atlantic from the second floor dining room is striking, and the Bajan buffet lunch includes fried fish and baked chicken accompanied by macaroni pie, salads, and vegetables fresh from the garden. Beer, rum punch, fresh fruit punch, and lime squash are refreshing choices to accompany your meal. ⊠ *Coast Rd., Bathsheba, St. Joseph* ☎ 246/433–9034 ☰ *AE, D, MC, V* ⊗ *Closed Sat. No dinner.*

$$–$$$ ✕ **Cliffside at New Edgewater.** *Caribbean.* The outdoor deck of this restaurant in the New Edgewater hotel provides one of the prettiest, breeziest ocean views in all Barbados and, therefore, is a good stop for lunch when touring the east coast. From noon to 3 PM, choose the Bajan buffet or select from the menu. Either way, you might enjoy fried flying fish, roast or stewed chicken, local lamb chops, rice and peas, steamed root vegetables, sautéed plantains, and salad. Afternoon tea with scones, pastries, and sandwiches is served from 3:30 to 6 PM. Dinner is also served but mostly to hotel guests and local residents, who are able to find their way home in the dark on the neighborhood's winding, often unmarked roads. ⊠ *New Edgewater Hotel, Bathsheba, St. Joseph* ☎ 246/433–9900 ⊕ *www.newedgewater.com* ⚘ *Reservations essential* ☰ *AE, MC, V.*

$$–$$$ ✕ **Naniki Restaurant.** *Caribbean.* Rich wooden beams and stone tiles, clay pottery, straw mats, colorful dinnerware, and fresh flowers from the adjacent anthurium farm set the style here. Huge picture windows and outdoor porch seating allow you to enjoy the exhilarating panoramic view of surrounding fields and hills and, when making the alfresco choice, a refreshing breeze along with your lunch of exquisitely prepared Caribbean standards. Seared flying fish, grilled dorado, stewed *lambi* (conch), curried chicken, and jerk chicken or pork are accompanied by cou-cou, peas and rice, or salad. Sunday brunch is a Caribbean buffet often featuring great jazz music by some of the Caribbean's best musicians. Vegetarian dishes are always available. ⊠ *Lush Life Nature Resort, Suriname, St. Joseph* ☎ 246/433–1300 ⊕ *www.lushlife.bb* ☰ *AE, MC, V* ⊗ *Closed Mon. No dinner.*

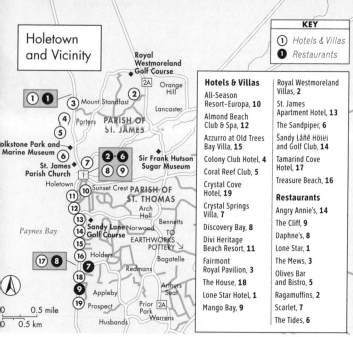

Holetown and Vicinity

KEY

① Hotels & Villas
❶ Restaurants

Royal Westmoreland Golf Course

Orange Hill

Mount Standfast

PARISH OF ST. JAMES

Porters

Lancaster

...lkstone Park and Marine Museum

St. James Parish Church

Sir Frank Hutson Sugar Museum

Holetown

Sunset Crest PARISH OF ST. THOMAS

Arch Hall

Paynes Bay

Sandy Lane Golf Course

Bennetts

Norwood

TO EARTHWORKS POTTERY

Holders

Bagatelle

Redmans

Arthurs Seat

Appleby

Prospect

Prior Park

Husbands

Warrens

0   0.5 mile
0   0.5 km

Hotels & Villas

All-Season Resort–Europa, **10**

Almond Beach Club & Spa, **12**

Azzurro at Old Trees Bay Villa, **15**

Colony Club Hotel, **4**

Coral Reef Club, **5**

Crystal Cove Hotel, **19**

Crystal Springs Villa, **7**

Discovery Bay, **8**

Divi Heritage Beach Resort, **11**

Fairmont Royal Pavilion, **3**

The House, **18**

Lone Star Hotel, **1**

Mango Bay, **9**

Royal Westmoreland Villas, **2**

St. James Apartment Hotel, **13**

The Sandpiper, **6**

Sandy Lane Hotel and Golf Club, **14**

Tamarind Cove Hotel, **17**

Treasure Beach, **16**

Restaurants

Angry Annie's, **14**

The Cliff, **9**

Daphne's, **8**

Lone Star, **1**

The Mews, **3**

Olives Bar and Bistro, **5**

Ragamuffins, **2**

Scarlet, **7**

The Tides, **6**

$$$ ✕ **Round House.** *Seafood.* Owners Robert and Gail Manley oversee an extensive menu for guests staying in their inn, tourists enjoying the east coast, and Bajans dining out. The lunch menu includes homemade soups and quiches, sandwiches, salads, and pasta. Dinner choices—served in the moonlight—extend from shrimp scampi, oven-baked dolphin steak, or grilled flying-fish fillet to baked ham, sirloin steak, or homemade pasta specials. Some people come just for the flying-fish pâté. Rolls and breads (whether for sandwiches or dessert), along with apple and coconut pies, are personally made by the owners. The Round House is an ocean-facing manse-turned-inn built in 1832. The view of the rugged coastline from the outside dining deck is mesmerizing. ⊠ *Bathsheba Beach, Bathsheba, St. Joseph* ☎ *246/433-9678* ⊕ *www.roundhousebarbados.com* ⌂ *Reservations essential* ▭ *MC, V* ⊘ *No dinner Sun. (except for inn guests).*

WEST COAST

If you are looking for a quick bite, Chefette is the island's homegrown fast-food restaurant chain. You can get bagels for breakfast, and chicken, burgers, pizza, rotis, ice cream, and more all throughout the afternoon and evening. Chefette has more than a dozen outlets strategically located throughout Barbados, including one at the airport.

Restaurant locations on the west coast are plotted on the Northern Barbados and Holetown and Vicinity maps.

$$-$$$ ✕ **Angry Annie's.** *Caribbean.* You can't miss this place. Outside and inside, everything's painted in cheerful Caribbean pinks, blues, greens, and yellows—and it's just steps from the main road. The food is just as lively: great barbecued "jump-up" ribs and chicken (as tasty as the roadside barbecue sold at street jump-ups in the Gap), grilled fresh fish or juicy steaks, "Rasta pasta" for vegetarians, and several spicy curries. Eat inside on gaily colored furniture, outside under the stars, or take it away with you. ✉ *1st St., Holetown, St. James* ☎ *246/432–2119* ▭ *AE, DC, MC, V* ⊘ *No lunch.*

★ **Fodor'sChoice**✕ **The Cliff.** *Eclectic.* Chef Paul Owens's mastery
$$$$ is the foundation of one of the finest dining experiences in the Caribbean, with prices to match. Steep steps hug the cliff on which the restaurant sits to accommodate those arriving by yacht, and every candlelit table has a sea view. Starters include smoked salmon ravioli with garlic sauce or grilled portobello mushroom on greens with truffle vinaigrette; for the main course, try Caribbean shrimp with a Thai green-curry coconut sauce, veal chop with a mustard-and-tarragon sauce, or red snapper fillet on a baked potato cake. Dessert falls into the sinful category, and service is impeccable. The prix-fixe menu will set you back $125 per person for a two-course meal (starter–main course or main course–dessert) or $150 per person for a three-course meal. Reserve days or even weeks in advance to snag a table at the front of the terrace for the best view. ✉ *Hwy. 1, Derricks, St. James* ☎ *246/432–1922* ⊕ *www.thecliffbarbados.com* ⚑ *Reservations essential* ▭ *AE, DC, MC, V* ⊘ *Closed Sun. (Apr. 15–Dec. 15). No lunch.*

★ **Fodor'sChoice** ✕ **Daphne's.** *Italian.* The beachfront restaurant
$$$$ of The House, Daphne's is the chic Caribbean outpost of the famed London eatery, Daphne's of Chelsea. The chef whips up contemporary Italian cuisine. Dine à la carte or choose the table d'hote menu ($55 for two courses or $65

Dessert at Daphne's Restaurant in The House

for three courses). Grilled mahimahi, for example, becomes "modern Italian" when combined with marsala wine, *peperonata* (stewed peppers, tomatoes, onions, and garlic), and zucchini. Perfectly prepared *melanzane* (eggplant) and zucchini parmigiana is a delicious starter, while a half portion of risotto with porcini mushrooms, green beans, and Parma ham is fabulously rich. Pappardelle with braised duck, red wine, and oregano is a sublime pasta choice. Light meals, salads, and half portions of pasta are available at lunch. The extensive wine list features both regional Italian and fine French selections. ⊠ *Paynes Bay, St. James* ☎ *246/432–2731* ⊕ *www.daphnesbarbados.com* ⚑ *Reservations essential* ☰ *AE, MC, V* ⊗ *Closed Mon. (May–Oct.).*

★ **Fodor's** Choice ✕ **Fish Pot.** *Mediterranean.* Just north of the
$$$–$$$$ little fishing village of Six Men's Bay, toward the far northern west coast of Barbados, this attractive seaside restaurant serves excellent Mediterranean cuisine and some of the island's freshest fish. Gaze seaward through windows framed with pale green louvered shutters while lunching on a seafood crepe, a grilled panini, or perhaps pasta with seafood or puttanesca sauce; in the evening, the menu may include panfried red snapper with caper-and-thyme mashed potatoes, seared herb-crusted tuna on garlic and spinach polenta, sun-dried tomato risotto tossed with vegetables, or cracker-crusted rack of lamb with thyme jus on roasted ratatouille. Bright and cheery by day and relaxed and cozy by night, the Fish Pot offers a tasty dining expe-

rience in a setting that's more classy than its name might suggest. ⊠ *Little Good Harbour Hotel, Shermans, St. Peter* ☎ 246/439–3000 ⊕ *www.littlegoodharbourbarbados.com* ⌂ *Reservations essential* ☰ *MC, V.*

¢–$ ✕ **Fisherman's Pub.** *Caribbean.* This is as local as local gets. For years, fishermen and other locals have come here daily for the inexpensive, authentic creole buffet served at lunch-time. For $10 or less, you can soak up the atmosphere and fill your plate with fried flying fish, stewed chicken or pork, curried goat or lamb, macaroni pie, fried plantain, cou-cou, and crisp green salad. In the evening, choose from the bar menu and dance (or simply listen) to catchy calypso music. Fisherman's Pub is an open-air, waterfront restaurant built on stilts just a stone's throw from the Speightstown fish market. ⊠ *Queen's St., Speightstown, St. Peter* ☎ 246/422–2703 ⌂ *Reservations not accepted* ☰ *MC, V.*

$$$$ ✕ **Lone Star.** *Continental.* In the 1940s this was the only commercial garage on the west coast; today, it's a snazzy restaurant in the tiny but chic Lone Star Hotel, where top chefs in the open-plan kitchen turn the finest local ingredients into gastronomic delights. The menu is extensive but pricey, even for lunch. All day, such tasty dishes as fish soup with rouille, Caesar or Thai chicken salad, tuna tartare, rotisserie chicken, and linguine with tomato-basil sauce and feta cheese are served in the oceanfront beach bar. At sunset, the casual daytime atmosphere turns trendy. You might start with an Oriental tasting plate or a half dozen oysters, followed by crispy roast duckling, grilled fish of the day, or lamb cutlets—or choose from one of dozens of other tasty land, sea, and vegetarian dishes. ⊠ *Lone Star Hotel, Hwy. 1, Mount Standfast, St. James* ☎ 246/419–0599 ⊕ *www.thelonestar.com* ☰ *AE, MC, V.*

$$$–$$$$ ✕ **The Mews.** *Continental.* Dining at the Mews is like being invited to a very chic friend's home for dinner. This restaurant once was, in fact, a private home. The front room is now an inviting bar, and an interior courtyard is an intimate, open-air dining area. The second floor is a maze of small dining rooms and dining balconies, but you've come for the food, after all. The international cuisine is presented with contemporary flair. A plump chicken breast, for example, will be stuffed with cream cheese, smoked salmon, and herb pâté and served on a garlic-and-chive sauce. A braised lamb shank is presented on a bed of cabbage with a port-thyme jus and creamed potatoes, and fillet of mahimahi is poached in a lemongrass, ginger, and cilantro broth. The warm molten chocolate cake is a must

for dessert. Some call the atmosphere avant-garde; others call it quaint. Everyone calls the food delicious. But don't stop at dinner; by about 10 PM, the bar begins to bustle. On weekends, the fun spills out into the street. ⊠ *2nd St., Holetown, St. James* ☎ *246/432–1122* ⚊ *Reservations essential* ⊟ *AE, MC, V* ⊘ *Closed Sun. No lunch.*

$$$-$$$$ ✕ **Olives Bar and Bistro.** *Caribbean.* This intimate restaurant, in a quaint Bajan residence in the center of Holetown, is a favorite west-coast dining spot of local professionals and visitors alike. Mediterranean and Caribbean flavors enliven inventive thin-crust pizzas and tasty salads; the dinner menu also includes fresh seafood, such as seared yellowfin tuna with ratatouille or pan-seared sea scallops with basmati rice and steamed greens. Vegetarian selections are always available. Dine inside, accompanied by the hint of soothing light jazz music, or in the courtyard; the upstairs bar is a popular spot to mingle over coffee, refreshing drinks, or snacks (pizza, pastas, salads). ⊠ *2nd St., Holetown, St. James* ☎ *246/432–2112* ⊟ *AE, D, MC, V* ⊘ *No lunch.*

$$-$$$ ✕ **Ragamuffins.** *Caribbean.* The only restaurant on Barbados in an authentic chattel house, Ragamuffins is tiny, funky, lively, and informal. The menu offers seafood, perfectly broiled T-bone steaks, West Indian curries, and vegetarian dishes such as Bajan stir-fried vegetables with noodles. Dine inside or out. The kitchen is within sight of the bar—which is a popular meeting spot most evenings for vacationers and locals alike. ⊠ *1st St., Holetown, St. James* ☎ *246/432–1295* ⊕ *www.ragamuffinsbarbados.com* ⚊ *Reservations essential* ⊟ *AE, D, MC, V* ⊘ *No lunch.*

$$-$$$ ✕ **Scarlet.** *Caribbean.* When you see a bright red building on the side of the road, you'll know you've found Scarlet. Movers and groovers come here in the evening to chill over a martini and share nibbles, such as a plate of flying-fish lollipops; or settle in after cocktails for a burger with sophisticated toppings, Bajan ham with corn pancakes, or perhaps Baxter's Road chicken. Enjoy your meal sitting at the large bar—the centerpiece of this casual but stylish watering hole—or at a nearby table. Specialty of the house: Scarlet Rocks (vodka, raspberry schnapps, strawberries, cranberry juice, basil, and black pepper!). ⊠ *Hwy. 1, Paynes Bay, St. James* ☎ *246/432–3663* ⚊ *Reservations essential* ⊟ *AE, MC, V* ⊘ *Closed Sun. and Mon. No lunch.*

★ Fodor'sChoice✕ **The Tides.** *Continental.* Local residents and $$$$ repeat visitors agree that the Tides is one of the island's best restaurants. Enter into a pretty courtyard and have a cocktail at the cozy bar or the coral-stone lounge in what was once a private mansion, then proceed to your seaside table. Perhaps the most intriguing feature of this stunning setting—besides the sound of waves crashing onto the shore just feet away—is the row of huge tree trunks growing right through the dining room. The food is equally dramatic. Chef Guy Beasley and his team give a contemporary twist to fresh seafood, fillet of beef, rack of lamb, and other top-of-the-line main courses by adding inspired sauces and delicate vegetables and garnishes. Save room for the sticky toffee pudding—definitely worth the calories. ⊠ *Balmore House, Hwy. 1, Holetown, St. James* ☎ *246/432–8356* ⊕ *www.tidesbarbados.com* ⚖ *Reservations essential* ⊟ *MC, V* ☻ *No lunch weekends.*

WHERE TO STAY

Most visitors stay on either the fashionable west coast, north of Bridgetown, or on the action-packed south coast. On the west coast, the beachfront resorts in St. Peter and St. James parishes are mostly luxurious, self-contained enclaves. Highway 1, a two-lane road with considerable traffic, runs past these resorts, which can make casual strolling to a nearby bar or restaurant difficult. Along the south coast, in Christ Church Parish, many hotels are clustered near the busy strip known as St. Lawrence Gap, convenient to dozens of small restaurants, bars, and nightclubs. On the much more remote east coast, a few small inns offer oceanfront views, cool breezes, and get-away-from-it-all tranquillity.

The lodgings listed below all have air-conditioning, telephones, and TVs in guest rooms unless otherwise noted.

VILLA AND CONDO COMPLEXES

Villa communities and condominium complexes, which are continually cropping up along the south and west coasts of Barbados, can be an economical option for families, groups, or couples vacationing together. Vacationers can rent individual units directly from property managers, just as you would reserve a hotel room. Units with fully equipped kitchens, two to six bedrooms, and as many baths run anywhere from $200 to $2,500 per night in the off-season—double that in winter.

Best Bets for Barbados Lodging

Fodor's offers a selective listing of quality lodging experiences, from the island's best boutique hotel to its most luxurious beach resort. Here, we've compiled our top recommendations based on the different types of lodging found on the island. The very best properties—in other words, those that provide a particularly remarkable experience—are designated in the listings with the Fodor's Choice logo.

Fodor's Choice: Accra Beach Hotel and Spa, Almond Beach Club and Spa, Almond Beach Village, Coral Reef Club, Hilton Barbados, Peach and Quiet, Sandpiper, Sandy Lane Hotel and Golf Club, Sweetfield Manor

Best Budget Stay: Accra Beach Hotel and Spa, Discovery Bay, Peach and Quiet, Round House, Sandy Bay Beach Club, Sea-U Guest House

Best Boutique Hotels: Cob-blers Cove Hotel, The House, Little Arches, Sweetfield Manor, Treasure Beach

Best Beachfront Resorts: Accra Beach Hotel and Spa, Almond Beach Village, Almond Casuarina Beach Resort, The Crane, Hilton Barbados, Sandy Lane Hotel and Golf Club, The Savannah, Silver Point, Tamarind Cove Hotel, Turtle Beach Resort

Best for Honeymooners: Almond Beach Club and Spa, Coral Reef Club, Fairmont Royal Pavilion, Sandy Lane Hotel and Golf Club

Best for Families: Almond Beach Village, Almond Casuarina Beach Resort, Barbados Beach Club, Bougainvillea Beach Resort, Hilton Barbados, Royal Westmoreland Villas, Sandy Lane Hotel and Golf Club, South Beach Resort, Tamarind Cove Hotel, Turtle Beach Resort

PRIVATE VILLAS AND CONDOS

Local real-estate agencies will arrange holiday rentals of privately owned villas and condos along the west coast in St. James and St. Peter. All villas and condos are fully furnished and equipped, including appropriate staff depending on the size of the villa or unit—which can range from one to eight bedrooms. Villa staffs usually works six days a week. Most villas have TVs, DVDs and/or VCRs, and CD players; all properties have telephones, and some have Internet access. International telephone calls are usually blocked; plan on using a phone card or calling card. Vehicles are generally not included in the rates, but rental cars can be arranged and delivered to the villa upon request. Linens and basic supplies (e.g., bath soap, toilet tissue, dishwashing detergent) are included.

Units with one to six bedrooms and as many baths run $200 to $2,500 per night in summer, and double that in winter. Rates include utilities and government taxes. The only additional cost is for groceries and staff gratuities. A security deposit is required upon booking and refunded seven days after departure less any damages or unpaid miscellaneous charges.

VILLA RENTAL AGENCIES

Altman Real Estate (⊠ Hwy. 1, Derricks, St. James ☎ 246/432–0840 or 866/360–5292 ⊕ www.aaaltman.com).

Bajan Services (⊠ Newton House, Battaleys, St. Peter ☎ 246/422–2618 or 866/978–5239 ⊕ www.bajanservices.com).

Island Villas (⊠ Trents Bldg., Holetown, St. James ☎ 246/432–4627 ⊕ www.island-villas.com).

PRIVATE APARTMENT RENTAL SOURCES

Apartments are available for holiday rentals in buildings or complexes that can have as few as 3 or 4 units or as many as 30 to 40 units—or even more. Prices range from $30 to $300 per night. The **Barbados Tourism Authority** (☎ 246/427–2623 ⊕ www.barbados.org) on Harbour Road in Bridgetown has a listing of apartments in prime resort areas on both the south and west coasts, complete with facilities offered and rates.

SOUTH COAST

Hotel locations in southern Barbados are plotted on the Southern Barbados map as well as the St. Lawrence Gap map.

★ Fodor's Choice ⚟ **Accra Beach Hotel and Spa.** *Resort.* An excel-
$$–$$$ lent choice if you prefer a full-service resort in the middle of the busy south coast, the Accra is large, it's modern, it faces a great beach, and it's competitively priced. Eight duplex penthouse suites—the priciest accommodations—face the sea. Most rooms overlook the large cloverleaf pool or the beach—and some of the oceanfront suites have hot tubs on the balconies. The more budget-minded can opt for the less-expensive "island-view" rooms, which face the street. It's not unusual to witness a local couple being married here, and the hotel is a popular meeting venue for local businesspeople. That shouldn't interrupt your

day lazing on the beach, mingling at the poolside swim-up bar, being pampered at the spa, or dining sumptuously at Wytukai (pronounced Y2K)—the island's only (so far) Polynesian restaurant. **Pros:** right on a great beach and, on the street side, near shopping, restaurants, and nightspots; terrific value; friendly staff. **Cons:** standard rooms are fairly ordinary—at least opt for accommodations with a pool or ocean view. ⊠ *Hwy. 7, Box 73W, Rockley, Christ Church BB15139* ☎ *246/435–8920* ⊕ *www.accrabeachhotel.com* ⇆ *188 rooms, 36 suites* ⚭ *In-room: safe, refrigerator (some), Internet. In-hotel: 3 restaurants, room service, bars, pool, gym, spa, beachfront, water sports, laundry service, Internet terminal* ⊟ *AE, D, MC, V.* ⦿ *EP.*

$$–$$$ 🖼 **Allamanda Beach Hotel.** *Hotel.* Located just opposite Hast-
☾ ings Plaza, a shopping center that has some duty-free shopping and a few eateries, all rooms at Allamanda Beach Hotel accommodate up to three people; the one-bedroom suites accommodate two adults and two children. All 50 units have good-size kitchenettes for preparing meals, making this a great choice for families. Units all have balconies with an ocean view, and most also overlook the pool. Guests may use the gym and spa at Amaryllis Beach Resort, a sister property just three minutes away in the Garrison area via the hotel's free shuttle. That resort also offers scuba diving, snorkeling, and nonmotorized water sports on beautiful Palm Beach that guests may use in addition to the pool and rather rocky beach at Allamanda. Guests can purchase one of the resort's meal plans, which range from a Continental or full breakfast each day to the full American plan (three meals a day) with or without beverages included. Those on a meal plan can also enjoy meals at Amaryllis at no extra charge. **Pros:** reasonably priced; self-catering option; friendly atmosphere. **Cons:** rooms (especially the kitchenettes) are ready for some attention; beach is better at sister hotel. ⊠ *Main Rd., Hastings, Christ Church* ☎ *246/438–1000* ⊕ *www.allamandabeach.com* ⇆ *48 rooms, 2 suites* ⚭ *In-room: kitchen, Wi-Fi. In-hotel: restaurant, room service, bar, pool, beachfront, laundry facilities, Internet terminal, Wi-Fi hotspot* ⊟ *AE, MC, V* ⦿ *EP.*

$$$$ 🖼 **Almond Casuarina Beach Resort.** *All-Inclusive.* One of three
☾ all-inclusive Almond properties in Barbados, this is the only one on the south coast. Blocks of accommodations surround a lush 8-acre garden of mature bamboo, palm, and fruit trees (and a few resident green monkeys). Rooms in a new beachfront building offer mesmerizing sea views; opportunities for dining, socializing, and water- and land

sports abound. Everything is included in the room rate—even windsurfing or sailing lessons and an all-day, every day Kids' Club. Guests also have full access to the dining, recreational, and entertainment facilities at Almond Beach Village in Speightstown and Almond Beach Club in St. James. **Pros:** great beach and beautiful garden; every amenity you could imagine; wonderful for kids. **Cons:** lots of good restaurants to try in nearby St. Lawrence Gap, but you've paid for an all-inclusive. ⊠ *St. Lawrence Gap, Dover, Christ Church* ☎ *246/428–3600* ⊕ *almondresorts.com* ➾ *280 rooms* ঙ *In-room: safe, Internet. In-hotel: 3 restaurants, room service, bars, tennis court, pools, gym, spa, beachfront, water sports, children's programs (ages infant–12), laundry service, Internet terminal, Wi-Fi hotspot* ⊟ *AE, MC, V* ⊙ *AI.*

$$$–$$$$ ⊡ **Barbados Beach Club.** *All-Inclusive.* Designed with families
ঙ in mind, this four-story hotel (with elevators) sits on a beautiful stretch of south-coast beach—and it offers tremendous value. For the price of your room, you get everything from beach volleyball to miniature golf and nature walks. If you like real golf, special packages are offered in conjunction with the nearby Barbados Golf Club. So grab a boogie board or a kayak and hit the water or take a scuba-diving lesson in the pool. Join the aerobics class in the pool or in the gym. Or sit by one of three pools (one for kids) and socialize while working on your tan. Meals are leisurely and informal at the Poolside Restaurant. At night the Sea Rocks Restaurant specializes in Caribbean seafood with a Mediterranean influence, while Veneto's is pure Italian. Children can eat early, and a staff member will watch the kids if parents want a special dinner alone at one of the restaurants. **Pros:** great beach; good value; wonderful for kids; golf package. **Cons:** limited access to fine-dining restaurants. ⊠ *Maxwell Coast Rd., Maxwell, Christ Church* ☎ *246/428–9900* ⊕ *www.barbadosbeachclub.com* ➾ *105 rooms, 2 penthouse suites* ঙ *In-room: safe, refrigerator, Wi-Fi. In-hotel: 3 restaurants, bars, tennis court, pool, gym, beachfront, diving, water sports, laundry service, children's program (ages 4–11), Internet terminal, Wi-Fi hotspot* ⊟ *AE, MC, V* ⊙ *AI.*

$$$ ⊡ **Bougainvillea Beach Resort.** *Vacation Rental.* Attractive
ঙ seaside town houses, with separate entrances, wrap around the pool or face the beachfront. Most important, the suites are huge compared to hotel suites elsewhere in this price range, are decorated in appealing Caribbean pastels, and have full kitchens. Each has a sitting area with a pullout

sofa—great for families with small kids. All suites have balconies or terraces that overlook either the pool and gardens or the sea. St. Lawrence Gap is a 15-minute westward stroll along the beach or a 20-minute walk along the road. The picturesque fishing village of Oistins is about the same distance in the opposite direction. Guests may have groceries delivered to their room or pre-stocked before arrival. You can even arrange a private cook, who will prepare Bajan specialties. Children under 15 stay free when sharing a room with adults. The minimum stay in high season is seven nights. **Pros:** great for families; easy stroll to St. Lawrence Gap or to Oistins; groceries pre-stocked upon request. **Cons:** bathrooms could use updating; sea can be rough for swimming. ⊠ *Maxwell Coast Rd., Maxwell, Christ Church* ☎ *246/418–0990* ⊕ *www.bougainvilleare-sort.com* ⇨ *138 suites* ⚹ *In-room: Internet, Wi-Fi. In-hotel: 2 restaurants, room service, bars, tennis court, pools, gym, spa, beachfront, water sports, children's programs (ages 3–12), laundry service, Internet terminal, Wi-Fi hotspot* ⊟ *D, MC, V* ⦿*EP.*

$–$$ ⊞ **Coconut Court Beach Hotel.** *Hotel.* This beachfront hotel is
♣ popular among families, particularly British families, who especially love the welcoming atmosphere, the activities room for kids, and the fact that children under 16 stay free (although there is also a maximum of three people to a room). What it really has going for it, though, is a marvelous location. Rooms stretch right along the beach, so the views and ocean breezes from the private balconies—all day and into the evening—are nothing short of spectacular. Accommodations are designated either rooms or studios—the main difference being that the rooms have a fridge, microwave, toaster, and electric kettle, while the studios have a full kitchenette with all the accouterments found in the rooms plus an oven and stove. **Pros:** beautiful beachfront; cooking facilities handy for snacks and light meals; Room 21 has the best ocean view. **Cons:** nothing luxurious here; rooms are rather simply decorated; restricted view in "west-wing" rooms. ⊠ *Main Rd., Hastings, Christ Church* ☎ *246/427–1655* ⊕ *www.coconut-court.com* ⇨ *112 rooms* ⚹ *In-room: safe (some), refrigerator (some), kitchen (some). In-hotel: restaurant, bars, pool, beachfront, children's program (ages 4–12), laundry service* ⊟ *AE, MC, V* ⦿*BP.*

$$$$ ⊞ **The Crane.** *Vacation Rental.* Hugging a seaside bluff on the southeast coast, the Crane is the island's oldest hotel in continuing operation. Today, the original coral-stone hotel building (1887) is the centerpiece of a luxurious,

40-acre villa complex that includes pools, restaurants, bars, and even a little village. Historic hotel rooms and apartments are decorated with original antiques, and corner suites have walls of windows and wraparound patios or balconies with panoramic views. The upscale private residences—in a half dozen modern high-rise buildings—are spacious, individually owned condos with hardwood floors, hand-carved four-poster beds, multiple bathrooms with spa showers, fully equipped kitchens, and private plunge pools. The Crane's original pool is a frequent backdrop for photo shoots, while a huge pool complex closer to the villas includes a spa pool, built in a cliff-top ruin with a 360-degree view, and a half dozen connecting pools and other water features. The adjacent old stable serves as a pool bar. Reef-protected Crane Beach is 98 steps (or an elevator ride) down the cliff. You'll need to rent a car if you expect to spend much time away from the resort grounds. The minimum stay is seven nights in high season; three nights during the rest of the year. **Pros:** enchanting view; lovely beach; fabulous suites; great restaurants. **Cons:** remote location; rental car recommended; service tends to be aloof. ⊠ *Crane Bay, St. Philip* ☎ *246/423–6220* ⊕ *www. thecrane.com* ⇨ *4 rooms, 14 suites, 202 villas* ⚭ *In-room: safe, kitchen (some), refrigerator, DVD (some), Internet, Wi-Fi (some). In-hotel: 3 restaurants, room service, bars, tennis courts, pools, gym, spa, beachfront, laundry facilities (some), laundry service, Internet terminal, Wi-Fi hotspot* ⊟ *AE, MC, V* ⏏ *EP.*

$$$$ ⛶ **Divi Southwinds Beach Resort.** *Resort.* The all-suites Divi
☾ Southwinds is situated on 20 acres of lawn and gardens bisected by action-packed St. Lawrence Gap. The bulk of the suites are north of the Gap in a large, unspectacular three-story building offering garden and pool views. The property south of the Gap wraps around a stunning 0.5 mi (1 km) of Dover Beach, where 16 beach villas provide an intimate setting steps from the sand. Whichever location you choose, all suites have separate bedrooms, sofa beds in the sitting room, and full kitchens. It's all within walking distance of lots of shops, restaurants, and nightspots. Kids under 15 stay free in their parents' suite. **Pros:** beautiful beach; beach villas are the best value; close to shopping, restaurants, and nightspots. **Cons:** few water sports available and none included; some rooms aching for renovations; comparatively pricey for the value received. ⊠ *St. Lawrence Main Rd., Dover, Christ Church* ☎ *246/428–7181* ⊕ *www. divisouthwinds.com* ⇨ *121 1-bedroom suites, 12 2-bed-*

room suites ⅋ *In-room: kitchen. In-hotel: 2 restaurants, bars, tennis courts, pools, gym, beachfront, laundry facilities, Internet terminal* ⊟ *AE, D, DC, MC, V* ⏀ *EP.*

★ Fodor'sChoice ⊠ **Hilton Barbados.** *Resort.* Beautifully situated on
$$$$ the sandy Needham's Point peninsula, the Hilton Barbados
☾ is minutes from Bridgetown. All 350 rooms and suites in this high-rise have private balconies overlooking either the ocean or Carlisle Bay; 77 rooms are on executive floors, with a private lounge and concierge services. Meetings are big business here, as the property has the largest hotel meeting space in Barbados. The broad white-sand beach, the sprawling bi-level pool complex, and a host of activities on land and sea make this a hit with vacationing families as well. Children under 18 stay free in a room with adults, children ages 4–12 get a break on meals, and children under 5 eat for free—and parents get one complimentary night of babysitting with a three-night stay. **Pros:** great location near town and on a beautiful beach; excellent accommodations; lots of services and amenities; frequent promotional deals provide real value. **Cons:** huge convention hotel; attracts groups; not much island flavor. ⊠ *Needham's Point, Aquatic Gap, St. Michael* ☎ *246/426–0200* ⊕ *www.hiltoncaribbean. com* ⫷*317 rooms, 33 suites* ⅋ *In-room: safe, Internet, Wi-Fi. In-hotel: 3 restaurants, room service, bars, tennis courts, pools, gym, water sports, children's programs (ages 4–12), some pets allowed, Internet terminal, Wi-Fi hotspot* ⊟ *AE, D, MC, V* ⏀ *EP.*

$$ ⊠ **Hotel PomMarine.** *Hotel.* And now for something completely different—Hotel PomMarine is part of the Hospitality Institute of Barbados Community College and staffed by its students. The 20 simple yet comfortable rooms and one self-catering suite here are obviously a popular choice of visiting parents, but also of local businesspeople who know value when they see it. You're wondering about the unusual name? The hotel sits on the former site of the Marine and Pomeroy hotels. The goal in building it was to combine hands-on student training with a functioning hotel, and so Hotel PomMarine opened in 1997. Enjoy the pool, tennis court, a light meal at the Golden Apple Café, exquisite dining at Muscovado Restaurant—and perhaps observe students working in a demo kitchen. Hastings Beach is across the street. **Pros:** cooking demonstrations; great restaurant; a whole different hotel experience. **Cons:** five-minute walk to the beach; rooms are rather ordinary; no "vacation" atmosphere. ⊠ *Barbados Community College, Marine Gardens, Hastings, Christ Church* ☎ *246/228–0900*

⊕ *www.pommarine.com* ⌁ *20 rooms, 1 suite* ⌂ *In-room: safe, kitchen (1). In-hotel: 2 restaurants, bars, pool, tennis court, Internet terminal* ▭ *AE, D, DC, MC, V* ⊚*EP.*

$$$ ⊡ **Little Arches Hotel.** *Hotel.* Just east of the picturesque fishing village of Oistins, this classy boutique hotel has a distinctly Mediterranean ambience and a perfect vantage point overlooking the sea. Beautifully appointed rooms are decorated with Italian fabrics, local pottery, and terrazzo flooring. Bathrooms have showers only, but the sinks are locally made earthenware. The pool is on the roof, alongside the open-air Café Luna restaurant. The Union Island and Palm Island suites each have a kitchen and a large, oceanfront patio with a private hot tub. Guests who book a 10-day stay are entitled to a choice of a complimentary round of golf at the Barbados Golf Club, an in-room champagne breakfast and massage, or a fully catered day sail. We recommend you leave the kids home if you're staying here, as Little Arches offers pure romance. **Pros:** stylish accommodations; great restaurant; across from fabulous Miami Beach. **Cons:** fairly remote; rental car advised. ⊠ *Enterprise Coast Rd., Enterprise, Christ Church* ☎ *246/420–4689* ⊕ *www.littlearches. com* ⌁ *8 rooms, 2 suites* ⌂ *In-room: safe, kitchen (some), Internet. In-hotel: restaurant, bar, pool, bicycles, laundry service, Internet terminal* ▭ *MC, V* ⊚*EP.*

★ **Fodor's**Choice⊡ **Peach and Quiet.** *Inn.* Forego the flashy accou-
$ trements of a resort and, instead, claim one of the stylish suites in this small seaside inn. With no in-room noisemakers and no children around, the only sounds you will hear are the gentle surf and your own conversations. Hands-on British owners Adrian and Margaret Loveridge have been running Peach since 1988 and are constantly renovating and refurbishing the property—perhaps one reason it's closed half the year. Decor in the spacious suites, arranged in whitewashed Mykonos-inspired buildings, is elegantly spare. Cooled by ceiling fans, each suite also has a large terrace or balcony; however, bathrooms have showers only. Besides lazing in the freshwater pool and windsurfing at nearby beaches (a five-minute walk), guests enjoy swimming and snorkeling in a natural "rock pool," joining early-morning or late-afternoon walks, and stargazing at night. You're advised to rent a car. **Pros:** the rates alone make this inn a great choice; peace and quiet; adults-only environment; engaging owners; stargazing and nature walks are special treats. **Cons:** inn is closed half of the year; remote location requires a rental car. ⊠ *Inch Marlow Main Rd., Inch Marlow, Christ Church* ☎ *246/428–5682*

⊕ *www.peachandquiet.com* ⇆ *22 suites* ⚹ *In-room: no a/c, no phone, safe, refrigerator, no TV. In-hotel: restaurant, bar, pool, beachfront, Wi-Fi, no kids under 12* ⊟ *D, MC, V* ⊙ *Closed May–Oct.* ⦿*EP.*

$$ ⊡ **Sandy Bay Beach Club.** *All-Inclusive.* Broad Sandy Beach is the main attraction here, along with the resort's close proximity to south-coast shops, restaurants, nightspots, and attractions. The hotel is within walking distance of St. Lawrence Gap. Guest rooms are in three buildings, arranged in a horseshoe around a large freshwater pool. Most rooms have an ocean view; end units face the broad white-sand beach and have an extraordinary view of the sea. The beach is protected by an offshore reef, so the sea is usually very calm. A full-time activities director will make sure you have plenty to do—or you can opt to have do nothing but relax and soak up the sun. Guests have breakfast, lunch, and dinner at the Quartermaster, a casual restaurant by day and informal eatery at night. In addition, they may reserve one dinner per week at Hidden Treasure, which offers an à la carte menu of international cuisine and Bajan specialties. Sandy Bay is on a main bus route, making it easy to get to Bridgetown and back or to any spot along the south coast. The hotel's parent company is part-owner of the Barbados Golf Club, an 18-hole public golf course that's a 12-minute drive from Sandy Bay, and guests get a discount on green fees there. The 9-hole Rockley Golf Course, however, is just two minutes away. **Pros:** on one of the best south-coast beaches; plenty of water sports; golf discounts; interesting sightseeing within walking distance. **Cons:** limited access to fine-dining restaurant; definitely don't confuse this hotel with Sandy Lane! ⊠ *Main Rd., Worthing, Christ Church* ☎*246/435–8000* ⊕ *www.sandybaybeachclub.com* ⇆*41 rooms, 89 suites* ⚹ *In-room: safe, refrigerator, kitchen (some), Internet. In-hotel: 2 restaurants, bars, pool, beachfront, water sports, Internet terminal* ⊟*AE, MC, V* ⦿*AI.*

$$$ ⊡ **The Savannah.** *Hotel.* Convenient, comfortable, and appealing to independent travelers who don't need organized entertainment, the Savannah is nevertheless perfectly situated for walks to the Garrison historic area, the Barbados Museum, and the racetrack—and minutes from Bridgetown by car or taxi. Two modern wings spill down to the beach from the main building, once the historic Sea View Hotel. Definitely opt for a room in one of the modern wings, which overlook a lagoon-style pool that flows between them in graduated steps, from a waterfall at the

Coral Reef Club, luxury cottage

Sweetfield Manor

Peach and Quiet

Hilton Barbados Executive Lounge

Sandy Lane Hotel

higher end to a more traditional pool by the beach; the oceanfront duplex suites at each end are superb. A favorite of local businesspeople, Boucan Restaurant is a buzz of activity at lunchtime. **Pros:** right on the beach; inviting pool; convenient to Bridgetown and sites. **Cons:** not a good choice for kids; rather dreary interior hallways. ⊠ *Garrison Main Rd., Hastings, Christ Church* ☎ *246/435–9473* ⊕ *www. gemsbarbados.com* ⊐ *90 rooms, 8 suites* ⚹ *In-room: safe, refrigerator, Wi-Fi. In-hotel: 2 restaurants, room service, bars, pools, gym, spa, beachfront, laundry service, Internet terminal, Wi-Fi hotspot* ⊟ *AE, D, MC, V* ⦿*CP.*

$$$ ⊺ **Silver Point.** *Vacation Rental.* This gated community of modern condos at Silver Sands–Silver Rock Beach is operated as a trendy boutique hotel. Suites are decorated in sleek, neutral colors with dark mahogany furnishings. Each unit has coral-stone accents, cedar closets, and an iPod dock; kitchens and baths have granite and marble countertops. Guests may also mingle at the bar and dine on Caribbean cuisine at the two-story, open-deck bar and restaurant. Silver Point is perfect for those who like something chic yet fairly remote and secluded—and for those who know that Silver Sands–Silver Rock Beach is the best place for windsurfing and kite surfing. The hotel, which overlooks the beach, offers a special windsurfing package that includes lessons and plenty of time on the water. **Pros:** stylish suites; perfect location for windsurfers; gated community. **Cons:** not within walking distance of anything except the beach; sea can be rough for swimming; rental car recommended. ⊠ *Silver Sands-Silver Rock Beach, Christ Church* ☎ *246/420–4416* ⊕ *www.silverpointhotel.com* ⊐ *58 suites* ⚹ *In-room: kitchen (some), DVD, Wi-Fi. In-hotel: 2 restaurants, bar, pools, gym, spa, beachfront, water sports, laundry facilities, Internet terminal, Wi-Fi hotspot* ⊟ *AE, MC, V* ⦿*EP.*

$$ ⊺ **Silver Sands Hotel.** *Hotel.* The sometimes congested lobby is a little deceiving, for Silver Sands sprawls out over 12 acres of gardens and along a significant strip of Silver Sands Beach. But back to the busy lobby—British tour groups of 100 or more arrive twice a month for two-week holidays—and they are a rather young, beach-loving crowd. Many guests choose this location for its proximity to optimum windsurfing beaches. This is also a favorite layover hotel for the airlines because it's so convenient to the airport. So even though the accommodations themselves are rather ordinary, the hotel is often full of guests—who all seem to be enjoying themselves to the fullest. Families enjoy the suites and studios, because they have kitchens and kids under 12 share the accommodations for free. Guests can purchase a SmartCard to use in the restaurants, bar, beauty salon, boutique, and minimart. **Pros:** tour groups and young people love this place; great windsurfing venue; nice pool and beach. **Cons:** basic accommodations; very busy place. ⊠ *Silver Sands, Christ Church* ☎ *246/428–6001* ⊕ *www. silversandsbarbados.com* ⇋ *41 rooms, 89 suites* ⌂ *In-room: kitchen (some), Wi-Fi. In-hotel: 2 restaurants, bar, tennis court, pools, gym, beachfront, laundry facilities, Internet terminal, Wi-Fi hotspot* ⊟ *AE, MC, V* ⊚ *EP.*

$$–$$$ ⊡ **South Beach Resort.** *Vacation Rental.* This resort is actually ⟳ a time-share vacation club, but it's run like a hotel—a very cool hotel indeed. The entrance here is certainly dramatic— and very much in the style of South Beach (although the one in Miami). To enter the sleek lobby, guests cross a double-wide lap pool via a footbridge. Rooms are decorated with quality furniture and fabrics, and the bathrooms are ultramodern. All rooms and suites have an eating area and a pullout sofa in the sitting area, making the accommodations suitable for parents and a couple of kids. Children under 12 are free when staying in the same room as adults. Accra (Rockley) Beach is just across the street, where beach chairs, water-sports equipment, and other beach toys—as well as drinks and snacks—can be rented or purchased. The restaurant serves breakfast only—either indoors or poolside. For other meals, the surrounding area is filled with restaurants offering everything from fast food to fine dining. And, of course, each unit has a kitchen. **Pros:** beautiful bathrooms; Accra Beach is great for families; Wi-Fi everywhere. **Cons:** more a hotel than a resort; on-site restaurant only serves breakfast; beach is across the street. ⊠ *Main Rd., Rockley, Christ Church* ☎ *246/435–8561* ⊕ *www.southbeachbarbados.com* ⇋ *22 rooms, 25 suites* ⌂ *In-room: kitchen, Wi-Fi. In-hotel: restaurant, room service, bar, pool, laundry facilities, Internet terminal, Wi-Fi hotspot* ⊟ *AE, MC, V* ⊚ *EP.*

$$$ ⊡ **Southern Palms Beach Club.** *Resort.* This resort is pretty ⟳ in pink, you might say. The pink, plantation-style main building opens onto an inviting pool area and 1,000 feet of white sandy beach. Rooms and suites are attractive and spacious. The duplex suites are a good choice for families, as kids under 12 stay free. All accommodations have either a balcony or patio, where you can enjoy the ocean breeze or simply stare out to sea. Friendly, low-key, and peaceful are good descriptions of the day-to-day atmosphere. Play miniature golf or shuffleboard with the kids, learn to windsurf, take a scuba lesson in the pool, join a beach volleyball game, grab a boogie board or perhaps a tennis racquet, or hit the gym—you choose. In the evening, live local bands entertain the after-dinner crowd, and a steel band accompanies the Sunday buffet lunch. **Pros:** friendly and accommodating staff; close to lots of restaurants and entertainment; nice beach. **Cons:** rooms are large and clean but dated; beach vendors can be a nuisance (not the hotel's fault). ⊠ *St. Lawrence Gap, Dover, Christ Church* ☎ *246/428–7171* ⊕ *www. southernpalms.net* ⬐ *72 rooms, 20 suites* ⌂ *In-room: safe, kitchen (some), Wi-Fi. In-hotel: restaurant, room service, bar, tennis courts, pools, gym, beachfront, water sports, laundry facilities, laundry service, Internet terminal, Wi-Fi hotspot* ⊟ *AE, MC, V* ⌾ *EP.*

★ **Fodor's** Choice ⛤ **Sweetfield Manor.** *B&B.* George and Ann
$$–$$$ Clarke transformed a decrepit manse (circa 1900) perched on a ridge about 1 mi (2 km) from Bridgetown—the former residence of the Dutch ambassador to Barbados—into the island's most delightful bed-and-breakfast inn. The main rooms, which are all available to guests along with the six guest rooms and carriage house suite, are individually furnished with antiques and art—much of it the work of Ann Clarke. She also prepares a fabulous gourmet breakfast each morning—fresh-squeezed juices, tasty egg dishes, and home-baked treats—served either in the large formal dining room, on the sunporch, or under a leafy mahogany tree in the garden. Tropical trees and plans surround a small pool tucked into the broad lawn. Enjoy the view, read a book, play cards or games, have a pleasant conversation. It's a perfect setting to just relax. **Pros:** peaceful enclave primarily suitable for adults; inviting pool and gardens; friendly innkeepers; delicious gourmet breakfast; perfect wedding venue. **Cons:** long walk to beach; rental car advised; not the best choice for kids. ⊠ *Britton New Rd., Brittons Hill, St. Michael* ☎ *246/429–8356* ⊕ *www.sweetfieldmanor.com* ⬐ *6 rooms, 4 with baths; 1 suite* ⌂ *In-room: no phone, safe, no TV, Wi-Fi (some). In-hotel: bar, pool, Wi-Fi hotspot* ⊟ *AE, D, MC, V* ⌾ *BP.*

$$$$ ⛤ **Turtle Beach Resort.** *All-Inclusive.* Families flock to Turtle
☾ Beach because it offers large, bright suites and enough all-included activities for everyone to enjoy. The Tommy Turtle Kids' Club keeps children busy with treasure hunts, supervised swims, games, and other activities from 9 AM to 9 PM each day. That gives parents a chance to play tennis, learn to windsurf or sail, relax at the beach, join the daily

2

shopping excursion to Bridgetown, or enjoy a dinner for two at Asagio's Restaurant. Families also have good times together—cooling off in the three pools, riding the waves on boogie boards, dining buffet style at open-to-the-view Chelonia Restaurant, or having a casual meal at the Waterfront Grill. **Pros:** perfect for family vacations; nice pools, roomy accommodations, lots of services and amenities. **Cons:** beach is fairly narrow and congested compared to other south-coast resorts; open vent between room and hallway can be noisy at night. ⊠ *St. Lawrence Gap, Dover, Christ Church* ☎ *246/428–7131* ⊕ *www.turtlebeachresort-barbados.com* ⇆ *164 suites* ⌂ *In-room: safe, refrigerator, Internet. In-hotel: 3 restaurants, room service, bars, tennis courts, pools, gym, spa, beachfront, diving, water sports, bicycles, children's programs (ages 3–12), laundry service, Internet terminal* ⊟ *AE, MC, V* ⼝ *AI.*

DID YOU KNOW? Portuguese explorer Pedro a Campos is credited with naming Barbados. In 1536, when he stopped by the island en route to Brazil, he and his crew were intrigued by the bearded appearance of the indigenous fig trees. "Os Barbados," or "the bearded ones," he proclaimed—and the name stuck.

EAST COAST

Hotel locations on the east coast are plotted on the Central Barbados map.

$–$$ ▦ **New Edgewater Hotel.** *Hotel.* This seaside outpost overlooking a 9-mi (14-km) stretch of the stunning east coast has been a cliffside retreat since the 1700s. Today the hotel is comparatively rustic and attracts guests who are content with taking a walk or curling up with a good book, as well as surfers who like the location near Bathsheba Beach and its famous Soup Bowl. As if that's not enough natural beauty, the western side of the hotel backs up against Joe's River and the 85-acre Joe's River Tropical Rainforest, complete with trails through the hills, gullies, and dense foliage. All but two rooms have a partial or full ocean view, and many have balconies. The view from Room 222 is particularly amazing. A previous owner made, by hand, all of the sturdy mahogany furniture in the hotel—and there's lots of it. You'll marvel at the parquet ceilings and magnificent leaded-glass windows throughout the hotel—and the pool that's shaped like Barbados. **Pros:** spectacular setting; surfers' paradise; quite and peaceful; nice pool area. **Cons:** remote location; no nearby beach for

swimming; don't expect luxury; public bathroom needs some attention. ⊠ *Bathsheba Beach, Bathsheba, St. Joseph* ☎ *246/433–9900* ⊕ *www.newedgewater.com* ⌁ *20 rooms, 4 suites* ⌂ *In-room: refrigerator, Internet. In-hotel: restaurant, bar, pool* ⊟ *AE, MC, V* ⍾ *CP.*

$–$$ ⛫ **Round House Inn.** *Inn.* It's hard to tell which is more appealing: the view of the rugged coastline or the magnificent historic (1832) manse strategically perched on the cliff to take advantage of the view. Guest rooms are tastefully decorated in subdued colors and furnished in a simple style—a clean, contemporary look without being "moderne." Each room has a great view of the ocean, and some rooms look out onto the pretty courtyard. Room No. 3 opens to a large sundeck with a small plunge pool. Although few activities are offered on the property itself, snorkeling, diving, horseback riding, hiking, and, of course, surfing at nearby Bathsheba Soup Bowl can be arranged. This cozy little enclave is owned and operated by Robert and Gail Manley, who also oversee what has become one of the most popular dining establishments on the east coast. **Pros:** beautiful east-coast views; lovely accommodations; waterfront; excellent restaurant; small and intimate. **Cons:** remote location; no TV (if you care); walk to the beach, where you can only surf or wade. ⊠ *Bathsheba, St. Joseph* ☎ *246/433–9678* ⊕ *www. roundhousebarbados.com* ⌁ *6 rooms* ⌂ *In-room: no a/c, no phone (some), safe, no TV (some). In-hotel: restaurant, bar, pools* ⊟ *AE, D, MC, V* ⍾ *EP.*

$–$$ ⛫ **Sea-U Guest House.** *Inn.* Uschi Wetzels, a German travel writer in an earlier life, became smitten with the wild and woolly east coast of Barbados while on assignment and returned in 1999 to build this tiny guesthouse. The main house, where she also lives with her daughter, is built in the traditional wooden colonial style. Its four simple guest rooms, each with a kitchenette, are cooled by ceiling fans and sea breezes. A cottage next door has two air-conditioned studios, also with kitchenettes, that can be connected to become a large suite. The property, perched on a cliff overlooking the sea, is thick with palm trees and other tropical foliage. A casual restaurant offers a full breakfast each day and a three-course, fixed-price (inexpensive) dinner three nights a week prepared by Wetzels and her Bajan chef. The honor bar, which you settle upon checkout, is a gathering place for guests each evening—and sometimes in the afternoon. During the day, though, guests are more likely to while away their time in a hammock, wander down to Bathsheba Beach for a dip in the tidal pools, or walk over to nearby Andromeda Botanical Gardens. **Pros:** peaceful and relaxing; couldn't be friendlier; there's Wi-Fi. **Cons:** simple accommodations; few amenities; remote location. ⊠ *Tent Bay, Bathsheba, St. Joseph* ☎ *246/433–9450* ⊕ *www.seaubarbados.com* ⌁ *6 rooms* ⚭ *In-room: no a/c (some), no phone, kitchen, no TV, Wi-Fi. In-hotel: restaurant, bar, Wi-Fi hotspot* ⊟ *MC, V* ⓘ⃝ *BP.*

WEST COAST

Hotel locations on the west coast are plotted on the Holetown and Vicinity and Northern Barbados maps.

$$ 🏨 **All Seasons Resort–Europa.** *Vacation Rental.* In the middle of Sunset Crest, a cottage community originally developed as an inexpensive holiday village for Canadian vacationers, All Seasons Resort–Europa is a group of duplex self-catering cottages that surround a large grassy lawn, a pool with three Jacuzzis, a recreation room, and a restaurant and bar. Accommodations are rather simple and priced accordingly. Shuttle service to the beach and shops is free. The hotel boasts a huge number of repeat guests, some who have been coming back for 10 or 15 years and who stay for several weeks and even months at a time. They obviously like the friendly, holiday camp atmosphere. **Pros:** inexpensive; good for long stays; congenial atmosphere, like a holiday camp. **Cons:** must shuttle to beach and to Holetown; rooms are simple but have kitchens and sitting areas. ⊠ *Palm Ave., Sunset Crest, St. James* ☎ *246/432–5046* ⊕ *www.allseasonsresort.bb* ⌁ *48 apartments* ⚭ *In-room: safe, kitchen, Wi-Fi. In-hotel: restaurant, bar, tennis court, pool, laundry service, Internet terminal, Wi-Fi hotspot* ⊟ *MC, V* ⓘ⃝ *EP.*

★ Fodor'sChoice 🏨 **Almond Beach Club and Spa.** *All-Inclusive.*
$$$$ Among several similar beachfront resorts south of Holetown, Almond Beach Club distinguishes itself as an adults-only environment with all-inclusive rates (only spa and salon services are extra) and reciprocal guest privileges (including shuttle service) at its enormous sister resorts, Almond Beach Village and Almond Casuarina. A horseshoe of rooms and suites faces the sea, although most units overlook the pools and gardens. Some suites facing the sea have no fourth wall, creating an airy, open-to-the-view environment. Lavish breakfast buffets, four-course lunches, afternoon teas, and intimate dinners are served in the main dining room—or you can dine on seafood at Water's Edge or West Indian cuisine at Enid's, the colorful Bajan restau-

rant that also offers free cooking classes. **Pros:** adults only; intimate atmosphere; short walk to Holetown; next door to Sandy Lane Beach. **Cons:** beach erodes to almost nothing at certain times of the year—usually the result of fall storms. ✉ *Hwy. 1, Vauxhall, St. James* ☎ *246/432–7840* ⊕ *www. almondresorts.com* ⤺ *133 rooms, 28 suites* ⚐ *In-room: safe, refrigerator (some). In-hotel: 3 restaurants, room service, bars, pools, gym, spa, beachfront, water sports, Wi-Fi hotspot, no kids under 16* ⊟ *AE, MC, V* ⦿ *AI.*

★ **Fodor's**Choice ⛬ **Almond Beach Village.** *All-Inclusive.* Barbados's
$$$$ premier family resort is massive enough to be a popular
☾ conference venue and romantic enough to host intimate weddings. Situated on an 18th-century sugar plantation north of Speightstown, the Village's 32 acres front a mile-long, powdery beach. Rooms and pools at the north end of the property, near a historic sugar mill, are reserved for adults; at the south end, junior and one-bedroom suites targeted to families with children are close to special facilities for kids and teens. A plethora of activities—golf (on the resort's 9-hole executive course), sailing, waterskiing, shopping excursions to Bridgetown, an off-site Bajan picnic, and more—are all included. Not enough? Hop the shuttle to Almond Beach Club and enjoy the (adults-only) facilities there—or venture to the south coast and spend the day at Almond Casuarina. **Pros:** family resort with certain areas for adults only; lots to do and all included, including complimentary Bajan cooking lessons; sugar mill is a picturesque wedding venue. **Cons:** it's huge; more emphasis might be placed on room renovations and less on expansion. ✉ *Hwy. 1B, Heywoods, St. Peter* ☎ *246/422–4900* ⊕ *www. almondresorts.com* ⤺ *373 rooms, 29 suites* ⚐ *In-room: safe, refrigerator. In-hotel: 4 restaurants, room service, bars, golf course, tennis courts, pools, gym, spa, beachfront, water sports, children's programs (ages infant–17), laundry facilities, laundry service, Internet terminal, Wi-Fi hotspot* ⊟ *AE, MC, V* ⦿ *AI.*

$$$$ ⛬ **Azzurro at Old Trees Bay.** *Private Villa.* The west coast of Barbados is alive with condo construction, and Old Trees Bay has a spot-on beachfront location just south of Sandy Lane Hotel. Azzurro is a spacious, two-bedroom Old Trees Bay residence with magnificent water views from the living room, dining room, and master bedroom terraces. The second bedroom has two double beds, so the apartment sleeps four very comfortably. It's fully equipped with all the comforts of home—plus a private plunge pool incorporated into the living room. In addition, the garden

area has a communal swimming pool. The staff, which includes a cook and a maid/laundress, works mornings and evenings. The residence is managed and rented by Altman Real Estate. **Pros:** lovely location with beautiful water views; close to shopping and restaurants. **Cons:** beach can be narrow at certain times of year. ⊠ *Hwy. 1, Paynes Bay, St. James* ⊕ *www.aaaltman.com* ➘ *2 bedrooms, 2 baths* ⚷ *Safe, dishwasher, VCR, daily maid service, cook, on-site security, pools, beachfront, laundry facilities* ⊟ *AE, MC, V* ⏐⊙⏐ *EP.*

$$$$ ⛱ **Cobblers Cove Hotel.** *Resort.* "English Country" best describes the style of this lovely resort favored by British sophisticates. Flanked by tropical gardens on one side and the sea on the other, each elegant suite has a comfy sitting room with a sofa bed and a wall of louvered shutters that open onto a patio, a trouser press, and a small library of books. For all-out luxury, the sublime (and enormous) Colleton and Camelot penthouse suites each have a richly decorated sitting room, king-size four-poster bed, dressing room, whirlpool bath, private sundeck, and large plunge pool. Socializing occurs in the library, which doubles as a TV lounge, and at the alfresco restaurant, which receives well-deserved raves for superb dining. **Pros:** very classy establishment; lovely grounds; the penthouse suites are amazing; very quiet. **Cons:** too quiet for some; only bedrooms have a/c. ⊠ *Road View, Speightstown, St. Peter* ☎ *246/422–2291* ⊕ *www.cobblerscove.com* ➘ *40 suites* ⚷ *In-room: safe, refrigerator, no TV, Internet, Wi-Fi. In-hotel: restaurant, room service, bar, tennis court, pool, gym, spa, beachfront, water sports, children's programs (ages 2–12), Internet terminal, Wi-Fi hotspot, no kids under 12 (Jan.–Mar.)* ⊟ *AE, D, MC, V* ⏐⊙⏐ *BP.*

$$$$ ⛱ **Colony Club Hotel.** *Resort.* As the signature hotel of five Elegant Hotel properties on Barbados, the Colony Club is certainly elegant—but with a quiet, friendly, understated style. A lagoon pool meanders through 7 acres of gardens, and 20 rooms have private access to the lagoon directly from their patios. Relax on the beach, soak in one of four pools, and enjoy an exquisite meal in the air-conditioned Orchids restaurant or a more informal repast at the open-air Laguna Restaurant. Nonmotorized water sports, an in-pool scuba-diving lesson, and tennis are all included. A free water taxi provides transportation to two sister hotels located along the west coast. **Pros:** clubby atmosphere; some rooms open directly onto the lagoon pool. **Cons:** relatively pricey; beach comes and goes depending on storms. ⊠ *Hwy.*

1, Porters, St. James ☎ *246/422–2335* ⊕ *www.colonyclub-hotel.com* ↩ *64 rooms, 32 junior suites* ⅃ *In-room: safe, refrigerator, DVD. In-hotel: 2 restaurants, room service, bars, tennis courts, pools, gym, spa, beachfront, water sports, laundry service, Internet terminal, no kids under 12 (Feb.)* ⊟ *AE, MC, V* ⊚ *EP.*

★ Fodor'sChoice ⛱ **Coral Reef Club.** *Resort.* The upscale Coral Reef
✪✪✪✪ Club offers the epitome of elegance and style, along with a welcoming, informal atmosphere. Individually designed suites are in pristine coral-stone manses and cottages scattered over 12½ acres of flower-filled gardens; the public areas ramble along the waterfront. Spend your days at the beach or around the pool, taking time out for afternoon tea. Garden rooms suit one or two guests and have a small patio or balcony, while junior suites have sitting areas and larger patios or balconies. Luxury cottage suites each have a plunge pool, bedroom, and separate living room with a sofa bed, making them perfect for families. After 7:30 PM, however, kids are not welcome in the dining room. The five pricey Plantation suites and two villas have spacious living rooms, private sundecks and plunge pools, and stereos— and are the only accommodations here that come with TVs (though you can get one for an added charge). Mingle at the bar before dining in the excellent terrace restaurant. **Pros:** absolutely delightful; elegant yet informal; beautiful suites with huge verandahs; delicious dining; six computers available to guests for free Internet access. **Cons:** no room TVs (if that matters); narrow beach sometimes disappears depending on the seasonal weather. ✉ *Hwy. 1, Porters, St. James* ☎ *246/422–2372* ⊕ *www.coralreefbarbados.com* ↩ *29 rooms, 57 suites, 2 villas* ⅃ *In-room: safe, refrigerator, no TV (some), Internet, Wi-Fi. In-hotel: restaurant, room service, bar, tennis courts, pools, gym, spa, beachfront, diving, water sports, children's programs (ages 2–8), Internet terminal, Wi-Fi hotspot, no kids under 12 (Jan. 15–Mar. 15)* ⊟ *AE, MC, V* ⊘ *Closed June* ⊚ *BP.*

$$$$ ⛱ **Crystal Cove Hotel.** *All-Inclusive.* Crystal Cove is a colony of attached duplex whitewashed cottages that are trimmed in the perky pastels typical of the Caribbean. Each room is bright and spacious with a balcony or patio. Most have hammocks and a water view; some are literally inches from the beach. Winding garden paths connect the units, which spill down a hillside to the beach where you can swim, sail, snorkel, water-ski, windsurf, or kayak to your heart's content—or play tennis, dip in the pool, or take advantage of preferred tee times at Royal Westmoreland

Golf Course and Country Club. Meals are bountiful and delicious—buffets and snacks at Drifters Beach Bar and a table-d'hôte menu at Reflections Restaurant. Each night there's entertainment in the form of a steel band or other live music. For change of scene, a free water taxi travels all day long (weather permitting) between the three sister properties on the west coast. Crystal Cove guests can also participate in a dine-around program with those resorts. **Pros:** rooms are large and comfortable; good food; nice beach; exchange dining program with sister resorts. **Cons:** not much available immediately outside the resort. ⊠ *Hwy. 1, Appleby, St. James* ☎ *246/432–2683* ⊕ *www.crystalcove-hotelbarbados.com* ⇨ *62 rooms, 26 suites* ⚬ *In-room: safe, refrigerator. In-hotel: 2 restaurants, room service, bars, tennis courts, pools, gym, beachfront, water sports, children's programs (ages 3–11), laundry service, Internet terminal* ⊟ *AE, DC, MC, V* ⋈ *AI.*

$$$$ ⊡ **Crystal Springs.** *Private Villa.* Ideal for a large group or
⟳ family reunion, Crystal Springs is a fabulous beachfront estate near Holetown that sleeps 16 people in the main house and several outbuildings. This is one of the few remaining properties that were redesigned by Britain's celebrated theatrical designer Oliver Messel in the 1960s. Elegant murals grace the ceiling of the dining terrace, which opens to the garden and is perfect for alfresco meals. This villa has a separate home theater and a game room with a mini gym. A private beach cove is excellent for swimming and snorkeling. Rentals include the use of a speedboat equipped for waterskiing; a 32-foot Boston Whaler is available for an additional fee. The staff includes a butler, housekeeper, laundress, gardener, night watchman, cooks, maids, and even a boatman. Children are welcome if accompanied by a nanny. This villa is managed and rented by Bajan Services. **Pros:** big enough to host a large group without tripping over each other; every feature and amenity you could imagine; that speedboat—and a boatman, to boot. **Cons:** nothing—unless you can't afford it. ⊠ *The Garden, Holetown, St. James* ⊕ *www.bajanservices. com* ⇨ *8 bedrooms, 8 baths* ⚬ *Dishwasher, DVD, VCR, fully staffed, gym, beachfront, water toys, laundry facilities* ⊟ *AE, MC, V* ⋈ *EP.*

$$ $$$ ⊡ **Discovery Bay.** *Resort.* This large plantation-style building just off the roadside has deluxe and club rooms that overlook the beach, while superior and garden-view rooms overlook the pool and gardens. The good-size rooms are rather basic in terms of style, but the price is right considering the beachfront location and convenience to the shopping, restaurants, and nightlife opportunities in Holetown—a five-minute walk from your room. The hotel offers accommodation-only rates, but most guests choose to pay about $50 more per day for the all-inclusive meal plan, which includes three meals a day, afternoon tea, beverages, and some activities. The food is pretty good—buffet breakfast and lunch are served by the pool; dinner, often themed, in the restaurant. **Pros:** great Holetown location; good beach; good value. **Cons:** rooms are basic. ⊠ *Hwy. 1, Holetown, St. James* ☎ *246/432–1301* ⊕ *www.rexresorts. com* ⇝ *79 rooms, 9 suites* ⚭ *In-room: safe, refrigerator, Internet. In-hotel, 2 restaurants, room service, bars, tennis court, gym, pool, beachfront, diving, water sports, laundry service* ▤ *AE, MC, V* ⊙ *EP.*

$$$–$$$$ ⛱ **Divi Heritage Beach Resort.** *Resort.* This small oceanfront enclave—a home away from home for adults only—is intentionally quiet. On-site activities are limited to tennis, snorkeling, and the beach, although day passes are available to guests who wish to use the pools, gym, water sports, spa, and restaurants at Almond Beach Club right next door. All suites, whether studio-size or one bedroom, are airy and spacious, with fully equipped kitchens, king-size beds, sleeper sofas in the sitting area, clay-tile floors, and arched doorways opening onto a patio or balcony. Oceanfront studios each have a private hot tub on the patio. Sunset Crest shopping mall (with a supermarket) is directly across the street, and it's a short walk to the restaurants, shops, and sights in the center of Holetown. **Pros:** great location; walk to shopping and restaurants; access to pool and activities next door. **Cons:** tiny beach; rooms are due for an overhaul. ⊠ *Hwy. 1, Sunset Crest, St. James* ☎ *246/432–2968* ⊕ *www. diviresorts.com* ⇝ *22 suites* ⚭ *In-room: kitchen. In-hotel: tennis court, beachfront, water sports, no kids under 16* ▤ *AE, D, DC, MC, V* ⊙ *EP.*

$$$$ ⛱ **Fairmont Royal Pavilion.** *Resort.* Every suite in this adults-oriented resort has a view of the sea from its broad balcony or patio. From ground-floor patios, in fact, you can step directly onto the sand. In the style of a Barbadian plantation house, the rooms have rich mahogany furniture and sisal rugs on ceramic-tile floors. The resort's traditional, personalized service continues on the beach, where "Beach Butlers" cater to your every seaside whim. Breakfast and lunch are served alfresco near the beach; afternoon tea and dinner, in the exquisite Palm Terrace. **Pros:** beautiful resort; excellent service—everyone remembers your

name; dining is excellent. **Cons:** dining is expensive; in fact everything here is expensive. ⌂ *Hwy. 1, Porters, St. James BB24051* ☎ *246/422–5555* ⊕ *www.fairmont.com* ⇨ *72 suite, 1 3-bedroom villa* ⌂ *In-room: safe, refrigerator, Internet. In-hotel: 2 restaurants, room service, bars, tennis courts, pool, gym, beachfront, diving, water sports, laundry service, Internet terminal, no kids under 12 (Nov–Apr)* ▤ *AE, D, MC, V* |◎| *EP.*

\$\$\$–\$\$\$\$ ⊞ **High Constantia Cottage.** *Private Villa.* Perched on a ridge overlooking Golden Mile Beach, High Constantia Cottage is a delightful Spanish-style villa with two air-conditioned double bedrooms, each with a private bath; and spectacular views of the sea from the living and dining rooms and patio. The hillside location catches every breeze, but each room has a ceiling fan just in case. You can also take a refreshing dip in the pool or soothe yourself in the Jacuzzi. The cook/housekeeper is available mornings through lunch and again in the evening. This cottage is managed and rented by Altman Real Estate. **Pros:** private and secluded; lovely views. **Cons:** not on the beach; only the bedrooms are air-conditioned. ⌂ *Coleridge Parry Rd., Heywood, St. Peter* ⊕ *www.aaaltman.com* ⇨ *2 bedrooms, 2 baths* ⌂ *Dishwasher, VCR, daily maid service, cook, pool, laundry facilities* ▤ *AE, MC, V* |◎| *EP.*

\$\$\$\$ ⊞ **The House.** *Resort.* Privacy, luxury, and service are hallmarks of this intimate adult sanctuary next door to sister resort Tamarind Cove. The 34 junior and one-bedroom suites wrap around a central courtyard filled with tropical trees, plants, and water features. Guest rooms are simply but elegantly decorated in tranquil white, ivory, and cream with splashes of dark and azure blue to highlight the Caribbean Sea just beyond the terrace. Beds and pillows are big, soft, and fitted with luxurious Egyptian cotton linens. This may not be home, but guests are certainly made to feel welcome with the service, the personalized attention, and the privacy. A 24-hour "ambassador" service caters to your every whim. Dine on the beachfront in a private cabana or at Daphne's Restaurant. Guests can enjoy the pools, restaurants, and water-sports opportunities—including complimentary windsurfing, boogie boarding, kayaking, waterskiing, tube rides, banana boats, and sailing on a Hobie Cat—at Tamarind Cove, a sister property just next door. Preferred tee times can be arranged at Royal Westmoreland Golf and Country Club, just a 10-minute ride away. Champagne breakfast, afternoon tea, and canapés at sundown make the House a home. But perhaps most

appreciated, a complimentary "jet-lag massage" is yours upon arrival. **Pros:** trendy and stylish; privacy assured; pure relaxation. **Cons:** the resort can be a little stuffy, but you can always head next door to Tamarind Cove. ⊠ *Hwy. 1, Paynes Bay, St. James* ☎ *246/432–5525* ⊕ *www.thehouse-barbados.com* ⊲ *34 suites* � *In-room: safe, refrigerator, DVD (some), Internet. In-hotel: restaurant, gym, beach-front, Internet terminal, no kids under 18, Wi-Fi hotspot* ⊟ *AE, MC, V* ⦿ *BP.*

$$$$ 🏠 **Jacaranda.** *Private Villa.* A family-friendly villa, Jaca-
☉   randa is located in a residential area that's a short walk from lovely Gibbs Beach. The home is designed around a central atrium with a large and inviting plunge pool. A spacious living room opens to a partially covered sundeck filled with comfortable furniture and loungers, and an outdoor swimming pool. The surrounding gardens create a peaceful retreat and provide privacy. Villa staff includes a cook (who specializes in preparing vegetarian meals), a maid/laundress, and a night watchman. This villa is man-aged and rented by Bajan Services. **Pros:** big sundeck with comfy furniture, children are welcome, vegetarians will love the cook. **Cons:** not on the beach; watch the kids around that plunge pool. ⊠ *Gibbs Glade, Speightstown, St. Peter* ⊕ *www.bajanservices.com* ⊲ *3 bedrooms, 4 baths* � *Dish-washer, DVD, VCR, Wi-Fi, daily maid service, cook, on-site security, pools, laundry facilities* ⊟ *AE, MC, V* ⦿ *EP.*

$$$$ 🏠 **Little Good Harbour.** *Vacation Rental.* This cluster of mod-
☉   ern, spacious self-catering cottages with one-, two-, and three-bedroom duplex suites overlooks a narrow strip of beach in the far north of Barbados—just beyond the pic-turesque fishing village of Six Men's Bay. Built in updated chattel-house style, with gingerbread balconies, this little enclave is a perfect choice for self-sufficient travelers who don't need the hand-holding that resorts provide and rel-ish the chance to experience a delightful slice of Bajan vil-lage life nearly at the front door. Some suites are directly on Shermans Bay beach, sharing a building—an old stone fort with louvered shutters on the windows—with the excellent hotel restaurant, the Fish Pot. You can arrange for a personal cook from the restaurant, if you wish, and stocked groceries upon arrival. Most suites are across the road in a grouping of cottages surrounded by palms and facing a pair of pools. All but a few suites have ocean views. While you're mostly on your own in terms of entertain-ment, the hotel will arrange activities and tours. It also has snorkeling equipment that you can use at the beach. **Pros:**

laid-back atmosphere; good for families; individualized experience. **Cons:** busy road; tiny beach; remote location. ⊠ *Hwy. 1B, Shermans, St. Peter* ☎ *246/439–3000* ⊕ *www. littlegoodharbourbarbados.com* ⇨ *21 suites* ⌂ *In-room: safe, kitchen. In-hotel: restaurant, room service, pools, gym, beachfront, water sports, laundry facilities* ⊟ *MC, V* ⊘ *Closed Sept.* ⦾ *EP.*

$$$$ ⊡ **Lone Star Hotel.** *B&B.* British owners transformed this 1940s-era service station into a sleek four-suite boutique hotel that—fortunately or unfortunately—has been discovered by celebrities. Four large, architecturally fascinating suites with shady terraces—two of which are at beach level—are beautifully decorated in elegant neutral colors and furnished in minimalist style with enormous Bajan mahogany beds, chic Italian-designed upholstered furniture, and Phillipe Starck fixtures in the bathrooms. The Lincoln Bedroom is named for the car, not the American president. Other suites are appropriately dubbed Buick, Cord, and Studebaker. Each suite has its own communications and entertainment center, with a TV, stereo/CD player, and DVD. The Beach House, a separate coral-stone villa, can be rented in its entirety or as one- or two-bedroom private suites. Its Caribbean-style decor is quite different from the hotel rooms, with comfy furniture, antiques, and tasteful artwork from the owners' personal collection. The beach is at your door; golf, tennis, fishing, snorkeling, scuba diving, and horseback riding are available nearby. The restaurant is extraordinary—both in terms of cuisine and atmosphere. **Pros:** rub shoulders and chill with celebs (perhaps); enjoy great cuisine; you'll love the decor. **Cons:** rubbing shoulders and chilling with celebs can get very expensive. ⊠ *Hwy. 1, Holetown, St. James* ☎ *246/419–0599* ⊕ *www.thelonestar. com* ⇨ *4 rooms, 2 suites* ⌂ *In-room: safe, refrigerator, DVD, Wi-Fi. In-hotel: restaurant, room service, bar, beachfront, Internet terminal, Wi-Fi hotspot* ⊟ *AE, MC, V* ⊘ *Closed June and Sept.* ⦾ *BP.*

$$$$ ⊡ **Mango Bay.** *All-Inclusive.* Located in the heart of Holetown, this convenient boutique resort is within walking distance of shops, restaurants, nightspots, historic sites, and the public bus to either Bridgetown or Speightstown. All-inclusive rates include accommodations, meals, brand-name beverages, and a host of water sports (including waterskiing), as well as off-property sightseeing experiences such as a glass-bottom boat trip, a shopping excursion to Bridgetown, and a catamaran day sail along the coast. A partially enclosed dining room provides both alfresco and

Port Charles Marina in Bridgetown, the island's capital

air-conditioned dining options. **Pros:** nice rooms; great food; friendly staff; walk to Holetown shopping and entertainment. **Cons:** although heroic measures continue to try to address the problem, a natural drainage stream on the north side of the property can sometimes become odoriferous. ✉ *2nd St., Holetown, St. James* ☎ *246/432–1384* ⊕ *www.mangobaybarbados.com* ➟ *64 rooms, 10 suites, 2 penthouse suites* ⚒ *In-room: safe, refrigerator (some), Internet. In-hotel: restaurant, bar, pool, beachfront, water sports, Internet terminal, Wi-Fi hotspot* ▭ *AE, D, DC, MC, V* ⊙*AI.*

$$$$ ⛴ **Port St. Charles.** *Vacation Rental.* A luxury residential marina development near historic Speightstown on the northwest tip of Barbados, Port St. Charles is a perfect choice for boating enthusiasts who either arrive on their own yacht or plan to charter one during their stay. Each villa is an intimate private home, decorated by the individual owners, and its own mega yacht berth on the property's picturesque lagoon. Port St. Charles also serves as a customs and immigration port of entry for boaters. Villas have one, two, or three bedrooms that surround a man-made lagoon or face the beach. Many have their own private plunge pools. Complimentary water taxis ferry guests around the property during the day—including over to the pool and pool bar at Sunset Island in the middle of the lagoon. **Pros:** a boater's dream; well-appointed units with beautiful views; friendly and safe; great restaurant. **Cons:** not the

best spot for little kids. ✉ *Hwy. 1B, Heywoods, St. Peter* ☎ *246/419–1000* ⊕ *www.portstcharles.com* ⤿ *31 villas* ⚹ *In-room: kitchen, DVD, Internet. In-hotel: 2 restaurants, bars, tennis court, pools, gym, beachfront, water sports, laundry facilities, Internet terminal* ⊟ *AE, MC, V* ⓋⓄⓁ *EP.*

$$$$ 🖼 **Royal Westmoreland Villas.** *Vacation Rental.* Located on ⟳ a ridge overlooking the sea, this villa community was the first of its kind in Barbados, built on a 500-acre estate in the mid-1990s adjoining the Royal Westmoreland Golf Club. Owners and guests value privacy and exclusivity, so access is granted by appointment only. Villas have two, three, or four bedrooms and fully equipped kitchens and dining areas. Cassia Heights Resort Club villas are modern, two-bedroom town houses located in the center of the estate near the clubhouse; Forest Hills Resort Club villas are two-bedroom houses with a common pool for the exclusive use of Forest Hills guests. Royal villas have vaulted ceilings, three large bedrooms with en suite bathrooms, and enormous sitting rooms with French doors that open to a terrace and, in some cases, a private swimming pool. When they're not golfing or playing tennis, villa guests can laze around the pool, chill at the spa, or head for the beach at the nearby Colony Club. Only a few are rented to vacationers through Royal Westmoreland; some owners use property management services and outside real estate agencies. **Pros:** nirvana for golfers; huge accommodations with every possible modern convenience; lots of activities and amenities for families; private and safe. **Cons:** very expensive; not on or close to the beach. ✉ *Hwy. 2A, Westmoreland, St. James* ☎ *246/422–4653* ⊕ *www.royal-westmoreland.com* ⤿ *5 villas* ⚹ *In-room: kitchen. In-hotel: 3 restaurants, bars, golf course, tennis courts, pools, gym, spa, children's programs (ages 4–12), laundry facilities* ⊟ *AE, MC, V* ⓋⓄⓁ *EP.*

★ Fodor'sChoice 🖼 **The Sandpiper.** *Resort.* This little gem just $$$$ north of Holetown is every bit as elegant as its sister hotel, Coral Reef Club, yet the atmosphere is more like a private hideaway. Guest rooms and suites are arranged in a loose "S" shape on 7 acres of gardens. One- and two-bedroom suites have a separate living room and full kitchen. All rooms have a toaster to ensure freshly made, warm toast with your room-service breakfast. Each unit has a CD player; those who can't live without TV can rent one by the week. Two beachfront Tree Top Suites are luxuriously spacious—with bathrooms as big as some Manhattan apartments; each Tree Top Suite has a wraparound terrace with a wet bar and plunge pool. Water sports, including waterskiing, are complimentary. Scuba diving, a children's playground, massage, and other personal services are available at the Coral Reef Club, which is nearby. **Pros:** chic and sophisticated, the Tree Top Suites are fabulous; the bathrooms are amazing. **Cons:** beach is small—typical of west-coast beaches; hotel is small and many guests return year after year, so reservations can be hard to get. ⊠ *Hwy. 1, Holetown, St. James* ☎ *246/422–2251* ⊕ *www.sandpiperbarbados.com* ⊅ *22 rooms, 25 suites* ⚭ *In-room: safe, kitchen (some), refrigerator, no TV, Internet, Wi-Fi. In-hotel: restaurant, room service, bars, tennis courts, pool, gym, beachfront, water sports, Internet terminal, Wi-Fi hotspot, no kids under 12 (Jan. 15–Mar. 15)* ⊟ *AE, MC, V* ⊗ *Closed Sept.* ⦿ *BP.*

★ **Fodor'sChoice**⬚ **Sandy Lane Hotel and Golf Club.** *Resort.* Few
$$$$ places on Earth can compare to Sandy Lane's luxurious
🕑 facilities and ultrapampering service—or to its astronomical prices. But for the few who can afford to stay here, it's an unparalleled experience. The main building of this exquisite resort is a coral-stone, Palladian-style mansion facing a sweeping stretch of beach shaded by mature trees. Guest accommodations, sumptuous in every detail, include three flat-screen TVs with DVD players, full in-room wet bar, a personal butler, and remote-controlled everything—even the draperies! The world-class spa, housed in a magnificent Romanesque building, is a vacation in itself. Add elegant dining, the Caribbean's best golf courses, a tennis center, a full complement of water sports, a special lounge for teenagers, incomparable style. You get the picture. **Pros:** top of the line, cream of the crop—no debate about that; the spa is amazing. **Cons:** over the top for most mortals; very formal—you feel the need to dress up just to walk through the lobby. ⊅ *Hwy. 1, Paynes Bay, St. James BB24024* ☎ *246/444–2000* ⊕ *www.sandylane.com* ⊅ *96 rooms, 16 suites, 1 5-bedroom villa* ⚭ *In-room: safe, refrigerator, DVD, Internet, Wi-Fi. In-hotel: 3 restaurants, room service, bars, golf courses, tennis courts, pool, spa, beachfront, water sports, children's programs (ages 3–12), laundry service, Internet terminal, Wi-Fi hotspot* ⊟ *AE, D, MC, V* ⦿ *BP.*

$$$–$$$$ ⬚ **St. James Apartment Hotel.** *Vacation Rental.* These apartments are perfectly situated right on Paynes Bay beach, one of the best on the west coast. The real appeal in staying in these elegant apartments is the self-catering aspect. For golfers, Sandy Lane Country Club is just 0.5 mi (1 km) north; for everyone else, Holetown and all the shopping,

restaurants, and entertainment there are just 1 mi (2 km) north, and a half dozen excellent restaurants are within walking distance. The hotel has three studios, two one-bedroom units, and six two-bedroom apartments. All have fully equipped, Italian-design, open-plan kitchens. Spacious sitting rooms have cushy seating and a large dining table, with French doors that open to a substantial patio or balcony—a perfect place for breakfast or cocktails at sunset. Each bedroom has its own private bath. Want to get to know your neighbors? Step through the lobby to a sundeck, available to all guests, and the powdery sand and the sea. **Pros:** save money by cooking some meals yourself; great quarters for independent travelers and long stays; great beach and sundeck; convenient to shopping and restaurants. **Cons:** no pool; no organized activities. ⊠ *Hwy. 1, Paynes Bay, St. James* ☎ *246/432–0489* ⊕ *www.the-stjames. com* ⌑ *11 apartments* ⚲ *In-room: safe, kitchen, Internet. In-hotel: beachfront, laundry service* ⊟ *MC,* V ⌑*EP.*

$$$$ ⛱ **Tamarind Cove Hotel.** *Resort.* This Mediterranean-style resort sprawls along 750 feet of prime west-coast beachfront and is large enough to cater to sophisticated couples and active families while, at the same time, offering cozy privacy to honeymooners. Most rooms provide a panoramic view of the sea. Four-poster beds in 10 luxury oceanfront suites add a touch of romance. Junior suites are great for couples or families with one or two small children; families with older kids might prefer the space and privacy of a one-bedroom suite. Tamarind offers an array of water sports, as well as golf privileges at the Royal Westmoreland Golf Club. A free water taxi shuttles to two sister hotels on the west coast. **Pros:** central location right on Paynes Bay beach; lots of free water sports. **Cons:** some rooms could use a little TLC; uninspired buffet breakfast. ⊠ *Hwy. 1, Paynes Bay, St. James* ☎ *246/432–1332* ⊕ *www.tamarindcovehotel. com* ⌑ *58 rooms, 47 suites* ⚲ *In-room: safe, refrigerator, Internet. In-hotel: 2 restaurants, room service, bars, pools, gym, beachfront, water sports, laundry service, Internet terminal* ⊟ *AE, MC,* V ⌑*EP.*

$$$$ ⛱ **Treasure Beach.** *Hotel.* Quiet, upscale, and intimate, this boutique all-suites hotel has a residential quality. Many guests—mostly British—are regulars, suggesting that the ambience here is well worth the price. Two floors of one-bedroom suites form a horseshoe around a small garden and pool. Most have a sea view, but all are just steps from the strip of sandy beach. The superdeluxe Hemmingway Suite blends antiques with modern luxury, an enormous

Turtle Time

Along Casuarina Beach, which stretches in front of both Almond Casuarina Resort and the aptly named Turtle Beach Resort, mother hawksbill turtles dig a pit in the sand, lay 100 or more eggs, cover the nest with sand, and then return to the sea. The eggs, which look just like Ping-Pong balls, are usually deposited between May and November and take about 60 days to hatch. If you happen to be strolling along the beach at the time they emerge, you'll see a mass of newborn turtles scrambling out of the sand and making a dash (at turtle speed, of course) for the sea. While the journey takes only a few minutes, this can be a very dangerous time for the tiny turtles. They are easy prey for gulls and large crabs. Meantime, the folks involved in the Barbados Sea Turtle Project (☎ 246/230–0142) at the University of the West Indies are working hard to protect and conserve the marine turtle populations in Barbados through educational workshops, tagging programs, and other research efforts.

---

terrace, and a whirlpool tub. All suites have comfortable sitting rooms with ceiling fans, plasma TVs, shelves of books, and open-air fourth walls that can be shuttered at night for privacy. Only the bedrooms are air-conditioned. The hotel's restaurant enjoys a well-deserved reputation among guests and locals alike for its fine cuisine and pleasant atmosphere. **Pros:** quiet retreat; congenial crowd; swimming with the turtles just offshore. **Cons:** narrow beach; only bedrooms are air-conditioned; offshore turtles attract boatloads of tourists. ☞ *Hwy. 1, Paynes Bay, St. James BB24009* ☎ *246/432–1346* ⊕ *www.treasurebeachhotel. com* ➪ *35 suites* ⚲ *In-room: safe, refrigerator, Wi-Fi. In-hotel: restaurant, room service, bar, pool, gym, beachfront, laundry service, Internet terminal, Wi-Fi hotspot, no kids under 12 (Jan.–Mar.)* ⊟ *AE, MC, V* ☯ *Closed Sept. and Oct.* ⊠*BP.*

$$$$ ⬚ **Turtle Nest.** *Private Villa.* Location is the drawing card for Turtle Nest. Walk through your private tropical garden and step directly onto the south end of Mullins Beach, one of the best beaches on the west coast. In addition, it's a short walk to the popular Mannie's Suga Suga restaurant and beach bar and all the water toys that are for rent there. The Suga Suga spa, just across the street, is also very inviting. This tastefully furnished beachfront cottage is fully air-conditioned, with fans in each room as well. The living

Beware the Dreaded Manchineel Tree

Large, leafy manchineel trees grow along many of the west-coast beaches. Although they look like perfect shade trees, just touching a leaf or the bark can cause nasty blisters. And don't seek refuge under the tree during a rain shower, as even drips from its leaves can affect sensitive skin. The fruit of the tree, which looks like a tiny green apple, is toxic. Most of the manchineels are marked with signs or with red bands painted on the trunk. Why not just cut them all down? Their root systems are extremely important for preventing beach erosion.

room opens onto a dining verandah with a sweeping view of Mullins Bay. Both bedrooms have sea views, too. The cottage is fully enclosed, and its entrance is controlled by electronic security gates. This villa is managed and rented through Island Villas. **Pros:** right on the beach; lots of action nearby; safe and secure. **Cons:** if you need electronic toys other than a TV, bring your own. ⊠ *Mullins Beach, Speightstown, St. Peter* ⊕ *www.island-villas.com* ⇆ *2 bedrooms, 2 baths* ⚬ *Dishwasher, Internet, daily maid service, cook, on-site security, beachfront, laundry facilities* ⊟ *AE, MC, V* ❍❙ *EP.*

BEACHES

Bajan beaches have fine white sand, and all are open to the public. Most are accessible from the road, so nonguest bathers don't have to pass through hotel properties. When the surf is too high and swimming is dangerous, a red flag will be hoisted on the beach. A yellow flag—or a red flag at half-mast—means swim with caution. Topless sunbathing—on the beach or at the pool—is not allowed anywhere in Barbados by government regulation.

BEACH MASSAGE, LADY? The latest trend among beach vendors is offering massage services—sometimes including what they call reflexology—to sunbathers. While a beach massage sounds refreshing and may even feel good, these people are certainly not trained therapists. At best, you'll get a soothing back or foot rub. Be advised, though, that they use raw aloe vera as their massage oil, which can permanently stain clothing, towels, and chair cushions.

SOUTH COAST

A young, energetic crowd favors the south-coast beaches, which are broad and breezy, blessed with powdery white sand, and dotted with tall palms. The reef-protected areas with crystal-clear water are safe for swimming and snorkeling. The surf is medium to high, and the waves get bigger and the winds stronger (windsurfers take note) the farther southeast you go.

Accra Beach. This popular beach, also known as Rockley Beach, is next to the Accra Hotel. Look forward to gentle surf and a lifeguard, plenty of nearby restaurants for refreshments, a children's playground, and beach stalls for renting chairs and equipment for snorkeling and other water sports. Parking is available at an on-site lot. ✉ *Hwy. 7, Rockley, Christ Church.*

★ **Bottom Bay.** Popular for fashion and travel-industry photo shoots, Bottom Bay is the quintessential Caribbean beach. Surrounded by a coral cliff, studded with a stand of palms, and an endless ocean view, this dreamy enclave is near the southeasternmost tip of the island. Swimming is not recommended, as the waves can be very strong, but it's the picture-perfect place for sunbathing, having a picnic lunch, or simply enjoying the view. Park at the top of the cliff and follow the steps down to the beach. ✉ *Dover, St. Philip.*

Carlisle Bay. Adjacent to the Hilton Barbados hotel just south of Bridgetown, this broad half circle of white sand is one of the island's best beaches—but it can become crowded on weekends and holidays. Park at Harbour Lights or at the Boatyard Bar and Bayshore Complex, both on Bay Street, where you can also rent umbrellas and beach chairs and buy refreshments. ✉ *Aquatic Gap, Needham's Point, St. Michael.*

★ **Casuarina Beach.** Stretched in front of the Almond Casuarina Resort, where St. Lawrence Gap meets the Maxwell Coast Road, this broad strand of powdery white sand is great for both sunbathing and strolling. The sea ranges from turquoise to azure; the surf from low to medium. Find public access and parking on Maxwell Coast Road, near the Bougainvillea Resort. ✉ *Maxwell Coast Rd., Dover, Christ Church.*

★ **Crane Beach.** An exquisite crescent of pink sand on the southeast coast, Crane Beach is protected by steep cliffs on the land side and a reef on the water side. As attractive as this location is now, it was named not for the elegant long-legged wading birds but for the crane used for hauling and loading cargo when this area was a busy port. Crane Beach usually has a steady breeze and lightly rolling surf that is great for bodysurfing. A lifeguard is on duty. Changing rooms are available at the Crane resort for a small fee (which you can apply toward drinks or a meal at the restaurant). Access is through the hotel and down to the beach via either a cliff-side elevator or 98 steps. ⌂ *Crane Bay, St. Philip.*

★ **Fodor's Choice Miami Beach.** Also called Enterprise Beach, this isolated spot on Enterprise Coast Road, just east of Oistins, is a picturesque and underrated slice of pure white sand with cliffs on either side and crystal-clear water. You can find a palm-shaded parking area, snack carts, and chair rentals. Bring a picnic or have lunch across the road at Café Luna in Little Arches Hotel. ⌂ *Enterprise Beach Rd., Enterprise, Christ Church.*

Sandy Beach. Next to the Sandy Bay Beach Resort, this beach has shallow, calm waters and a picturesque lagoon, making it an ideal location for families with small kids. Park right on the main road. You can rent beach chairs and umbrellas, and plenty of places nearby sell food and drinks. ⌂ *Hwy. 7, Worthing, Christ Church.*

Silver Sands–Silver Rock Beach. Nestled between South Point, the southernmost tip of the island, and Inch Marlowe Point, Silver Sands–Silver Rock is a beautiful strand of white sand that always has a stiff breeze. That makes this beach the best in Barbados for intermediate and advanced windsurfers and, more recently, kite surfers. ⌂ *Off Hwy. 7, Christ Church.*

EAST COAST

With long stretches of open beach, crashing ocean surf, rocky cliffs, and verdant hills, the Atlantic (windward) side of Barbados is where Barbadians spend their holidays. But be cautioned: swimming at east-coast beaches is treacherous, even for strong swimmers, and is *not* recommended. Waves are high, the bottom tends to be rocky, the currents are unpredictable, and the undertow is dangerously strong.

Barclays Park. Serious swimming is unwise at this beach, which follows the coastline in St. Andrew, but you can take a dip, wade, and play in the tide pools. A lovely shaded area with picnic tables is directly across the road. ⊠ *Ermy Bourne Hwy., north of Bathsheba, St. Andrew.*

★ **Bathsheba/Cattlewash.** Although it's not safe for swimming, the miles of untouched, windswept sand along the East Coast Road in St. Joseph Parish are great for beachcombing and wading. As you approach Bathsheba Soup Bowl, the southernmost stretch just below Tent Bay, the enormous mushroomlike boulders and rolling surf are uniquely impressive. This is also where expert surfers from around the world converge each November for the Independence Classic Surfing Championship. ⊠ *East Coast Rd., Bathsheba, St. Joseph.*

WEST COAST

Gentle Caribbean waves lap the west coast, and its stunning coves and sandy beaches are shaded by leafy mahogany trees. The water is perfect for swimming and water sports. An almost unbroken chain of beaches runs between Bridgetown and Speightstown. Elegant homes and luxury hotels face much of the beachfront property in this area, dubbed Barbados's "Platinum Coast."

West-coast beaches are considerably smaller and narrower than those on the south coast. Also, prolonged stormy weather in September and October may cause sand erosion, temporarily making the beach even narrower. Even so, west-coast beaches are seldom crowded. Vendors stroll by, selling handmade baskets, hats, dolls, jewelry, even original watercolors; owners of private boats offer waterskiing, parasailing, and snorkeling excursions. There are no concession stands, but hotels and beachside restaurants welcome nonguests for terrace lunches (wear a cover-up), and you can buy picnic items at supermarkets in Holetown.

Brighton Beach. Calm as a lake, this is where you can find locals taking a quick dip on hot days. Just north of Bridgetown, Brighton Beach is also home to the Malibu Beach Club. ⊠ *Spring Garden Hwy., Brighton, St. Michael.*

★ Fodor's Choice **Mullins Beach.** This lovely beach just south of Speightstown is a perfect place to spend the day. The water is safe for swimming and snorkeling, there's easy parking on the main road, and Mullins Restaurant serves snacks, meals, and drinks—and rents chairs and umbrellas. ⊠ *Hwy. 1, Mullins Bay, St. Peter.*

Cricket, a popular sport because of the island's British heritage

Paynes Bay. The stretch of beach just south of Sandy Lane is lined with luxury hotels. It's a very pretty area, with plenty of beach to go around and good snorkeling. Public access is available at several locations along Highway 1; parking is limited. Grab liquid refreshments and a bite to eat at Bomba's Beach Bar. ⊠ *Hwy. 1, Paynes Bay, St. James.*

SPORTS AND ACTIVITIES

Cricket, football (soccer), polo, and rugby are extremely popular sports in Barbados among participants and spectators alike, with local, regional, and international matches held throughout the year. Contact the Barbados Tourism Authority or check local newspapers for information about schedules and tickets.

DIVING AND SNORKELING

More than two dozen dive sites lie along the west coast between Maycocks Bay and Bridgetown and off the south coast as far as St. Lawrence Gap. Certified divers can explore flat coral reefs and see sea fans, huge barrel sponges, and more than 50 varieties of fish. Nine sunken wrecks are dived regularly, and at least 10 more are accessible to experts. Underwater visibility is generally 80 to 90 feet. The calm waters along the west coast are also ideal for snorkeling. The marine reserve, a stretch of protected reef between

Sandy Lane and the Colony Club, contains beautiful coral formations accessible from the beach.

On the west coast, **Bell Buoy** is a large, dome-shape reef where huge brown coral-tree forests and schools of fish delight all categories of divers at depths ranging from 20 to 60 feet. At **Dottins Reef,** off Holetown, you can see schooling fish, barracudas, and turtles at depths of 40 to 60 feet. **Maycocks Bay,** on the northwest coast, is a particularly enticing site; large coral reefs are separated by corridors of white sand, and visibility is often 100 feet or more. The 165-foot freighter *Pamir* lies in 60 feet of water off Six Men's Bay; it's still intact, and you can peer through its portholes and view dozens of varieties of tropical fish. **Silver Bank** is a healthy coral reef with beautiful fish and sea fans; you may get a glimpse of the *Atlantis* submarine at 60 to 80 feet. Not to be missed is the *Stavronikita,* a scuttled Greek freighter at about 135 feet; hundreds of butterfly fish hang out around its mast, and the thin rays of sunlight filtering down through the water make fully exploring the huge ship a wonderfully eerie experience.

Farther south, **Carlisle Bay** is a natural harbor and marine park just below Bridgetown. Here you can retrieve empty bottles thrown overboard by generations of sailors and see cannons and cannonballs, anchors, and six unique shipwrecks lying in 25 to 60 feet of water, all close enough to visit on the same dive (*Berwyn, Fox, CTrek, Eilon,* the barge *Cornwallis,* and the island's newest wreck, *Bajan Queen,* a cruise vessel that sank in 2002).

Dive shops provide a two-hour beginner's "resort" course ($75–$80) followed by a shallow dive, or a weeklong certification course (about $380). Once you're certified, a one-tank dive runs about $50–$55; a two-tank dive is $75–$90. All equipment is supplied, and you can purchase multidive packages. Gear for snorkeling is available (free or for a small rental fee) from most hotels. Snorkelers can usually accompany dive trips for $20 for a one- or two-hour trip. Most dive shops have relationships with several hotels and offer special dive packages, with transportation, to hotel guests.

On the west coast, **Dive Barbados** (⊠ *Mount Standfast, St. James* ☎ *246/422–3133* ⊕ *www.divebarbados.net*), on the beach next to the Lone Star Hotel, offers all levels of PADI instruction, two or three reef and wreck dives daily for up to six divers each time, snorkeling with hawksbill turtles

Sports Legend: Sir Garfield Sobers

Cricket is more than a national pastime in Barbados. It's a passion. And no one is more revered than Sir Garfield Sobers, the greatest sportsman ever to come from Barbados and globally acknowledged as the greatest all-round cricketer the game has ever seen. Sobers played his first test match in 1953 at the age of 17 and continually set and broke records until his last test match in 1973. He was an equally accomplished batsman and bowler. He was knighted by Queen Elizabeth II in 1974 for his contributions to the sport and honored as a national hero of Barbados in 1999.

just offshore, as well as underwater camera rental and free transportation.

On the south coast, the **Dive Shop, Ltd** (⊠ *Bay St., Aquatic Gap, St. Michael* ☎ *246/426–9947, 888/898–3483 in U.S., 888/575–3483 in Canada* ⊕ *www.divebds.com*), the island's oldest dive shop, offers daily reef and wreck dives, plus beginner classes, certification courses, and underwater photography instruction. Underwater cameras are available for rent.

Hightide Watersports (⊠ *Coral Reef Club, Holetown, St. James* ☎ *246/432–0931, 800/970–0016, or 800/513–5763* ⊕ *www.divehightide.com*) offers three dive trips—one- and two-tank dives and night reef/wreck/drift dives—daily for up to eight divers, along with PADI instruction, equipment rental, and free transportation.

FISHING

Fishing is a year-round activity in Barbados, but its prime time is January through April, when game fish are in season. Whether you're a serious deep-sea fisher looking for marlin, sailfish, tuna, and other billfish or you prefer angling in calm coastal waters where wahoo, barracuda, and other small fish reside, you can choose from a variety of half- or full-day charter trips departing from the Careenage in Bridgetown. Expect to pay $175 per person for a shared charter; for a private charter, expect to pay $500–$600 per boat for a four-hour half-day or $950–$1,000 for an eight-hour full-day charter. Spectators are welcome for $50 per person if you don't fish.

Billfisher II (☎ 246/431–0741), a 40-foot Pacemaker, accommodates up to six passengers with three fishing chairs and five rods. Captain Winston ("The Colonel") White has been fishing these waters since 1975. His full-day charters include a full lunch and guaranteed fish (or a 25% refund); all trips include drinks and transportation to and from the boat.

Blue Jay (☎ 246/429–2326 ⊕ *www.bluemarlinbarbados. com*) is a spacious, fully equipped, 45-foot Sport Fisherman with a crew that knows the water's denizens—blue marlin, sailfish, barracuda, and kingfish. Four to six people can be accommodated—it's the only charter boat on the island with four chairs. Most fishing is done by trolling. Drinks, snacks, bait, tackle, and transfers are provided.

Cannon II (☎ 246/424–6107), a 42-foot Hatteras Sport Fisherman, has three chairs and five rods and accommodates six passengers; drinks and snacks are complimentary, and lunch is served on full-day charters.

GOLF

Barbadians love golf, and golfers love Barbados. In addition to the courses listed below, Almond Beach Village has a 9-hole, par-3 executive course open only to guests. **Barbados Golf Club** (⊠ *Hwy. 7, Durants, Christ Church* ☎ 246/428–8463 ⊕ *www.barbadosgolfclub.com*), the first public golf course on Barbados, is an 18-hole championship course (6,805 yards, par 72) redesigned in 2000 by golf course architect Ron Kirby. Green fees are $135 for 18 holes, plus a $20 per-person cart fee. Unlimited three-day and seven-day golf passes are available. Several hotels offer preferential tee-time reservations and reduced rates. Club and shoe rentals are available.

★ **Fodor's**Choice At the prestigious **Country Club at Sandy Lane** (⊠ *Hwy. 1, Paynes Bay, St. James* ☎ 246/444–2500 ⊕ *www. sandylane.com/golf*), golfers can play on the Old Nine or on either of two 18-hole championship courses: the Tom Fazio–designed Country Club Course or the spectacular Green Monkey Course, reserved for hotel guests and club members only. Golfers have complimentary use of the club's driving range. The Country Club Restaurant and Bar, which overlooks the 18th hole, is open to the public. Green fees in high season are $150 for 9 holes ($130 for hotel guests) or $235 for 18 holes ($200 for hotel guests). Golf carts, caddies, or trolleys are available for hire, as are clubs and shoes. Carts are equipped with GPS, which alerts you to upcoming traps and hazards, provides tips on how to play the hole, and allows you to order refreshments!

Rockley Golf and Country Club (⊠ *Golf Club Rd., Worthing, Christ Church* ☎ *246/435–7873* ⊕ *www.rockleygolfclub. com*), on the southeast coast, has a challenging 9-hole course (2,800 yards, par 35) that can be played as 18 from varying tee positions. Club and cart rentals are available. Green fees are $55 for 18 holes and $45 for 9 holes.

★ The **Royal Westmoreland Golf Club** (⊠ *Westmoreland, St. James* ☎ *246/422–4653* ⊕ *www.royal-westmoreland.com*) has a world-class Robert Trent Jones Jr.–designed, 18-hole championship course (6,870 yards, par 72) that meanders through the 500-acre property. This challenging course is primarily for villa renters, with a few mid-morning tee times for visitors subject to availability; green fees for villa renters are $250 for tee times before 10 AM or $300 after 10 AM for 18 holes; for visitors, $250 for 18 holes (tee times, Sunday–Friday 10–11 AM only). Green fees include use of an electric cart (required); club rental is available.

GUIDED TOURS

Taxi drivers will give you a personalized tour of Barbados for about $25 per hour for up to three people. Or you can choose an overland horseback or mountain bike journey, a 4x4 safari expedition, or a full-day bus excursion. The prices vary according to the mode of travel and the number and kind of attractions included. Ask your hotel to help you make arrangements.

Highland Adventure Centre (⊠ *Cane Field, St. Thomas* ☎ *246/438–8069 or 246/438–8928*) offers beautiful horseback or mountain bike tours for $50 per person, including transportation, guides, and refreshments. The mountain bike tour is an exhilarating 7.5-mi (12-km) ride (15% uphill) through the picturesque heart of northern Barbados, ending up at Barclays Park on the east coast. **Island Safari** (⊠ *Main Rd., Bush Hall, St. Michael* ☎ *246/429–5337* ⊕ *www.islandsafari.bb*) will take you to all the popular spots via a 4x4 Land Rover—including some gullies, forests, and remote areas that are inaccessible by conventional cars and buses. The cost for half-day or full-day tours ranges $50–$80 per person, including snacks or lunch.

The Sandy Lane Gold Cup at the Barbados Turf Club

HIKING

Hilly but not mountainous, the northern interior and the east coast are ideal for hiking.

The **Arbib Heritage and Nature Trail** (⊠ *Speightstown, St. Peter* ☎ *246/426–2421* ⊕ *www.nationaltrustbarbados.com*), maintained by the Barbados National Trust, is actually two trails—one offers a rigorous hike through gullies and plantations to old ruins and remote north-country areas; the other is a shorter, easier walk through Speightstown's side streets and past an ancient church and chattel houses. Guided hikes take place on Wednesday, Thursday, and Saturday at 9 AM (book by 3 PM the day before) and cost $7.50.

The **Barbados National Trust** (⊠ *Wildey House, Wildey, St. Michael* ☎ *246/426–2421* ⊕ *www.nationaltrustbarbados.com*) sponsors free walks, called **Hike Barbados,** year-round on Sunday from 6 AM to about 9 AM and from 3:30 PM to 6 PM; once a month, a moonlight hike substitutes for the afternoon hike and begins at 5:30 PM (bring a flashlight). Experienced guides group you with others of similar levels of ability. Stop and Stare hikes go 5–6 mi (8–10 km); Here and There, 8–10 mi (13–16 km); and Grin and Bear, 12–14 mi (19–23 km). Wear loose clothes, sensible shoes, sunscreen, and a hat, and bring your camera and a bottle of water. Routes and locations change, but each hike is a loop, finishing in the same spot where it began. Check local newspapers, call the Trust, or check online for the full hike schedule or the scheduled meeting place on a particular Sunday.

HORSE RACING

Horse racing is administered by the **Barbados Turf Club** (☎246/426–3980 ⊕ www.barbadosturfclub.com) and races take place on alternate Saturdays throughout the year at the Garrison Savannah, a 6-furlong grass oval in Christ Church, about 3 mi (5 km) south of Bridgetown. The important races are the Sandy Lane Barbados Gold Cup, held in late February or early March, and the United Insurance Barbados Derby Day in August. Post time is 1:30 PM. General admission is $5, $10 for grandstand seats and $20 for the clubhouse. (Prices are higher on Gold Cup day.)

SEA EXCURSIONS

Mini-submarine voyages are enormously popular with families and those who enjoy watching fish but who don't wish to snorkel or dive. Party boats depart from Bridgetown's Deep Water Harbour for sightseeing and snorkeling or romantic sunset cruises. Prices are $60–$80 per person for daytime cruises and $35–$65 for three-hour sunset cruises, depending on the type of refreshments and entertainment included; transportation to and from the dock is provided. For an excursion that may be less splashy in terms of a party atmosphere—but definitely splashier in terms of the actual experience—turtle tours allow participants to feed and swim with a resident group of hawksbill and leather-back sea turtles.

☾ The 48-passenger **Atlantis Submarine** (⌧ Shallow Draught, Bridgetown, St. Michael ☎246/436–8929 ⊕ www.atlantisadventures.com) turns the Caribbean into a giant aquarium. The 45-minute underwater voyage aboard the 50-foot submarine ($100 per person, including transportation) takes you to wrecks and reefs as deep as 150 feet. Children love the adventure, but they must be at least 3 feet tall to go on board.

☾ Five-hour daytime cruises along the west coast on the 100-foot **MV Harbour Master** (☎246/430–0900 ⊕ www.tallshipscruises.com) stop in Holetown and land at beaches along the way; evening cruises are shorter but add a buffet dinner and entertainment. Day or night you can view the briny deep from the ship's onboard 34-seat semisubmersible.

A daytime cruise on the 57-foot catamaran **Heatwave** (☎ 246/826–4447 ⊕ *www.heatwavesailingcruises.com*) includes stops along the coast for swimming and snorkeling and a barbecue lunch. The sunset cruise includes dinner.

☾ **Just Breezing Water Sports** (☎ 246/262–7960 ⊕ *www.justbreez-*
★ *ingwatersports.com*), based in Holetown, has a 32-foot glass-bottom boat from which guests can view, snorkel, and swim with the turtles. The cruise is particularly fun for families with young children. Two trips depart daily, at 10 AM and 2 PM. They cover about 6 mi (10 km) of coastline along the west coast, cost $45 per adult, and last two hours each. Hotel transportation, cool drinks, snorkels, and masks are all included.

The 44-foot CSY sailing yacht **Limbo Lady** (☎ 246/420–5418) sails along the captivating west coast, stopping for a swim, snorkeling, and a Bajan buffet lunch on board. Sunset cruises are another option.

The 53-foot catamaran **Tiami** (☎ 246/430–0900 ⊕ *www. tallshipscruises.com*) offers a luncheon cruise to a secluded bay or a romantic sunset and moonlight cruise with special catering and live music.

SURFING

The best surfing is on the east coast, at Bathsheba Soup Bowl, but the water on the windward side of the island is safe only for the most experienced swimmers. Surfers also congregate at Surfer's Point, at the southern tip of Barbados near Inch Marlow, where the Atlantic Ocean meets the Caribbean Sea.

The Independence Classic Surfing Championship (an international competition) is held at Bathsheba Soup Bowl every November—when the surf is at its peak. For information, contact the **Barbados Surfing Association** (☎ 246/228–5117).

Dread or Dead Surf Shop (✉ *Hastings Main Rd., Hastings, Christ Church* ☎ 246/228–4785 ⊕ *www.dreadordead.com*) promises to get beginners from "zero to standing up and surfing" in a single afternoon. The four-hour course—"or until you stand up or give up"—costs $75 per person and includes a board, wax, a rash guard (if necessary), a ride

. . . and the Black Spiny Sea Urchins!

Black spiny sea urchins lurk in the sand on the shallow sea bottom and near reefs. Should you step on one, its sharp venom-filled spines will cause a painful wound. They've even been known to pierce wet suits, so divers should be careful when brushing up against submerged rock walls. Getting several stings at once can cause muscle spasms and breathing difficulties for some people, so victims need to get help immediately. Clean the wound before carefully removing the stinger(s). Some say ammonia (aka urine) is the best remedy. We say it's lime and alcohol. So should the worst happen, find the nearest bartender.

to and from the surf break, and an instructor; additional lessons cost $37.50. Intermediate or experienced surfers can get all the equipment and the instructor for a full day of surfing for $150.

Zed's Surfing Adventures (⊠ *Surfer's Point, Inch Marlow, Christ Church* ☎ *246/428–7873* ⊕ *www.barbadossurf.com*) rents surfboards, offers lessons, and offers surf tours—which include equipment, a guide, and transportation to surf breaks appropriate for your experience.

WINDSURFING

Barbados is on the World Cup Windsurfing Circuit and is one of the prime locations in the world for windsurfing. Winds are strongest November through April at the island's southern tip, at Silver Sand–Silver Rock Beach, which is where the Barbados Windsurfing Championships are held in mid-January. Use of boards and equipment is often among the amenities included at larger hotels; equipment can usually be rented by nonguests.

More-experienced windsurfers congregate at **Silver Rock Windsurfing Club** (⊠ *Silver Sands–Silver Rock Beach, Christ Church* ☎ *246/428–2866*), where the surf ranges from 3 to 15 feet and provides an exhilarating windsurfing experience.

The Oistins Fish Fry, held every night in the south coast fishing village

NIGHTLIFE

When the sun goes down, the people come out to "lime" (which may be anything from a "chat-up" to a full-blown "jump-up"). Performances by world-renowned stars and regional groups are major events, and tickets can be hard to come by—but give it a try. Most resorts have nightly entertainment in season, and nightclubs often have live bands for listening and dancing. The busiest bars and dance clubs rage until 3 AM. On Saturday nights some clubs—especially those with live music—charge a cover of about $15.

★ Fodor's Choice The **Oistins Fish Fry** (⊠ *Oistins, Christ Church*) is the place to be on Friday evenings, when the south-coast fishing village becomes a convivial outdoor street fair. Barbecued chicken and a variety of fish are served right from the grill and consumed at roadside picnic tables; servings are huge, and prices are inexpensive—about $10. Drinks, music, and dancing add to the fun.

DID YOU KNOW? BAXTER'S ROAD IS SOMETIMES CALLED "THE STREET THAT NEVER SLEEPS." Night owls head for Baxter's Road, in Bridgetown, any night of the week for after-hours fun and food. The strip of rum shops begins to hit its stride at 11 PM, but locals usually show up around 3 AM. Street vendors sell freshly made "Baxter's Road" fried chicken and other snacks all night long, but Enid's is the place to see and be seen.

Nightspots A-Plenty

St. Lawrence Gap, the narrow waterfront byway with restaurants, bars, and nightclubs one right after another, is where the action is on the south coast. In Holetown, on the west coast, the restaurants and clubs on 1st and 2nd streets are giving "the Gap" a run for its money. Along with a half dozen or so restaurants that offer fare ranging from ribs or pizza to elegant cuisine, a handful of nightspots and night "experiences" have cropped up recently. After-dinner drinks at the Mews or at Lexy Piano Bar are popular any evening, but on Sunday evenings locals and tourists alike descend on One Love Rum Shop for the karaoke and to Ragamuffin's restaurant, next door, for the after-dinner drag show.

BARS

Barbados supports the rum industry with more than 1,600 "rum shops," simple bars where men (mostly) congregate to discuss the world (or life in general), drink rum, and eat a "cutter" (sandwich). In more sophisticated establishments you can find world-class rum drinks made with the island's renowned Mount Gay and Cockspur brands—and no shortage of Barbados's own Banks Beer.

The **Boatyard** (✉ *Bay St., Carlisle Bay, Bridgetown, St. Michael* ☎ *246/436–2622* ⊕ *www.theboatyard.com*) is a popular pub with both a DJ and live bands; from happy hour until the wee hours, the patrons are mostly local and visiting professionals.

On the south coast, **Bubba's Sports Bar** (✉ *Main Rd., Rockley, Christ Church* ☎ *246/435–6217* ⊕ *www.bubbassportsbar. net*) offers merrymakers and sports lovers live sports on three 10-foot video screens and a dozen TVs, along with a Bajan à la carte menu and, of course, drinks at the bar.

Jumbie's (✉ *Hwy. 1, Paynes Bay, St. James* ☎ *246/434– 3434*) has an open-air party room with either a DJ or live music Wednesday through Sunday from 4:30 PM to 4:30 AM. Happy hours run from 5 PM to 7 PM and again from 10 PM to 1 AM and all day Sunday! Obviously, it's a very happy place to congregate in the evening.

★ **Lexy Piano Bar** (✉ *2nd St., Holetown, St. James* ☎ *246/432– 5399* ⊕ *www.lexypianobar.com*) is a cool, trendy club named for owner Alex Santoriello, a transplanted Broadway singer and actor. A changing roster of singer-pianists play sing-along standards, classic rock, R&B, and Broadway tunes. Most any night, you'll find Santoriello there.

McBride's Pub (⊠ *St. Lawrence Gap, Christ Church* ☎ 246/436–6352 ⊕ *www.mcbridesbarbados.com*) is, as you night have guessed, an Irish pub with Irish beer on tap, pub grub from the kitchen, and Irish music, karaoke, reggae, rock, Latin, or techno music every night. Happy hour(s) run from 11 PM to 1 AM every night.

Upstairs at Olives (⊠ *2nd St., Holetown, St. James* ☎ 246/432–2112) is a sophisticated watering hole. Enjoy cocktails and conversation seated amid potted palms and cooled by ceiling fans—either before or after dinner downstairs.

Waterfront Cafe (⊠ *The Careenage, Bridgetown, St. Michael* ☎ 246/427–0093 ⊕ *www.waterfrontcafe.com.bb*) has live jazz in the evening, with a small dance floor for dancing. The picturesque location alongside the wharf is also a draw.

DANCE CLUBS

The open-air, beachfront **Harbour Lights** (⊠ *Upper Bay St., Bridgetown, St. Michael* ☎ 246/436–7225 ⊕ *www.harbourlightsbarbados.com*) claims to be the "home of the party animal" and has dancing under the stars most nights to live reggae and soca music.

★ The **Reggae Lounge** (⊠ *St. Lawrence Gap, Dover, Christ Church* ☎ 246/435–6462) is a popular open-air nightclub where live bands or DJs play the latest Jamaican hits and old reggae favorites.

The **Ship Inn** (⊠ *St. Lawrence Gap, Dover, Christ Church* ☎ 246/420–7447 ⊕ *www.shipinnbarbados.com*) is a large, friendly pub with local band music every night for dancing.

THEME NIGHTS

★ Fodor'sChoice On Wednesday and Friday evenings at the
♨ **Plantation Restaurant and Garden Theater** (⊠ *St. Lawrence Main Rd., Dover, Christ Church* ☎ 246/428–5048 ⊕ *www. plantationtheatre.com*) the Tropical Spectacular calypso cabaret presents "Bajan Roots and Rhythms," a delightful extravaganza that the whole family will enjoy. The show includes steel-band music, fire eating, limbo, and dancing to

the reggae, soca, and pop music sounds of popular Barbadian singer John King and the Plantation House Band. The fun begins at 6:30 PM. A Barbadian buffet dinner, unlimited drinks, transportation, and the show cost $97.50; for the show and drinks only, it's $57.50.

SHOPPING

Shoppers will find plenty of satisfaction in Barbados. There's something for everyone, whether you're interested in duty-free perfumes, china, and jewelry or are more enticed by handmade crafts made by local artisans—pottery, wood carvings, textiles, watercolors, sculptures, and more. And then there's rum. You'll definitely want to bring home a bottle. Maybe two.

AREAS AND MALLS

Bridgetown's **Broad Street** is the primary downtown shopping area. **DaCostas Mall,** in the historic Colonnade Building on Broad Street, has more than 25 shops that sell everything from Piaget to postcards; across the street, **Mall 34** has 22 shops where you can buy duty-free goods, souvenirs, and snacks. At the **cruise-ship terminal** shopping arcade, passengers can buy both duty-free goods and Barbadian-made crafts at more than 30 boutiques and a dozen vendor carts and stalls. **Pelican Craft Centre** is a cluster of workshops halfway between the cruise-ship terminal and downtown Bridgetown, where craftspeople create and sell locally made items.

Holetown and St. Lawrence Gap each have a **Chattel House Village,** a cluster of brightly colored shops selling local products, fashions, beachwear, and souvenirs. Also in Holetown, **Sunset Crest Mall** has two branches of the Cave Shepherd department store, a bank, a pharmacy, and several small shops; at **West Coast Mall** you can buy duty-free goods, island wear, and groceries. In Rockley, Christ Church, **Quayside Shopping Center** houses a small group of boutiques, restaurants, and services.

BRIDGETOWN SHOPPING SHUTTLE. **A free Bridgetown shuttle serves hotels on the south and west coasts, so guests can visit downtown shops, see the sites, and perhaps have lunch. The shuttle operates Monday through Saturday, departing from the hotels at 9:30 and 11 AM and returning from Bridgetown** at 1:30 and 3 PM. Reserve your seat with your hotel concierge a day ahead.

DEPARTMENT STORES

Cave Shepherd (⊠ *Broad St., Bridgetown, St. Michael* ☎ *246/431–2121* ⊕ *www.caveshepherd.com*) offers a wide selection of clothing and luxury goods; branch stores are in Holetown, at the airport, and at the cruise-ship terminal.

Harrison's (⊠ *Broad St., Bridgetown, St. Michael* ☎ *246/431–5500*) has 11 locations—including its two large stores on Broad Street and one each at the airport and the cruise-ship terminal—offering luxury name-brand goods from the fashion corners of the world.

SPECIALTY STORES

ANTIQUES

Although many of the private homes, greathouses, and museums in Barbados are filled with priceless antiques, you'll find few for sale—mainly British antiques and some local pieces, particularly mahogany furniture. Look especially for planters' chairs and the classic Barbadian rocking chair, as well as old prints and paintings.

Greenwich House Antiques (⊠ *Greenwich Village, Trents Hill, St. James* ☎ *246/432–1169*) fills an entire plantation house with vintage Barbadian mahogany furniture, art deco pieces, crystal, silver, china, books, and pictures; it's open daily from 10:30 to 5:30.

ART

Perhaps one of the most long-lasting souvenirs to bring home from Barbados is a piece of authentic Caribbean art. The colorful flowers, quaint villages, mesmerizing seascapes, and fascinating cultural experiences and activities that are endemic to the region and familiar to visitors have been translated by local artists onto canvas and into photographs, sculpture, and other media. Gift shops and even some restaurants display local artwork for sale, but the broadest array of artwork will be found in an art gallery.

Gallery of Caribbean Art (⊠ *Northern Business Centre, Queen St., Speightstown, St. Peter* ☎ *246/419–0858* ⊕ *www.artgallerycaribbean.com*) is committed to promoting Caribbean art from Cuba to Curaçao, including a number of pieces by

"Bajan Roots and Rhythms" at the Plantation Restaurant and Garden Theatre

Barbadian artists. A branch gallery is located at the Hilton Barbados hotel, Needham's Point.

On the Wall Art Gallery (⌧ *No. 2 Edgehill Heights, St. Thomas* ☎ *246/425–0223* ⊕ *www.onthewallartgallery.com*), next door to Earthworks Pottery, has an array of original paintings by Barbadian artists, along with arts and crafts products. Additional galleries are located in dedicated space at the Tides restaurant on the west coast and Champers restaurant on the south coast.

CLOTHING

Dingolay (⌧ *Bay St., Bridgetown, St. Michael* ☎ *246/436–2157* ⌧ *Hwy. 1, Holetown, St. James* ☎ *246/432–8709*) sells tropical clothing designed and made in Barbados for ladies and girls as well as shoes, handbags, and accessories from around the world.

Check out the colorful T-shirts from **Irie Blue** (⌧ *DaCostas Mall, Broad St., Bridgetown, St. Michael* ☎ *246/431–0017*), which are designed and made in Barbados. You can also find them in many gift shops.

DUTY-FREE GOODS

Duty-free luxury goods—china, crystal, cameras, porcelain, leather items, electronics, jewelry, perfume, and clothing—are found in Bridgetown's Broad Street department stores and their branches, at the cruise-ship-terminal shops (for passengers only), and in the departure lounge shops at

Grantley Adams International Airport. Prices are often 30%–40% less than at home. To buy goods at duty-free prices, you must produce your passport, immigration form, or driver's license, along with departure information (e.g., flight number and date) at the time of purchase—or you can have your purchases delivered free to the airport or harbor for pickup. Duty-free alcohol, tobacco products, and some electronic equipment *must* be delivered to you at the airport or harbor.

The anchor shop of **Little Switzerland** (⊠ *DaCostas Mall, Broad St., Bridgetown, St. Michael* ☎ *246/431–0030*) is at DaCostas Mall, with branches at the cruise-ship terminal and at West Coast Mall, Sunset Crest, in Holetown. Here you can find perfume, jewelry, cameras, audio equipment, Swarovski and Waterford crystal, and Wedgwood china.

The **Royal Shop** (⊠ *32 Broad St., Bridgetown, St. Michael* ☎ *246/429–7072*) carries fine watches and jewelry fashioned in Italian gold, Caribbean silver, diamonds, and other gems.

HANDICRAFTS

Typical crafts include pottery, shell and glass art, wood carvings, handmade dolls, watercolors, and other artwork (both originals and prints).

Best of Barbados (⊠ *Worthing, Christ Church* ☎ *246/421–6900* ⊕ *www.best-of-barbados.com*) was the brainchild of architect Jimmy Walker as a place to showcase the works of his artist wife. Now with seven locations, the shops offer products that range from Jill Walker's framable prints, housewares, and textiles to arts and crafts in both "native" style and modern designs. Everything is made or designed on Barbados.

★ Fodor'sChoice **Earthworks Pottery** (⊠ *No. 2, Edgehill Heights, Edgehill Heights, St. Thomas* ☎ *246/425–0223* ⊕ *www.earthworks-pottery.com*) is a family-owned and -operated pottery shop where you can purchase anything from a dish or knickknack to a complete dinner service or one-of-a-kind art piece. You can find the characteristically blue or green pottery decorating hotel rooms for sale in gift shops throughout the island, but the biggest selection (including some "seconds") is at Earthworks, where you also can watch the potters work.

Island Crafts (⊠ *5 Pelican Craft Centre, Bridgetown, St. Michael* ☎ *246/426–4391*) offers locally made pottery, wood carvings, straw items, glass art, batik, and wire sculptures. Additional shops are at Harrison's Cave, the airport courtyard, and the airport departure lounge.

★ **Pelican Craft Centre** (⊠ *Princess Alice Hwy., Bridgetown, St. Michael* ☎ *246/427–5350*) is a cluster of workshops halfway between the cruise-ship terminal and downtown Bridgetown where craftspeople create and sell locally made leather goods, batik, basketry, carvings, jewelry, glass art, paintings, pottery, and other items. It's open weekdays 9–5 and Saturday 9–2, with extended hours during holidays or cruise-ship arrivals.

Red Clay Pottery and Fairfield Gallery (⊠ *Fairfield House, Fairfield Cross Rd., Fairfield, St. Michael* ☎ *246/424–3800*) has been operated by potter Denis Bell all his life, "save a little time spent doing some engineering and raising a family." Visitors are welcome to watch the potters at work in the studio, which is in an old sugar-boiling house, and, in the adjacent shop, purchase plates, platters, bowls, place settings, and fine decorative items designed by Bell's daughter, Maggie.

☉ In the chattel houses at **Tyrol Cot Heritage Village** (⊠ *Codrington Hill, St. Michael* ☎ *246/424–2074*), you can watch local artisans make hand-painted figurines, straw baskets, clothing, paintings, and pottery—and, of course, buy their wares. The workshops are open primarily during the winter season and when cruise ships are in port.

St. Lucia

WORD OF MOUTH

"You must take a trip to The Pitons . . . they are incredible and truly worth the entire trip to St. Lucia."

—skinnyboy

By Jane E. Zarem

ALL EYES FOCUS ON ST. LUCIA FOR 10 DAYS EACH MAY, when the St. Lucia Jazz Festival welcomes renowned international musicians who perform for enthusiastic fans at Pigeon Island National Park and other island venues. St. Lucians themselves love jazz—and, of course, the beat of Caribbean music resonates through their very souls. The irony is that if you randomly ask 10 St. Lucians to name their favorite kind of music, most would say "country." One possible explanation is that many young St. Lucian men have taken short-term jobs overseas, cutting sugarcane in Florida and working on farms elsewhere in the South, where they inevitably hear country music. And while the work experience isn't something most remember fondly, the music apparently is.

The pirate François Le Clerc, nicknamed Jambe de Bois (Wooden Leg) for obvious reasons, was the first European "settler" in St. Lucia (pronounced *loo*-sha). In the late 16th century, Le Clerc holed up on Pigeon Island, just off the island's northernmost point, and used it as a staging ground for attacking passing ships. Now Pigeon Island is a national park, a playground for locals and visitors alike, and, as mentioned, a popular performance venue for the annual St. Lucia Jazz Festival. Several years ago a man-made causeway attached Pigeon Island to the mainland; today Sandals Grande St. Lucian Spa & Beach Resort, one of the largest resorts in St. Lucia, and the Landings, a luxury villa community with an 80-slip marina, are sprawled along that causeway.

St. Lucia has evolved over the years into one of the most popular vacation destinations in the Caribbean—particularly for honeymooners and other romantics, who are enticed by the island's striking natural beauty, its many splendid resorts and appealing inns, and its welcoming atmosphere. And the evolution continues. Renewed emphasis from both the public and private sectors is being placed on enhancing the island's tourism industry and supporting new and revamped lodgings, activities, and attractions. That's great news for visitors, who already appear delighted with St. Lucia.

A lush, mountainous island located between Martinique and St. Vincent, and 100 mi (160 km) due west of Barbados, the 27-mi by 14-mi (43½-km by 22½-km) St. Lucia easily earns the moniker "Helen of the West Indies." The capital city of Castries and nearby villages in the northwest are home to 40% of the population and, along with Rodney Bay farther north and Marigot Bay just south of the capital, are the destinations of most vacationers. In the central and southwestern parts of the island, dense rain forest, jungle-covered mountains, and vast banana plantations dominate the landscape. A torturously winding road follows most of the coastline, bisecting small villages, cutting through mountains and thick forests, and passing through fertile valleys. On the southwest coast, Petit Piton and Gros Piton, the island's unusual twin peaks that rise out of the sea to more than 2,600 feet, are familiar navigational landmarks for sailors and aviators alike. Divers are attracted to the reefs found just north of Soufrière, the quaint city that was the capital during French colonial times. Most of the natural tourist attractions are in this area, along with several more upscale resorts and inns. "If you haven't been to Soufrière," St. Lucians will tell you, "you haven't been to St. Lucia."

Like most of its Caribbean neighbors, St. Lucia was first inhabited by the Arawaks and then the Carib Indians. British settlers attempted to colonize the island twice in the early 1600s, but it wasn't until 1651, after the French West India Company secured the island from the Caribs, that Europeans gained a foothold. For 150 years the French and the British frequently battled for possession of the island, with a dizzying 14 changes in power before the British finally took possession in 1814. The Europeans established sugar plantations, using slaves from West Africa to work the fields. By 1838, when the slaves were emancipated, more than 90% of the population was of African descent—which is also the approximate proportion of today's 170,000 St. Lucians. Indentured East Indian laborers were brought over in 1882 to help bail out the sugar industry, which collapsed when slavery was abolished and then all but died in the 1960s, when bananas became the major crop.

On February 22, 1979, St. Lucia became an independent state within the British Commonwealth of Nations, with a resident governor-general appointed by the queen. Still, the island appears to have retained more relics of French influence—notably the patois, cuisine, village names, and surnames—than of the British. Most likely, that's because the British contribution primarily involved the English language, the educational and legal systems, and the political structure, while the French culture historically had more impact on the arts—culinary, dance, and all that jazz!

ST. LUCIA TOP REASONS TO GO

■ Magnificent, lush scenery, particularly in the south and around Soufrière, makes St. Lucia one of the Caribbean's most beautiful islands.

■ A popular honeymoon spot, St. Lucia is filled with romantic retreats.

■ Sybaritic lodging options include an all-inclusive spa resort with daily pampering on the menu, a posh dive resort sandwiched between a mountain and the beach, and two picturesque resorts optimally positioned right between the Pitons.

■ The St. Lucia Jazz Festival draws performers and listeners from all over the world.

■ The friendly St. Lucians love sharing their island and their cultural heritage with visitors.

EXPLORING ST. LUCIA

Except for a small area in the extreme northeast, one main route circles all of St. Lucia. The road snakes along the coast, cuts across mountains, makes hairpin turns and sheer drops, and reaches dizzying heights. It takes at least four hours to drive the whole loop. Even at a leisurely pace with frequent sightseeing stops, the curvy roads make it a tiring drive in a single outing.

The West Coast Road between Castries and Soufrière (a 1½- to 2-hour journey) has steep hills and sharp turns, but it's well marked and incredibly scenic. South of Castries, the road tunnels through Morne Fortune, skirts the island's largest banana plantation (more than 127 varieties of bananas, called "figs" in this part of the Caribbean, grow on the island), and passes through tiny fishing villages. Just north of Soufrière, the road passes through the island's fruit basket, where most of the mangoes, breadfruit, tomatoes, limes, and oranges are grown. In the mountainous region that forms a backdrop for Soufrière, you will notice 3,118-foot Mt. Gimie (pronounced Jimmy), St. Lucia's highest peak. As you approach Soufrière, you'll also have spectacular views of the Pitons. And that spume of smoke wafting out of the thickly forested mountainside just east of Soufrière emanates from La Soufrière Drive-In Volcano.

The landscape changes dramatically between the Pitons and Vieux Fort on the island's southeastern tip. Along the South

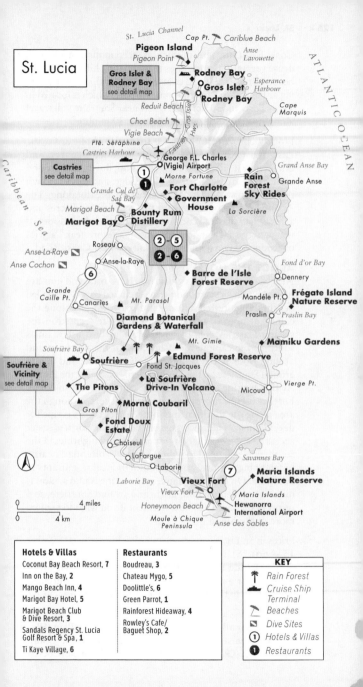

St. Lucia

St. Lucia Channel · Cap Pt. · Cariblue Beach
Pigeon Island
Pigeon Point
Anse Lavouette

**Gros Islet &
Rodney Bay**
see detail map
Rodney Bay
Gros Islet
Rodney Bay
Esperance Harbour
Cape Marquis

Reduit Beach
Choc Beach
Vigie Beach
Pte. Séraphine
Castries Harbour
Grand Anse Bay
George F.L. Charles (Vigie) Airport
Grande Anse
Morne Fortune
Rain Forest Sky Rides

Castries
see detail map
① ①
Fort Charlotte
Government House
La Sorcière

Grande Cul de Sac Bay
Bounty Rum Distillery
Marigot Beach
Marigot Bay

Caribbean Sea

Roseau ○
② – ⑤
② – ⑥

Anse-La-Raye
Anse Cochon
Anse-la-Raye
Fond d'or Bay

**Barre de l'Isle
Forest Reserve**
○ Dennery

Grande Caille Pt.
Canaries
Mt. Parasol
Mandèle Pt.
**Frégate Island
Nature Reserve**

⑥
Praslin ○ Praslin Bay

**Diamond Botanical
Gardens & Waterfall**
Mt. Gimie
Mamiku Gardens

Soufrière Bay
Soufrière
Fond St. Jacques
Edmund Forest Reserve

**Soufrière &
Vicinity**
see detail map
The Pitons
**La Soufrière
Drive-In Volcano**
Micoud
Vierge Pt.

Gros Piton
Morne Coubaril
**Fond Doux
Estate**
○ Choiseul

○ LaFargue
○ Laborie
Savannes Bay

Laborie Bay
Vieux Fort ⑦
**Maria Islands
Nature Reserve**

Vieux Fort
Maria Islands
**Hewanorra
International Airport**
Honeymoon Beach
Moule à Chique
Peninsula
Anse des Sables

ATLANTIC OCEAN

0 —— 4 miles
0 —— 4 km

Hotels & Villas
Coconut Bay Beach Resort, **7**
Inn on the Bay, **2**
Mango Beach Inn, **4**
Marigot Bay Hotel, **5**
Marigot Beach Club
& Dive Resort, **3**
Sandals Regency St. Lucia
Golf Resort & Spa, **1**
Ti Kaye Village, **6**

Restaurants
Boudreau, **3**
Chateau Mygo, **5**
Doolittle's, **6**
Green Parrot, **1**
Rainforest Hideaway, **4**
Rowley's Cafe/
Baguet Shop, **2**

KEY
⚓ Rain Forest
⚓ Cruise Ship
     Terminal
〰 Beaches
◣ Dive Sites
① Hotels & Villas
❶ Restaurants

Coast Road, the terrain starts as steep mountainside with dense vegetation, progresses to undulating hills, and finally becomes rather flat and comparatively arid. Anyone arriving at Hewanorra International Airport, which is located in Vieux Fort, and staying at a resort near Soufrière will travel along this route, a journey of about 30 minutes.

From Vieux Fort north to Castries, a 1½-hour drive, the East Coast Road twists through Micoud, Dennery, and other coastal villages. It then winds up, down, and around mountains, crosses Barre de l'Isle Ridge, and slices through the rain forest. Much of the scenery is breathtaking. The Atlantic Ocean pounds against rocky cliffs, and acres and acres of bananas and coconut palms blanket the hillsides. If you arrive at Hewanorra and stay at a resort near Castries or Rodney Bay, you'll travel along the East Coast Road.

ABOUT THE HOTELS
Nearly all of St. Lucia's villas, hotels, resorts, and inns are tucked into lush surroundings on secluded coves, unspoiled beaches, or forested hillsides in three locations along the calm Caribbean (western) coast. They're located in the greater Castries area between Marigot Bay, a few miles south of the capital, and Choc Bay in the north; in and around Rodney Bay and north to Cap Estate; and in and around Soufrière on the southwestern coast near the Pitons. At this writing, only one resort can be found in Vieux Fort, near Hewanorra International Airport, although the area along the southern and southeastern coasts is ripe for development. The advantage of being in the north is easier access to a wider range of restaurants and nightlife; in the south, you're limited to your own hotel's offerings, nearby hotel dining options, and a handful of local restaurants in Soufrière. On the other hand, many of the island's "don't-miss" natural attractions are in and around Soufrière, so a resort in the south can be convenient if you want to explore more of the island.

Prices in St. Lucia can be twice as high in-season (December 15–April 15) as during the quieter months. Most hotels don't include meals in their rates, but some will offer breakfast or a meal plan. Others require you to purchase a meal plan in the high season, and a few offer all-inclusive packages.

Assume that all hotels operate on the European Plan (**EP**— with no meals) unless we specify that they use the Continental Plan (**CP**—with a Continental breakfast), Breakfast

Plan (**BP**—with full breakfast), or the Modified American Plan (**MAP**—with breakfast and dinner). Other hotels may offer the Full American Plan (**FAP**—including all meals but no drinks) or may be All-Inclusive (**AI**—with all meals, drinks, and most activities.)

ABOUT THE RESTAURANTS

Bananas, mangoes, passion fruit, plantains, breadfruit, okra, avocados, limes, pumpkins, cucumbers, papaya, yams, christophenes (also called chayote), and coconuts are among the fresh local fruits and vegetables that grace St. Lucian menus. The French influence is strong, and most chefs cook with a creole flair. Resort buffets and restaurant fare run the gamut from steaks and chops to pasta and pizza. Every menu lists fresh fish along with the ever-popular lobster. Caribbean standards include calla-loo, stuffed crab back, pepper pot stew, curried chicken or goat, and *lambi* (conch). The national dish of salt fish and green fig—a stew of dried, salted codfish and boiled green banana—is, let's say, an acquired taste. Soups and stews are traditionally prepared in a coal pot, a rustic clay casserole on a matching clay stand that holds the hot coals. Chicken and pork dishes and barbecues are also popular here. Fresh lobster is available in season, which lasts from August through March each year. As they do throughout the Caribbean, local vendors who set up barbecues along the roadside, at street fairs, and at Friday-night "jump-ups" do a land-office business selling grilled fish or chicken legs, bakes (fried biscuits), and beer—you can get a full meal for less than $10. Most other meats are imported—beef from Argentina and Iowa, lamb from New Zealand. Piton is the local brew; Bounty, the local rum.

Dress on St. Lucia is casual but conservative. Shorts are usually fine during the day, but bathing suits and immod-est clothing are frowned upon anywhere but at the beach. In the evening the mood is casually elegant, but even the fanciest places generally expect only a collared shirt and long pants for men and a sundress or slacks for women. And any form of camouflage—even a baby's T-shirt—should not be worn anywhere in St. Lucia and may be confiscated by the police.

WHAT IT COSTS IN U.S. DOLLARS					
	¢	$	$$	$$$	$$$$
Restaurants	under $8	$8–$12	$12–$20	$20–$30	over $30
Hotels*	under $80	$80–$150	$150–$250	$250–$350	over $350
Hotels**	under $125	$125–$250	$250–$350	$350–$450	over $450

*EP, BP, CP **AI, FAP, MAP
Restaurant prices are for a main course at dinner and do not include 8% tax or customary 10% service charge. Hotel prices are per night for a double room in high season, excluding 8% tax and meal plans (except at all-inclusives).

SAFETY

Although crime isn't a significant problem in St. Lucia, take the same precautions you would at home—lock your door, secure your valuables, and don't carry too much money or flaunt expensive jewelry on the street. It's safe (not to mention convenient) to ride local buses in the Rodney Bay area. The Rapid Response Unit is a special police brigade dedicated to visitor security in and around Rodney Bay.

TIMING

St. Lucia is busiest in the high season, which runs from mid-December to mid-April, and during the annual St. Lucia Jazz Festival and Carnival events; at other times of year, the atmosphere is quieter and hotel rates can be significantly cheaper.

In April the **St. Lucia Golf Open** is an amateur tournament held at the St. Lucia Golf & Country Club in Cap Estate.

In early May the weeklong **St. Lucia Jazz Festival** is one of the premier events of its kind in the Caribbean. International jazz greats perform at outdoor venues on Pigeon Island and at various hotels, restaurants, and nightspots throughout the island; free concerts are also held at Derek Walcott Square in downtown Castries. Despite the fact that it's the beginning of the off-season, you may have trouble finding a hotel room at any price during Jazz Festival week.

St. Lucia's summer **Carnival** is a monthlong festival, with musical shows, road marches (parades), calypso, soca (Caribbean dance music), and panorama (steel drum) competitions, king and queen pageants, jump-ups (street dancing), and other events held in and around Castries from late June through early July. It is the island's biggest

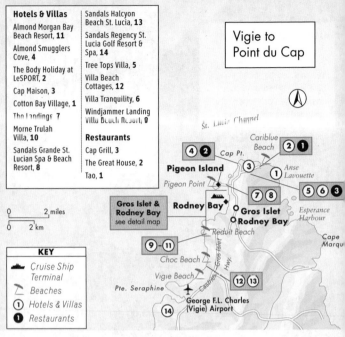

Hotels & Villas

Almond Morgan Bay Beach Resort, **11**

Almond Smugglers Cove, **4**

The Body Holiday at LeSPORT, **2**

Cap Maison, **3**

Cotton Bay Village, **1**

The Landings, **7**

Morne Trulah Villa, **10**

Sandals Grande St. Lucian Spa & Beach Resort, **8**

Sandals Halcyon Beach St. Lucia, **13**

Sandals Regency St. Lucia Golf Resort & Spa, **14**

Tree Tops Villa, **5**

Villa Beach Cottages, **12**

Villa Tranquility, **6**

Windjammer Landing Villa Beach Resort, **9**

Restaurants

Cap Grill, **3**

The Great House, **2**

Tao, **1**

Vigie to Point du Cap

Gros Islet & Rodney Bay
see detail map

0   2 miles
0   2 km

KEY

🚢 Cruise Ship Terminal

🏖 Beaches

① Hotels & Villas

❶ Restaurants

and most inclusive event—or, more appropriately, series of events.

The **St. Lucia Billfishing Tournament** is a three-day competition held in late September or early October, which attracts anglers from throughout the Caribbean who hope to catch the biggest fish. Marlin weighing less than 250 pounds are tagged and returned to the sea, so you can imagine the size of the winner—and even the runners-up. You can take a look at each day's catch at the weighing station at Rodney Bay Marina.

October is **Creole Heritage Month.** The monthlong series of cultural events, which are held in communities throughout the island, culminates on the last Sunday of the month with Jounen Kweyol Etenasyonnal (International Creole Day), a celebration that includes food, crafts, song, and dance.

In late November or early December, the finish of the **Atlantic Rally for Cruisers,** the world's largest ocean-crossing race, is marked by a week of concerts and other festivities at Rodney Bay. More than 200 yachts usually make the crossing each year.

NORTH OF VIGIE TO POINTE DU CAP

From Castries north toward Rodney Bay, Gros Islet, and Cap Estate, the roads are straight, flat, mostly flat, and easy to navigate. This is the most developed part of the island, and many of St. Lucia's resorts, restaurants, and nightspots can be found here. The beaches in the north are also some of the St. Lucia's best. Pigeon Island, one of the island's most important historical sites, is at the island's northwestern tip.

Sights North of Vigie are plotted on the Vigie to Pointe du Cap map.

RENT A CAR? Driving yourself is a fine idea if you want to do some exploring and try lots of restaurants during your visit. If you're staying at an all-inclusive beach resort and plan limited excursions off the property, taxis would be a better choice. The drive from Castries to Soufrière is magnificent, but the winding, mountainous coastal roads can be exhausting for the uninitiated; local drivers are accustomed to the trek.

WHAT TO SEE

☾ **Pigeon Island National Park.** Jutting out from the north-
★ west coast, Pigeon Island is connected to the mainland by a causeway. Tales are told of the pirate Jambe de Bois (Wooden Leg), who once hid out on this 44-acre hilltop islet—a strategic point during the French and British struggles for control of St. Lucia. Now it's a national park and a venue for concerts, festivals, and family gatherings. There are two small beaches with calm waters for swimming and snorkeling, a restaurant, and picnic areas. Scattered around the grounds are ruins of barracks, batteries, and garrisons that date from 18th-century French and English battles. In the Museum and Interpretative Centre, housed in the restored British officers' mess, a multimedia display explains the island's ecological and historical significance. ⊠ *Pigeon Island, St. Lucia National Trust, Rodney Bay* ☎ *758/452–5005* ⊕ *www.slunatrust.org* ⊠ *$5* ☾ *Daily 9–5.*

RODNEY BAY, THEN AND NOW. A mosquito-infested swamp near beautiful Reduit Beach was drained and opened up to the sea in the 1970s, creating a beautiful lagoon and ensuring the value of the surrounding real estate for tourism development. Today Rodney Bay Village is a hive of tourist activity, with hotels, res-

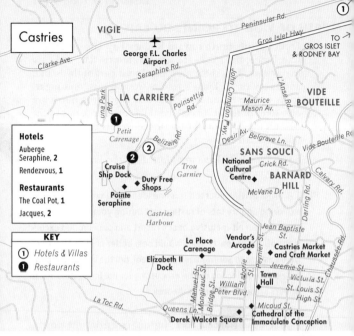

taurants, much of the island's nightlife, and, of course, Rodney
Bay Marina.

Rodney Bay. About 15 minutes north of Castries, the natural
bay and an 80-acre man-made lagoon—surrounded by hotels
and many popular restaurants—are named for Admiral
George Rodney, who sailed the British Navy out of Gros Islet
Bay in 1780 to attack and ultimately decimate the French
fleet. With 250 slips, Rodney Bay Marina is one of the Caribbean's premier yachting centers and the destination of the
Atlantic Rally for Cruisers (transatlantic yacht crossing) each
December. Yacht charters and sightseeing day trips can be
arranged at the marina. The Rodney Bay Ferry makes hourly
crossings between the marina and the shopping complex, as
well as daily excursions to Pigeon Island.

CASTRIES

Castries, the capital city, and the area north and just south
of it are the island's most developed areas. About 15 minutes south of Castries, lovely Marigot Bay is both a yacht
haven and a picture-pretty destination for landlubbers.

Dunstan St. Omer

The murals of Dunstan St. Omer, one of St. Lucia's leading artists—if not *the* leading artist—adorn many walls and churches throughout the island, and his paintings and portraits are prized both locally and internationally. St. Omer is best known locally for frescoing the walls of the **Cathedral of the Immaculate Conception,** in Castries, with the images of black saints just prior to a visit by Pope John Paul II in 1985. He also designed St. Lucia's national flag. A 2004 recipient of the St. Lucia Cross, the nation's highest award, he inspired generations of youngsters for more than 30 years as an art instructor in the public schools. St. Omer is also the father of nine children, two of whom—Luigi and Julio—inherited their father's talent and have followed in his footsteps.

The capital, a busy commercial city of about 65,000 people, wraps around a sheltered bay. Morne Fortune rises sharply to the south of town, creating a dramatic green backdrop. The charm of Castries lies almost entirely in its liveliness, since four fires that occurred between 1796 and 1948 destroyed most of the colonial buildings. Freighters (exporting bananas, coconut, cocoa, mace, nutmeg, and citrus fruits) and cruise ships come and go frequently, making Castries Harbour one of the Caribbean's busiest ports.

Sights in Castries are plotted on the Castries map.

WHAT TO SEE

★ **Castries Market.** At the corner of Jeremie and Peynier streets, spreading beyond its brilliant orange roof and full of excitement and bustle, the market is open every day except Sunday. It's liveliest on Saturday morning, when farmers bring their fresh produce and spices to town, as they have for more than a century. Adjacent to the produce market is the **craft market,** where you can buy pottery, wood carvings, and handwoven straw articles. ⊠ *Corner of Jeremie and Peynier Sts., Castries* ⊙ *Mon.–Sat. 6–5.*

Cathedral of the Immaculate Conception. Directly across Laborie Street from Derek Walcott Square stands Castries's Roman Catholic cathedral, which was built in 1897. Though it appears rather somber on the outside, the interior walls are decorated with colorful murals reworked by St. Lucian artist Dunstan St. Omer just prior to Pope John Paul II's visit in 1985. This church has an active parish and is open

daily for both public viewing and religious services. ☒ *Laborie St., Castries* ⊙ *Daily.*

Derek Walcott Square. The city's green oasis is bordered by Brazil, Laborie, Micoud, and Bourbon streets. Formerly Columbus Square, it was renamed to honor the hometown poet who won the 1992 Nobel prize for literature—one of two Nobel laureates from St. Lucia (the late Sir W. Arthur Lewis won the 1979 Nobel prize in economics). Some of the 19th-century buildings that have survived fire, wind, and rain can be seen on Brazil Street, the square's southern border. On the Laborie Street side there's a huge, 400-year-old samaan (monkey pod) tree with leafy branches that shade a good portion of the square. ☒ *Bordered by Brazil, Laborie, Micoud, and Bourbon Sts., Castries.*

La Place Carenage. On the south side of the harbor near the pier and markets is another duty-free shopping complex with a dozen shops and a café. ☒ *Jeremie St., Castries* ☏ *758/453–2451* ⊙ *Weekdays 9–4, Sat. 9–1.*

Pointe Seraphine. This duty-free shopping complex is on the north side of the harbor, about a 20-minute walk or 2-minute cab ride from the city center; a launch ferries passengers across the harbor when cruise ships are in port. Pointe Seraphine's attractive Spanish-style architecture houses more than 20 upscale duty-free shops, a tourist information kiosk, a taxi stand, and car-rental agencies. The shopping center is adjacent to the cruise-ship pier. ☒ *Castries Harbour, Castries* ☏ *758/452–3036* ⊙ *Weekdays 9–4, Sat. 9–1.*

Vendor's Arcade. Across Peynier Street from the craft market you'll find a maze of handicraft and souvenir vendors. ☒ *Corner of Jeremie and Peynier Sts., Castries* ⊙ *Mon.–Sat. 6–5.*

BETWEEN CASTRIES AND CANARIES

Just south and east of Castries are several of the island's popular sights.

Sights between Castries and Canaries are plotted on the St. Lucia map.

CLOSE UP

Plas Kassav

As you're traveling south to Soufrière, watch for Plas Kassav Bread Bakery in Anse La Verdure, a blink and-you'll-miss-it spot on the West Coast Road between Anse La Raye and Canaries. If you're there early enough, you can see the cassava roots being grated and processed into flour using traditional methods, and the cassava bread dough being mixed in huge copper caldrons. Cinnamon, cherries and raisins, coconut, and other flavorings are added, then the dough— 13 varieties in all—is formed into small buns, placed on banana leaves, and baked over hot coals. Plas Kassav (Creole for Cassava Place) began as a small family bakery in 1998 and has grown into a popular local enterprise simply by word of mouth. There is a large sign, but taxi drivers all know where it is and will not hesitate to stop so you can try a warm, mouthwatering treat that is a staple of St. Lucia's traditional cuisine.

WHAT TO SEE

Barre de l'Isle Forest Reserve. St. Lucia is divided into eastern and western halves by Barre de l'Isle Ridge. A mile-long (1½-km-long) trail cuts through the reserve, and four lookout points provide panoramic views. Visible in the distance are Mt. Gimie, immense green valleys, both the Caribbean Sea and the Atlantic Ocean, and coastal communities. The reserve is about a half-hour drive from Castries; it takes about an hour to walk the trail—an easy hike—and another hour to climb Mt. La Combe Ridge. Permission from the St. Lucia Forest and Lands Department is required to access the trail in Barre de l'Isle; a naturalist or forest officer guide will accompany you. ⊠ *Trailhead on East Coast Rd. near Ravine Poisson, midway between Castries and Dennery* ☎ *758/450–2231 or 758/450–2078* ☞ *Guide services $10* ☉ *Daily by appointment only.*

Bounty Rum Distillery. St. Lucia Distillers, which produces the island's own Bounty Rum, offers 90-minute Rhythm and Rum tours of its distillery, including information on the history of sugar, the background of rum, a detailed description of the distillation process, colorful displays of local architecture, a glimpse at a typical rum shop, Caribbean music, and, of course, a chance to sample the company's rums and liqueurs. The distillery is at the Roseau Sugar Factory in the Roseau Valley, on the island's largest banana plantation, a few miles south of Castries and not far from Marigot. Reservations for the tour are essential. ⊠ *Roseau Sugar Factory, West Coast Rd., Roseau* ☎ *758/451–4258* ⊕ *www.saintluciarums.com* ☎ *$5* ⊙ *Weekdays 9–3.*

Ft. Charlotte. Begun in 1764 by the French as the Citadelle du Morne Fortune, Ft. Charlotte was completed after 20 years of battling and changing hands. Its old barracks and batteries are now government buildings and local educational facilities, but you can drive around and look at the remains, including redoubts, a guardroom, stables, and cells. You can also walk up to the Inniskilling Monument, a tribute to the 1796 battle in which the 27th Foot Royal Inniskilling Fusiliers wrested the Morne from the French. At the military cemetery, which was first used in 1782, faint inscriptions on the tombstones tell the tales of French and English soldiers who died here. Six former governors of the island are buried here as well. From this point atop Morne Fortune you can view Martinique to the north and the twin peaks of the Pitons to the south. ⊠ *Morne Fortune.*

Government House. The official residence of the governor-general of St. Lucia, one of the island's few remaining examples of Victorian architecture, is perched high above Castries, halfway up Morne Fortune—the "Hill of Good Fortune"—which forms a backdrop for the capital city. Morne Fortune has also overlooked more than its share of *bad* luck over the years, including devastating hurricanes and four fires that leveled Castries. Within Government House itself is **Le Pavillon Royal Museum,** which houses important historical photographs and documents, artifacts, crockery, silverware, medals, and awards; original architectural drawings of Government House are displayed on the walls. However, you must make an appointment to visit. ⊠ *Morne Fortune, Castries* ☎ *758/452–2481* ☎ *Free* ⊙ *Tues. and Thurs. 10–noon and 2–4, by appointment only.*

★ **Fodor's Choice Marigot Bay.** This is one of the prettiest natural harbors in the Caribbean. In 1778, British admiral Samuel Barrington sailed into this secluded bay-within-a-bay and, the story goes, covered his ships with palm fronds to hide them from the French. Today this picturesque community—where parts of the original movie *Doctor Dolittle* were filmed in the late 1960s—is a favorite anchorage for boaters and a peaceful destination for landlubbers. The **Marigot Bay Hotel**—a luxury resort (formerly Discovery at Marigot Bay), marina, and marina village with restaurants, bars, grocery store, bakery, boutiques, and other services and activities—has totally revitalized the area, yet great pains were taken to protect both the beauty and the ecology of Marigot Bay. A 24-hour ferry ($2 round-trip) connects the bay's two shores—a voyage that takes about a minute each way.

☽ **Rain Forest Sky Rides.** Ever wish you could get a bird's-eye ★ view of the rain forest or experience it without hiking up and down miles of mountain trails? Here's your chance. Depending on your athleticism, choose the two-hour aerial tram ride, the zip-line experience, or both. Either guarantees a magnificent view as you peacefully slip above or actively zip through the canopy of the 3,442-acre Castries Waterworks Rain Forest in Babonneau, 30 minutes east of Rodney Bay. On the tram ride, eight-passenger gondolas glide slowly among the giant trees, twisting vines, and dense thickets of vegetation accented by colorful flowers as a tour guide explains and shares anecdotes about the various trees, plants, birds, and other wonders of nature found in the area. The zip line, on the other hand, is a thrilling experience in which you're rigged with a harness, helmet, and clamps that attach to cables strategically strung through the forest. Short trails connect the 10 lines, so riders come down to earth briefly and hike to the next station before speeding through the forest canopy to the next stop. Bring binoculars and a camera. ✉ *Chassin, Babonneau* ☏ *758/458–5151* ⊕ *www.rfat.com* ✆ *Tram $72, zip line $60, combo $85* ⊙ *Tues.–Sun. 9–4.*

THE "SNAKE MAN." Driving along the West Coast Road just north of Canaries, don't be surprised if you see a man selling coconuts on the northbound side of the road with a boa constrictor wrapped around his neck. The "snake man" has been a fixture here for years—usually from mid-morning to mid-afternoon—and we're sure the startled looks on tourists' faces give him a kick. Taxi drivers will stop if you want some coconut water or just a closer look. For a small tip, the "snake man" will let you take his picture—wearing his boa, of course.

DID YOU KNOW?

The Devaux family has owned Diamond Botanical Gardens since 1713; the sulfurous water has stained the surrounding rocks different colors.

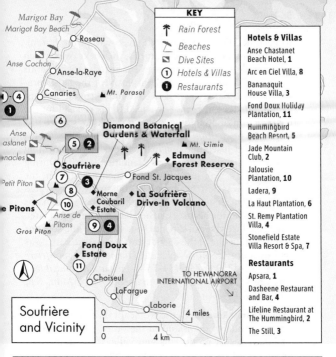

KEY

✝ Rain Forest
↘ Beaches
◩ Dive Sites
① Hotels & Villas
❶ Restaurants

Hotels & Villas

Anse Chastanet
Beach Hotel, **1**

Arc en Ciel Villa, **8**

Bananaquit
House Villa, **3**

Fond Doux Holiday
Plantation, **11**

Hummingbird
Beach Resort, **5**

Jade Mountain
Club, **2**

Jalousie
Plantation, **10**

Ladera, **9**

La Haut Plantation, **6**

St. Remy Plantation
Villa, **4**

Stonefield Estate
Villa Resort & Spa, **7**

Restaurants

Apsara, **1**

Dasheene Restaurant
and Bar, **4**

Lifeline Restaurant at
The Hummingbird, **2**

The Still, **3**

Marigot Bay
Marigot Bay Beach
Roseau
Anse Cochon
Anse-la-Raye
Canaries ▲ Mt. Parasol
Anse astanet
nacles
Soufrière
Petit Piton
e Pitons
Gros Piton
Anse de Pitons

Diamond Botanical
Gardens & Waterfall
▲ Mt. Gimie
Edmund
Forest Reserve
Fond St. Jacques
Morne ◆ La Soufrière
Coubaril Drive-In Volcano
Estate

Fond Doux
Estate
Choiseul
LaFargue
Laborie

TO HEWANORRA
INTERNATIONAL AIRPORT

Soufrière
and Vicinity

0   4 miles

0   4 km

SOUFRIÈRE AND THE SOUTH

Most sightseeing trips from the Rodney Bay area head south toward Soufrière. This is where you can view the landmark Pitons and explore the French-colonial capital of St. Lucia, with its drive-in volcano, botanical gardens, working plantations, and countless other examples of the natural beauty for which St. Lucia is deservedly famous.

Sights in this section are plotted in the Soufrière and Vicinity map.

WHAT TO SEE

★ ~~Fodor's~~Choice **Diamond Botanical Gardens and Waterfall.** These
☙ splendid gardens are part of Soufrière Estate, a 2,000-acre land grant presented by King Louis XIV in 1713 to three Devaux brothers from Normandy in recognition of their services to France. The estate is still owned by their descendants; Joan Du Bouley Devaux maintains the gardens. Bushes and shrubs bursting with brilliant flowers grow beneath towering trees and line pathways that lead to a natural gorge. Water bubbling to the surface from underground sulfur springs streams downhill in rivulets

to become Diamond Waterfall, deep within the botanical gardens. Through the centuries, the rocks over which the cascade spills have become encrusted with minerals and tinted yellow, green, and purple. Near the falls, curative mineral baths are fed by the underground springs. King Louis XVI of France provided funds in 1784 for the construction of a building with a dozen large stone baths to fortify his troops against the St. Lucian climate. It's claimed that Joséphine Bonaparte bathed here as a young girl while visiting her father's plantation nearby. During the Brigand's War, just after the French Revolution, the bathhouse was destroyed. In 1930 the site was excavated by André Du Boulay, and two of the original stone baths were restored for his use. Outside baths were added later. For a small fee you can slip into your swimsuit and soak for 30 minutes in one of the outside pools; a private bath costs slightly more. ⊠ *Soufrière Estate, Diamond Rd., Soufrière* ☎ *758/452–4759 or 758/454–7565* ⊕ *www.diamondstlucia. com* ⊡ *$5, outside bath $4, private bath $6* ⊗ *Mon.–Sat. 10–5, Sun. 10–3.*

Edmund Forest Reserve. Dense tropical rain forest stretches from one side of the island to the other, sprawling over 19,000 acres of mountains and valleys. It's home to a multitude of exotic flowers and plants, as well as rare birds—including the brightly feathered Jacquot parrot. The Edmund Forest Reserve, on the island's western side, is most easily accessible from just east of Soufrière, on the road to Fond St. Jacques. A trek through the lush landscape, with spectacular views of mountains, valleys, and the sea beyond, can take three or more hours. It takes an hour or so just to reach the reserve by car from the north end of the island. It's a strenuous hike, so you need plenty of stamina and sturdy hiking shoes. Permission from the Forest and Lands Department is required to access reserve trails, and the department requires that a naturalist or forest officer guide you because the vegetation is so dense. ⊠ *East of Fond St. Jacques* ☎ *758/450–2231, 758/450–2078 for Forest and Lands Department* ⊡ *Guide $10, guided tours that include round-trip transportation from your hotel $55–$85* ⊗ *Daily by appointment only.*

☾ **Fond Doux Estate.** One of the earliest French estates estab-
★ lished by land grant (1745 and 1763), this plantation still produces cocoa, citrus, bananas, coconut, and vegetables on 135 hilly acres; the restored 1864 plantation house is still in use as well. A 30-minute walking tour begins at the

cocoa fermentary, where you can see the drying process underway. You then follow a trail through the lush culti- vated area, where a guide points out the various fruit- or spice-bearing trees and tropical flowers. Additional trails lead to old military ruins, a religious shrine, and another vantage point for the spectacular Pitons. Cool drinks and a creole buffet lunch are served at the restaurant. Souvenirs, including just-made chocolate balls, are sold at the bou- tique. ⊠ *Chateaubelair, Soufrière* ☎ 758/459–7545 ⊕ *www. fonddouxestate.com* ☜ *Estate $30, includes buffet lunch* ⊙ *Daily 9–4.*

★ Fodor'sChoice **La Soufrière Drive-In Volcano.** As you approach, ☁ your nose will pick up the strong scent of the sulfur springs—more than 20 belching pools of muddy water, multicolor sulfur deposits, and other assorted minerals baking and steaming on the surface. Actually, you don't drive in. You drive up within a few hundred feet of the gur- gling, steaming mass, then walk behind your guide—whose service is included in the admission price—around a fault in the substratum rock. It's a fascinating, educational half hour, though it can also be pretty stinky on a hot day. ⊠ *Bay St., Soufrière* ☎ 758/459–5500 ☜ *$2* ⊙ *Daily 9–5.*

☁ **Morne Coubaril.** On the site of an 18th-century estate, a 250-acre land grant by Louis XIV of France in 1713, the original plantation house has been renovated and a farm worker's village has been re-created to show visitors what life was like for both the owners (a single family that owned the land until 1960) and those who did all the hard labor over the centuries producing cotton, coffee, sugarcane, and cocoa. Cocoa, coconuts, and manioc are still grown on the estate using traditional agricultural methods. Guides show how coconuts are opened and roasted for use as oil and animal feed and how cocoa is fermented, dried, crushed by dancing on the beans, and finally formed into chocolate sticks. Manioc roots (also called cassava) are grated, squeezed of excess water, dried, and turned into flour used in baking. The grounds are lovely for walking or hiking, and the views of mountains and sea beyond are spellbinding. The Pitt, a large, open-air restaurant, serves a creole buffet at lunchtime by reservation only. ⊠ *Soufrière* ☎ 758/459–7340 ⊕ *www.mornecoubarilestate.com* ☜ *$6, with lunch $10* ⊙ *Daily 9–4:30.*

★ Fodor'sChoice **The Pitons.** These two unusual mountains, which are, in fact, a symbol of St. Lucia and were named

a UNESCO World Heritage Site in 2004, rise precipitously from the cobalt-blue Caribbean Sea just south of Soufrière. Covered with thick tropical vegetation, the massive outcroppings were formed by lava from a volcanic eruption 30 to 40 million years ago. They are not identical twins since—confusingly—2,619-foot Petit Piton is taller than 2,461-foot Gros Piton, though Gros Piton is, as the word translates, broader. It's possible to climb the pitons as long as you have permission and use a guide, but it's a strenuous trip. Gros Piton is the easier climb, though the trail up even this shorter Piton is one very tough trek and requires the permission of the Forest and Lands Department and a knowledgeable guide. ☎ *758/450–2231, 758/450–2078 for St. Lucia Forest and Lands Department, 758/459–9748 for Pitons Tour Guide Association ✆ Guide services $45 ☉ Daily by appointment only.*

Soufrière. The oldest town in St. Lucia and the former French-colonial capital, Soufrière was founded by the French in 1746 and named for its proximity to the volcano of the same name. The wharf is the center of activity in this sleepy town (which currently has a population of about 9,000), particularly when a cruise ship is moored in pretty Soufrière Bay. French-colonial influences can be noticed in the architecture of the wooden buildings, with second-story verandahs and gingerbread trim that surround the market square. The market building itself is decorated with colorful murals. The **Soufrière Tourist Information Centre** (✉ *Bay St., Soufrière* ☎ *758/459–7200*) provides information about area attractions. Outside some of the popular attractions in and around Soufrière, souvenir vendors can be persistent. Be polite but firm if you're not interested in their wares.

VIEUX FORT AND THE EAST COAST

Vieux Fort is on the southeast tip of St. Lucia and is the location of Hewanorra International Airport, which serves all commercial jet aircraft arriving at and departing from St. Lucia. While less developed for tourism than the island's north and west (although that may change in coming years), the area around Vieux Fort and along the east coast is home to some of St. Lucia's unique ecosystems and interesting natural attractions.

Sights in this section are plotted on the St. Lucia map.

CLOSE UP

St. Lucia's Two Nobel Laureates

Sir W. Arthur Lewis won the Nobel Prize in Economics in 1979. Born in St. Lucia in 1915, Lewis graduated with distinction from the London School of Economics and went on to earn a PhD in industrial economics. His life interest—and his influence—was in economic development and the transformation and expansion of university education in the Caribbean. Lewis died in 1991 and was buried on the grounds of Sir Arthur Lewis Community College in St. Lucia.

Sir Derek Walcott was born in Castries in 1930. *Omeros*—an epic poem about his journey around the Caribbean, the American West, and London—contributed to his winning the Nobel Prize for Literature in 1992. Walcott is also a writer, playwright, and painter of watercolors. Today, in addition to spending time at his home in St. Lucia, he teaches poetry and drama at Boston University and lectures and gives readings throughout the world.

3

WHAT TO SEE

Frégate Island Nature Reserve. A 1-mi-long (1.5-km-long) trail encircles the nature reserve, which you reach from the East Coast Road near the fishing village of Praslin. In this area, boatbuilders still fashion traditional fishing canoes, called *gommiers* after the trees from which the hulls are made. The ancient design was used by the original Amerindian people who populated the Caribbean. A natural promontory at Praslin provides a lookout from which you can view the two small islets Frégate Major and Frégate Minor and—with luck—the frigate birds that nest here from May to July. The only way to visit is on a guided tour, which includes a ride in a gommier to Frégate Minor for a picnic lunch and a swim; all trips are by reservation only and require a minimum of two people. Arrange visits through your hotel, a tour operator, or the St. Lucia National Trust; many tours include round-trip transportation from your hotel as well as the tour cost. ⊠ *Praslin* ☎ *758/452–5005, 758/453–7656, 758/454–5014 for tour reservations* ⊕ *www.slunatrust.org* 🖃 *$18* ⊗ *Daily by appointment only.*

Mamiku Gardens. One of St. Lucia's largest and loveliest botanical gardens surrounds the hilltop ruins of the Micoud Estate. Baron Micoud, an 18th-century colonel in the French Army and governor general of St. Lucia, deeded the land to his wife, Madame de Micoud, to avoid confisca-

Embracing Kwéyòl

English is St. Lucia's official language, but most St. Lucians speak and often use Kwéyòl—a French-based Creole language—for informal conversations among themselves. Primarily a spoken language, Kwéyòl in its written version doesn't look at all like French; pronounce the words phonetically, though—*entenasyonnal* (international), for example, or the word *Kwéyòl* (Creole) itself—and you indeed sound as if you're speaking French.

Pretty much the same version of the Creole language, or patois, is spoken in the nearby island of Dominica. Otherwise, the St. Lucian Kwéyòl is quite different from that spoken in other Caribbean islands with a French and African heritage such as Haiti, Guadeloupe, and Martinique—or elsewhere, such as Louisiana, Mauritius, and Madagascar. Interestingly, the Kwéyòl spoken in St. Lucia and Dominica is mostly unintelligible to people from those other locations—and vice versa.

St. Lucia embraces its Creole heritage by devoting the month of October each year to celebrations that preserve and promote Creole culture, language, and traditions. In selected communities throughout the island, events and performances highlight Creole music, food, dance, theater, native costumes, church services, traditional games, folklore, native medicine—a little bit of everything, or *"tout bagay"* as you say in Kwéyòl.

Creole Heritage Month culminates during the last weekend of October with all-day events and activities on Jounen Kwéyòl Entenasyonnal, or International Creole Day, which is recognized by all countries that speak a version of the Creole language.

tion by the British during one of the many times when St. Lucia changed hands. Locals abbreviated her name to "Ma Micoud," which, over time, became "Mamiku." Nevertheless, the estate did become a British military outpost in 1796 but, shortly thereafter, was burned to the ground by slaves during the Brigand's War. The estate is now primarily a banana plantation, but the gardens themselves—including several secluded or "secret" gardens—are filled with tropical flowers and plants, including delicate orchids and fragrant herbs. Admission includes a guided tour. ⊠ *Vieux Fort Hwy., Praslin* ☎ *758/455–3729* ⌂ *$6* ☉ *Daily 9–5*.

Maria Islands Nature Reserve. Two tiny islands in the Atlantic Ocean, off St. Lucia's southeast coast, comprise the reserve, which has its own interpretive center. The 25-acre Maria Major and the 4-acre Maria Minor, its little sister, are inhabited by two rare species of reptiles (the colorful Zandoli Terre ground lizard and the harmless Kouwes grass snake) that share their home with frigate birds, terns, doves, and other wildlife. There's a small beach for swimming and snorkeling, as well as an undisturbed forest, a vertical cliff covered with cacti, and a coral reef for snorkeling or diving. Tours, including the boat trip to the islands, are offered by the St. Lucia National Trust by appointment only; you should bring your own picnic lunch, as there are no facilities. ✉ *St. Lucia National Trust Regional Office, Vieux Fort* ☎ *758/452–5005, 758/453–7656, 758/454–5014 for tour reservations* ⊕ *www.slunatrust.org* 🎫 *$35* ☼ *Aug.–mid-May, Wed.–Sun. 9:30–5, by appointment only.*

Vieux Fort. St. Lucia's second-largest town is where you'll find Hewanorra International Airport. From the Moule à Chique Peninsula, the island's southernmost tip, you can see all of St. Lucia to the north and the island of St. Vincent 21 mi (34 km) south. This is where the waters of the clear Caribbean Sea blend with those of the deeper blue Atlantic Ocean.

WHERE TO EAT

With so many popular all-inclusive resorts, guests take most meals at hotel restaurants—which are generally quite good and, in some cases, exceptional. It's fun when vacationing, however, to try some of the local restaurants, as well—for lunch when sightseeing or for a special night out.

NORTH OF VIGIE TO POINTE DU CAP

Restaurant locations can be found on the Rodney Bay and Vigie to Pointe du Cap maps.

$$–$$$ ✕ **Buzz.** *Seafood.* Longtime St. Lucian restaurateur Pat Bowden opened Buzz in "restaurant central"—busy Rodney Bay—opposite the Royal St. Lucian Hotel and Reduit Beach. Starting with cool drinks (maybe a Buzz cooler) and warm appetizers (perhaps lobster and crab cakes, crispy calamari, or tempura shrimp) at the friendly bar, diners make their way to the dining room or the garden for some serious seafood or a good steak, baby back ribs, West Indian pepper pot stew, or spicy lamb shanks. The seared yellowfin tuna, potato-crusted red snapper, and

Best Bets for St. Lucia Dining

With the many restaurants to choose from, how will you decide where to eat? Fodor's writers and editors have selected their favorite restaurants in the Best Bets lists below. The Fodor's Choice properties represent the "best of the best." Find specific details about a restaurant in the full reviews.

★ **Fodor's** Choice

Coal Pot, Dasheene Restaurant and Bar, The Edge, Jacques Waterfront Dining, Rainforest Hideaway, Tao, Ti Bananne

Best Waterfront Dining

Apsara, Boudreau, Chateau Mygo, Coal Pot, Jacques Waterfront Dining, Rainforest Hideaway, Rowley's Café/Baguet Shop

Best for Families

Chateau Myqo, Doolittle's, The Lime on the Bay, Rowley's Café/Baguet Shop

Most Romantic

Apsara, Coal Pot, Boudreau, Dasheene Restaurant and Bar, the Great House, Rainforest Hideaway, Tao

Best for Local St. Lucian Cuisine

Chateau Mygo, Lifeline Restaurant at the Humminghird, The Lime on the Bay, The Still

---

seafood creole are big hits, though. Fresh lobster is available in season (August–March). ⊠ *Reduit Beach, Rodney Bay, Gros Islet* ☎ *758/458–0450* ⊕ *www.buzzstlucia.com* ⚓ *Reservations essential* ▭ *AE, MC, V* ⊙ *Closed Mon., Apr.–Nov. No lunch.*

$$$–$$$$　✕ **Cap Grill.** *Steak.* If you're in the mood for a perfectly cooked steak—or seafood or pasta—head for the golf course. Cap Grill, in the impressive clubhouse of the St. Lucia Golf Club, serves breakfast and lunch daily, dinner from Thursday through Saturday, and Sunday brunch in air-conditioned comfort or alfresco on the dining porch. In either case, your table will overlook the golf course, which is floodlighted at night. Golfers come for an early breakfast or an after-the-round lunch of Black Angus burgers, baguette sandwiches, fresh salads, or pasta specials. The Sports Bar is busy all afternoon. And you don't have to be a golfer to come for dinner. Start with fillet of beef, fish carpaccio, or Caribbean ceviche, followed perhaps by garlic soup or shrimp and corn chowder, and then on to the steak: perfectly grilled 12- or 16-ounce New York strip or beautifully tender 8-ounce filet mignon. Or opt for roast duck breast, blackened mahimahi, rack of lamb, coconut shrimp, roasted pork tenderloin, or stuffed chicken breast.

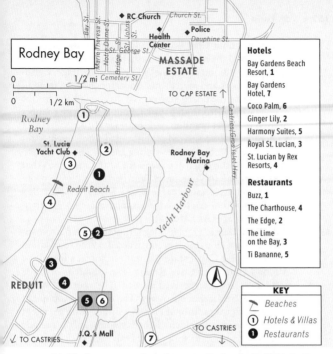

Rodney Bay

| 0 | 1/2 mi |
| 0 | 1/2 km |

RC Church — Church St.
Police — Dauphine St.
Health Center
Bay St. · Marie Theresa St. · Notre Dame St. · St. Johns · St. Georges St. · Bridge St.
Cemetery St.

MASSADE ESTATE

TO CAP ESTATE ↑

Castries/Gros Islet Hwy.

Rodney Bay

St. Lucia Yacht Club ◆

Rodney Bay Marina

Reduit Beach

Yacht Harbour

REDUIT

J.Q.'s Mall ◆

↙ TO CASTRIES

TO CASTRIES

Hotels
Bay Gardens Beach Resort, **1**
Bay Gardens Hotel, **7**
Coco Palm, **6**
Ginger Lily, **2**
Harmony Suites, **5**
Royal St. Lucian, **3**
St. Lucian by Rex Resorts, **4**

Restaurants
Buzz, **1**
The Charthouse, **4**
The Edge, **2**
The Lime on the Bay, **3**
Ti Bananne, **5**

KEY	
⌇	*Beaches*
①	*Hotels & Villas*
❶	*Restaurants*

It's like home away from home! ⊠ *St. Lucia Golf Club, Cap Estate* ☎ *758/450–8523* ⊕ *www.stluciagolf.com* ⌫ *Reservations essential* ⊟ *AE, MC, V* ⊘ *No dinner Sun.–Wed.*

\$\$\$–\$\$\$\$ ✕ **The Charthouse.** *Steak.* Since 1985 the Charthouse, part of the international chain, has been charcoal broiling U.S. Prime beefsteak and serving it up to hungry St. Lucians and vacationers in an open-air, waterfront location on Rodney Bay. Some prefer the hickory-smoked baby back ribs or the roast prime rib of beef—or even grilled seafood. In any case, it's all prepared and served by a friendly staff, many of whom have been with the restaurant since it opened. Fresh lobster is delivered daily in season. After dinner, gentlemen (and audacious ladies) can choose from a wide variety of Cuban cigars, if they wish. ⊠ *Rodney Bay Marina, Gros Islet* ☎ *758/459–8115* ⌫ *Reservations essential* ⊟ *AE, MC, V* ⊘ *No lunch.*

★ **Fodor'sChoice** ✕ **The Edge.** *Eclectic.* Innovative Swedish chef
\$\$\$–\$\$\$\$ Bobo Bergstrom, formerly the culinary director at Windjammer Landing and chef de cuisine at the famed Operakallaren in Stockholm, has brought "Eurobbean" cuisine to his own fine-dining establishment overlooking the harbor at Harmony Suites hotel. St. Lucian locals and visitors

alike rave about Chef Bobo's culinary feats, the excellent wine list, and the island's first sushi bar. The contemporary fusion style combines the chef's European heritage, Caribbean traditions and ingredients, and a touch of Asian influence. Among the dozen starters is a dreamy lobster bisque scented with saffron and paprika. Follow that with snapper braised in fennel bouillon, jerk-marinated and grilled beef tenderloin, or spice-glazed rabbit roulade. You might want to consider the five-course tasting menu. There's sure to be a dish on the extensive menu (or at the sushi bar) that suits everyone in your party, but be sure to leave room for a fabulous dessert. ⊠ *Harmony Suites, Rodney Bay* ☎ *758/450–3343* ⊕ *www.edge-restaurant.com* ⟐ *Reservations essential* ⊟ *AE, MC, V.*

$$$–$$$$ ✕**The Great House.** *French.* Elegant, gracious, and romantic, the Great House was reconstructed on the foundation of an original Cap Estate plantation house adjacent to Almond Smugglers Cove Resort. The grandeur of those early days has been revived as well. The waitstaff wears traditional St. Lucian costumes. The chef adds a piquant creole touch to traditional French cuisine—with excellent results. The menu, which changes nightly, might include pumpkin-and-potato soup, local crab back with lime vinaigrette, sautéed Antillean shrimp in a creole sauce, and broiled sirloin with thyme butter and sweet-potato chips. Cocktails at the open-air bar are especially enjoyable at sunset. The Derek Walcott Theatre is next door. ⊠ *Cap Estate* ☎ *758/450–0450 or 758/450–0211* ⟐ *Reservations essential* ⊟ *AE, D, DC, MC, V* ⊙ *No lunch.*

$$–$$$ ✕**The Lime on the Bay.** *Eclectic.* A casual bistro with lime-green gingham curtains, straw hats decorating the ceiling, and hanging plants, the Lime specializes in local dishes such as spicy jerk chicken or pork and breadfruit salad—as well as char-grilled steak and fresh-caught fish. The portions are plentiful, and the prices are reasonable, which is perhaps why you often see St. Lucians and visitors alike "liming" (an island term that means something akin to hanging around and relaxing) all day and most of the night at this popular restaurant. The Late Lime, a club where the crowd gathers as night turns to morning, is next door. ⊠ *Rodney Bay* ☎ *758/452–0761* ⊟ *D, MC, V* ⊙ *Closed Tues.*

★ Fodor'sChoice ✕**Tao.** *Asian.* For exquisite dining, head for Tao

$$$–$$$$ at the Body Holiday at LeSPORT. Perched on a second-floor balcony at the edge of Cariblue Beach, you're guaranteed a pleasant breeze and a starry sky while you enjoy fusion cuisine—a marriage of Asian tastes and a Caribbean touch.

European-inspired Caribbean cuisine at The Edge in Rodney Bay

Choose from appetizers such as seafood dumplings, sashimi salad, or miso eggplant timbale, followed by tender slices of pork loin teriyaki, twice-cooked duck, wok-seared calves' liver, or tandoori chicken—the results are mouthwatering. Fine wines accompany the meal, desserts are extravagant, and service is superb. Seating is limited; hotel guests have priority, so reserve early. ⌂ *The Body Holiday at LeSPORT, Cap Estate* ☎ *758/450–8551* ⊕ *www.thebodyholiday.com* ⌂ *Reservations essential* ▤ *AE, MC, V* ⊘ *No lunch.*

★ **Fodor's**Choice ✕ **Ti Bananne.** *Caribbean.* Poolside at the Coco
$$$–$$$$ Palm hotel in Rodney Bay, Ti Bananne is an airy Caribbean-style bistro and bar that serves breakfast, lunch, and dinner daily. Breakfast attracts mostly hotel guests, but the elegant yet casual restaurant has been positioned as an independent restaurant to attract both guests and nonguests for lunch and dinner. Lunch is a good bet if you're poking around Rodney Bay, need a break from Reduit Beach, or are just looking for a good meal in a friendly spot. On Wednesday there's a special creole lunch buffet; for Sunday brunch, a barbecue buffet. In the evening, stop first at the bar for a fruity rum drink, cold Piton beer, or something stronger—but the open-to-the-breeze dining room is where the magic really comes through. Executive chef Richardson Skinner and head chef Giancarlo Crumps, both natives of Trinidad and Tobago with extensive experience throughout the Caribbean, conjure up exquisite French-inspired, creole-influenced dishes such as panfried

The Coal Pot restaurant in Vigie Marina, Castries

snapper with orange and butter sauce and green fig Lyonnaise. Leave room for dessert—the trio of crèmes brûlées (mango and ginger, coconut, and sea moss and cinnamon) is the showstopper. And speaking of the show, a live band entertains every evening. ⊠ *Coco Palm, Rodney Bay, Gros Islet* ☎ *758/456–2828* ⊕ *www.coco-resorts.com* ⚑ *Reservations essential* ▭ *AE, MC, V.*

CASTRIES

Restaurant locations can be found on the St. Lucia and Castries maps.

★ Fodor'sChoice ✕ **Coal Pot.** *French.* Popular since the early
$$$–$$$$ 1960s, this tiny (only 10 tables) waterfront restaurant overlooking pretty Vigie Cove is managed by local artist Michelle Elliott and her French husband, Xavier Ribot, who is also the chef. For a light lunch, opt for a Greek or shrimp salad or, perhaps, broiled fresh fish with creole sauce. Dinner might start with divine lobster bisque, followed by fresh seafood accompanied by one (or more) of the chef's fabulous sauces—ginger, coconut-curry, lemon-garlic butter, or wild mushroom. Hearty eaters may prefer duck, lamb, beef, or chicken laced with peppercorns, red wine, and onion or Roquefort sauce. ⊠ *Vigie Marina, Castries* ☎ *758/452–5566* ⊕ *www.coalpotrestaurant.com* ⚑ *Reservations essential* ▭ *AE, D, MC, V* ⊗ *Closed Sun. No lunch Sat.*

$$$–$$$$ ✕ **Green Parrot.** *Caribbean.* One reason to dine in this English colonial–style hotel atop the Morne is the romantic view overlooking Castries Harbour and the twinkling lights of the city after dark. The food is good, too. Acclaimed chef Harry Edwards, who trained years ago at Claridge's Hotel in London, prepares a menu of St. Lucian specialties and international dishes—and you can count on a good steak. There's also lively entertainment—a floor show with a belly dancer on Wednesday night and limbo dancing on Saturday. On Monday night the tradition is that a lady who wears a flower in her hair and is accompanied by a "well-dressed" gentleman might receive a free dinner. ⊠ *Morne Fortune, Castries* ☎ *758/452–3399* ⚓ *Reservations essential* 🏛 *Jacket required* ⊟ *AE, MC, V.*

★ **Fodor's** Choice ✕ **Jacques Waterfront Dining.** *Eclectic.* Chef-owner
$$$–$$$$ Jacky Rioux creates magical dishes in his open-air garden restaurant (known for years as Froggie Jack's) overlooking Vigie Cove. The cooking style is decidedly French, as is Rioux, but fresh produce and local spices create a fusion cuisine that's memorable at either lunch or dinner. You might start with a bowl of creamy tomato-basil or pumpkin soup, a grilled portobello mushroom, or octopus and conch in curried coconut sauce. Main courses include fresh seafood, such as oven-baked kingfish with a white wine and sweet pepper sauce, or breast of chicken stuffed with smoked salmon in a citrus butter sauce. The wine list is also impressive. ⊠ *Vigie Marina, Castries* ☎ *758/458–1900* ⊕ *www.jacquesrestaurant.com* ⚓ *Reservations essential* ⊟ *AE, MC, V* ⊗ *Closed Sun.*

BETWEEN CASTRIES AND CANARIES

Restaurant locations can be found on the St. Lucia map.

$$$–$$$$ ✕ **Boudreau.** *Continental.* Simple and satisfying are words that come to mind when dining at Boudreau, the Marigot Bay Hotel's main dining room. The chef's passion for incorporating St. Lucian ingredients into the menu brings him to market regularly to choose the best fruits, roots, and greens to blend with fresh seafood and prime meats—or to create a vegetarian dish that's both filling and full of flavor. Seafood lovers may enjoy pan-roasted kingfish with tempura vegetables, mashed sweet potatoes, and maple mango sauce. Boudreau—which is rather casual at breakfast and lunch but becomes rather elegant at dinner—welcomes villa guests, yachties, and day-trippers alike. The open-air restaurant is named for Walter Boudreau, a schooner captain who sailed into

Marigot Bay more than 50 years ago and built the original hotel where the Marigot Bay Hotel is now located. Clearly, he would be impressed. ✉ *Marigot Bay Hotel, Marigot Bay* ☎ *758/458–5300* ⊕ *www.marigotbay.com* ⚓ *Reservations essential* ⊟ *AE, MC, V* ☉ *Closed Sept.*

$$–$$$ ✕ **Chateau Mygo.** *Seafood.* Walk down a garden path to ☺ Chateau Mygo (a corruption of the word "Marigot"), pick out a table on the dockside dining deck, pull up a chair, and soak up the waterfront atmosphere of what is arguably the prettiest bay in the Caribbean. The tableau is mesmerizing—and that's at lunch, when you can order a sandwich, burger, fish or chicken and chips, salads, or grilled fish or chicken with peas and rice and vegetables. At dinner, chef-owner Doreen Rambally—whose family has owned and operated this place since the mid-1970s—draws on three generations of East Indian and creole family recipes. Beautifully grilled fresh tuna, red snapper, kingfish, mahimahi, and local lobster are embellished with flavors such as ginger, mango, papaya, or passion fruit, and then dished up with regional vegetables—perhaps callaloo, okra, dasheen, breadfruit, christophene, or yams. Of course, you can also have roast pork, beef, a chicken dish, or even pizza, if you wish. This is a very casual restaurant where locals, yachties, and frequent visitors know they'll get a delicious, reasonably priced meal right on the waterfront. And oh, that view! ✉ *Marigot Bay* ☎ *758/451–4772* ⊟ *MC, V.*

$$–$$$ ✕ **Doolittle's.** *Continental.* Named for the protagonist in ☺ the original (1967) *Dr. Doolittle* movie starring Rex Harrison, part of which was filmed right here in Marigot Bay, Doolittle's is the inside/outside waterfront restaurant at the Marigot Beach Club & Dive Center on the north side of the bay. You can watch yachts quietly slip by as you enjoy your meal. The menu offers a broad range of choices—light meals such as sandwiches, burgers, grilled chicken, and salads at lunchtime and, in the evening, seafood, steak, chicken, and Caribbean specials such as curries and stews. Take the little ferry across the bay to reach Doolittle's. During the day, bring your bathing suit. The beach is just outside the restaurant's door. ✉ *Marigot Beach Club, Marigot Bay* ☎ *758/451–4974* ⊕ *www.marigotdiveresort. com* ⊟ *MC, V.*

★ Fodor'sChoice ✕ **Rainforest Hideaway.** *Eclectic.* Fabulous fusion
$$$–$$$$ fare—in this case, the exotic tastes and flavors influencing classical French cuisine—is presented by Chef Myron at this romantic fine-dining hideaway on the north shore of pretty Marigot Bay. It's definitely worth the 20-minute-or-so

drive from Castries. A little ferry whisks you to the alfresco restaurant, perched on a dock, where you're greeted with complimentary champagne. You'll be duly impressed by entrées such as balsamic-glazed roast quail, five-spice roast fillet of beef, or citrus-marinated wild salmon, accompanied by rich sauces, exotic vegetables, and excellent wines—not to mention the blanket of stars in the sky overhead and the live jazz several times a week. Sunday brunch is a special treat in this picturesque setting on the bay. ⊠ *Marigot Bay* ☎ *758/286–0511* ⊕ *www.rainforesthideawaystlucia.com* ⚮ *Reservations essential* ⊟ *AE, D, MC, V* ⊙ *No lunch.*

¢–$ ✕ **Rowley's Café/Baguet Shop.** *Café.* Join the yachties and
☕ Marigot Bay Hotel guests for breakfast, lunch, afternoon tea, an evening snack, or just dessert at this French bakery and café in the Marina Village on Marigot Bay. Open every day from 7 AM to 7 PM, it offers freshly baked French bread, crusty croissants, and delicious French pastries. Sandwiches are prepared on a baguette, croissant, or focaccia—your choice. Pair your favorite with a cup of cappuccino, mocha, or latte. Or hold the coffee until dessert, and pair your fruit tart, pain au chocolat, coconut flan, or another delicious pastry selection with a steaming cup of rich espresso. Eat in (well, outside on the dock) or take it out. Even if you eat in, you'll probably want a baguette—or a bagful—to take out, as well. ⊠ *Marina Village, Marigot Bay* ☎ *758/451–4275* ⚮ *Reservations not accepted* ⊟ *AE, MC, V.*

SOUFRIÈRE AND VICINITY

Restaurant locations can be found on the Soufrière and Vicinity map.

$$$–$$$$ ✕ **Apsara.** *Indian.* India has had an important historical impact on many islands in the Caribbean, from the heritage of its people—descendents of both indentured servants and wealthy businessmen—to the colorful Madras plaids that adorn national costumes and the curry flavoring that is a staple of Caribbean cuisine. At night, Anse Chastanet's Trou au Diable restaurant transforms itself into Apsara, an upscale dining experience where modern Indian cuisine is served in an extraordinarily romantic, candlelit, beachfront setting. Chef Hemant Dadlani, who hails from Mumbai, has created an innovative menu that fuses East Indian and Caribbean cooking. That translates to food that's full of flavor but not too spicy, although you can opt for some dishes that are hotter than others. You might start with mulligatawny soup with cumin yogurt or vegetable samosas,

followed by coconut-chili king prawns, pork vindaloo, or tandoori-roasted salmon, lamb chops, chicken, or lobster. Definitely order the naan bread, either plain or flavored with almond, coconut, or raisin. And for dessert, depending on your appetite, choose the mango, saffron, or sea moss *kulfi* (Indian-style ice cream) or go all the way with Apsara's Temptation (tandoori-baked pineapple with honey, saffron, and passion-fruit syrup, Indian ice cream, and sun-blushed chili). ⊠ *Anse Chastanet, Soufrière* ☎ *758/459–7354* ⊕ *www. ansechastanet.com* ⚲ *Reservations essential* ⊟ *AE, D, DC, MC, V* ☺ *Closed Tues. No lunch.*

★ Fodor's Choice ╳ **Dasheene Restaurant and Bar.** *Caribbean.* The
$$$–$$$$ terrace restaurant at Ladera resort has breathtakingly close-up views of the Pitons and the sea between them, especially beautiful at sunset. It's casual by day and magical at night. Executive chef Orlando Satchell describes his creative West Indian menu as "sexy Caribbean." Appetizers may include grilled crab claws with a choice of dips or silky pumpkin soup with ginger. Typical entrées are triggerfish seasoned and soaked in lime and fish stock and cooked in banana leaves, shrimp Dasheene (panfried with local herbs), seared duck breast with passion-fruit jus, or baron fillet of beef with sweet potato and green-banana mash. Light dishes, fresh salads, and sandwiches are served at lunchtime. ⊠ *Ladera resort, 2 mi (3 km) south of Soufrière* ☎ *758/459–7323* ⊕ *www.ladera.com* ⊟ *AE, D, DC, MC, V.*

$$–$$$ ╳ **Lifeline Restaurant at the Hummingbird.** *Caribbean.* The chef at this cheerful restaurant-bar in the Hummingbird Beach Resort specializes in French-creole cuisine, starting with fresh seafood or chicken seasoned with local herbs and accompanied by a medley of vegetables just picked from the Hummingbird's garden. Sandwiches and salads are also available. If you stop for lunch, sit outside by the pool for a magnificent view of the Pitons (you can also take a dip), and be sure to visit the batik studio and art gallery of proprietor Joan Alexander-Stowe, adjacent to the dining room. ⊠ *Hummingbird Beach Resort, Anse Chastanet Rd., Soufrière* ☎ *758/459–7232* ⊕ *www.istlucia.co.uk* ⊟ *AE, D, MC, V.*

$$ ╳ **The Still.** *Caribbean.* When you're visiting Diamond Waterfall, this is a great lunch spot. The two dining rooms seat up to 400 people, so it's a popular stop for tour groups and cruise passengers. The emphasis is on local cuisine using vegetables such as christophene, breadfruit, yam, and callaloo along with grilled fish or chicken, but there are also pork and beef dishes. All fruits and vegetables used in the

Amazing views at Dasheene Restaurant in the Ladera Resort

restaurant are organically grown on the estate. ✉ *The Still Plantation, Sir Arthur Lewis St., Soufrière* ☎ *758/459–7261* ▭ *MC, V.*

WHERE TO STAY

Most people—particularly honeymooning couples—choose to stay in one of St. Lucia's many beach resorts, the majority of which are upscale and fairly pricey. Several are all-inclusive, including the three Sandals resorts, two Almond resorts, and two resorts owned and/or managed by Sunswept (The Body Holiday at LeSPORT and Rendezvous).

If you're looking for lodgings that are more intimate and less expensive, St. Lucia has dozens of small inns and hotels that are often locally owned, always charming, and usually less expensive—but that may or may not be directly on the beach. Luxury villa communities and independent private villas are another alternative in St. Lucia. Most of the villa communities—which, as elsewhere in the Caribbean, continue to emerge in St. Lucia—are located in the north near Cap Estate.

The lodgings listed below all have air-conditioning, telephones, and TVs in guest rooms unless otherwise noted.

VILLA COMMUNITIES AND CONDOMINIUM COMPLEXES

Luxury villa communities are an important part of the accommodations mix in St. Lucia, as they can be an economical option for families, groups, or couples vacationing together. Several villa communities have opened in recent years, and more are on the way. The villas themselves are privately owned, but nonowners can rent individual units directly from the property managers for a vacation or short-term stay, the same as reserving hotel accommodations. Units with fully equipped kitchens, up to three bedrooms, and as many baths run $200–$2,500 per night, depending on the size and the season.

PRIVATE VILLAS AND CONDOS

Local real-estate agencies will arrange vacation rentals of privately owned villas and condos that are fully furnished and equipped. Most private villas are located in the hills of Cap Estate in the very north of the island, in Rodney Bay or Bois d'Orange amid all the tourist activity, or in Soufrière among all the natural treasures of St. Lucia. Some are within walking distance of a beach. All rental villas are staffed with a housekeeper and a cook who specializes in local cuisine; in some cases, a caretaker lives on the property and a gardener and/or night watchman are on staff. All properties have telephones, and some have Internet access and/or fax machines. Telephones may be barred against outgoing overseas calls; plan to use a phone card or calling card. Most villas have TVs, DVDs, and CD players. All private villas have a swimming pool; condos share a community pool. Vehicles are generally not included in the rates, but rental cars can be arranged and delivered to the villa upon request. Linens and basic supplies (e.g., bath soap, toilet tissue, dish detergent) are included. Pre-arrival grocery stocking can be arranged for a fee in addition to the cost of the groceries.

Units with one to nine bedrooms and as many baths run $200–$2,000 per night, depending on the size of the villa, the amenities, the number of guests, and the season. Rates include utilities and government taxes. Your only additional cost will be for groceries and staff gratuities. A security deposit is required upon booking and refunded after departure less any damages or unpaid miscellaneous charges.

VILLA RENTAL AGENCIES

Discover Villas of St. Lucia (☎ 758/484–3066 ⊕ www.a1stluciavillas.com). **Island Villas St. Lucia** (☎ 758/458–4903 ⊕ www.island-

Best Bets for St. Lucia Lodging

CLOSE UP

Fodor's offers a selective listing of quality lodging experiences, from the island's best boutique hotel to its most luxurious beach resort. Here, we've compiled our top recommendations based on the different types of lodging found on the island. The very best properties—in other words, those that provide a particularly remarkable experience—are designated in the listings with the Fodor's Choice logo.

★ **Fodor's**Choice

Anse Chastanet Beach Hotel, Bay Gardens Beach Resort, Body Holiday at LeSPORT, Cap Maison, Coco Palm, Cotton Bay Village, Jade Mountain Club, Jalousie Plantation, Ladera, the Landings, Marigot Bay Hotel, Royal St. Lucian, Sandals Grande St. Lucia Spa & Beach Resort, Sandals Halcyon Beach St. Lucia, Sandals Regency St. Lucia Golf Resort & Spa, Ti Kaye Village

BEST BEACHFRONT RESORTS
Almond Morgan Bay Beach Resort, Almond Smugglers Cove, Anse Chastanet Beach Hotel, Bay Gardens Beach Resort, Body Holiday at LeSPORT, Coconut Bay Beach Resort & Spa, Cotton Bay Village, Jalousie Plantation, Rendezvous,

Royal St. Lucian, St. Lucian by Rex Resorts, Sandals Grande St. Lucia Spa & Beach Resort, Sandals Halcyon Beach St. Lucia, Sandals Regency St. Lucia Golf Resort & Spa, Windjammer Landing Villa Beach Resort

BEST BOUTIQUE HOTELS
Bay Gardens Hotel, Coco Palm, Fond Doux Holiday Plantation, La Haut Plantation, Ladera, Ti Kaye Village

BEST FOR ROMANCE
Anse Chastanet Beach Hotel, Body Holiday at LeSPORT, Jade Mountain Club, Jalousie Plantation, Ladera, Marigot Bay Hotel, Royal St. Lucian, Sandals Grande St. Lucia Spa & Beach Resort, Sandals Halcyon Beach St. Lucia, Sandals Regency St. Lucia Golf Resort & Spa, Stonefield Estate Villa Resort & Spa, Ti Kaye Village

BEST FOR FAMILIES
Almond Morgan Bay Beach Resort, Almond Smugglers Cove, Bay Gardens Beach Resort, Coconut Bay Beach Resort & Spa, Cotton Bay Village, Jalousie Plantation, La Haut Plantation, the Landings, Mango Beach Inn, Royal St. Lucian, St. Lucian by Rex Resorts, Windjammer Landing Villa Beach Resort

3

---

villas.com/stlucia.php). **Tropical Villas** (🕿 758/452–8240 ⊕ www.tropicalvillas.net).

NORTH OF VIGIE TO POINTE DU CAP

Hotel locations can be found on the St. Lucia, Rodney Bay, and Vigie to Pointe du Cap maps.

$$$$ ⚀ **Almond Morgan Bay Beach Resort.** *All-Inclusive.* An all-inclusive resort appropriate for singles, couples, and families alike, Almond Morgan Bay offers both quiet seclusion on 22 acres surrounding a stretch of white-sand beach and tons of free sports and activities. Rooms, each with a private balcony or terrace, are in several buildings set among tropical gardens or facing the beachfront. The resort's four restaurants include waterfront Bambou, which serves a mouthwatering fusion of Caribbean and Asian cuisines; French-creole Le Jardin; and seafood restaurant Morgan's Pier, which stretches dramatically into the bay. Four swimming pools (two designated for adults only) and all manner of activities are available day and night. **Pros:** family-friendly; lots to do; three complimentary rounds of golf included; great atmosphere at Morgan's Pier. **Cons:** resort is huge and can be very busy, especially when all rooms are filled; beach is small. ✉ *Choc Bay, Gros Islet ⬧ Box 2167, Castries* ☎ *758/450–2511* ⊕ *www.almondresorts.com* ⤶ *340 rooms ⬧ In-room: safe. In-hotel: 4 restaurants, bars, tennis courts, pools, gym, spa, beachfront, water sports, children's programs (ages 3 months–16), laundry service, Internet terminal* ☰ *AE, D, MC, V* ⍥ *AI.*

$$$$ ⚀ **Almond Smugglers Cove.** *All-Inclusive.* This all-inclusive resort has more food, fun, and features than you'll have time to enjoy in a week. On 60 acres and overlooking a pretty bay at the island's northernmost point, basic but comfortable guest rooms are spread out over a broad hillside; golf cart transportation is available to get you from place to place. The resort has five swimming pools, a sandy beach, and a laundry list of water sports to enjoy. The world-class St. Lucia Racquet Club, with seven tennis courts and a squash court, is on-site, and guests get three free 18-hole rounds of golf at the nearby St. Lucia Golf Course. Four dining rooms offer as many cuisines, libations flow freely from four bars, and there's live entertainment nightly. The plethora of planned entertainment lends the resort a holiday camp atmosphere, but families with young children really love it. **Pros:** family rooms sleep five; excellent children's program; superlative tennis facilities; nightly entertainment is family-friendly. **Cons:** busy, busy, busy; not the place for a quiet getaway; guest rooms are spread far and wide on the hillside. ✉ *Smugglers Cove, Cap*

Estate, Gros Islet ☎ 758/450–0551 ⊕ www.almondresorts.
com ⇨ 257 rooms, 100 suites ⚙ In-room: safe. In-hotel: 4
restaurants, room service, bars, tennis courts, pools, gym,
spa, beachfront, water sports, children's programs (ages
3 months–16), laundry service, Internet terminal, Wi-Fi
hotspot ⊟ AE, D, MC, V ⊠ AI.

★ Fodor'sChoice ⊞ **Bay Gardens Beach Resort.** *Resort.* One of three
$$ Bay Gardens properties in Rodney Bay Village, the beach
ⓒ resort has a prime location directly on beautiful Reduit
Beach. The six three-story buildings wrap around a large,
lagoon-style pool. Water sports and diving are available
on the beach, or you can arrange a massage in one of the
poolside cabanas. All suites have living and dining areas,
full kitchens, and modern baths; most have views of the
sea from the balcony or terrace. Rooms and suites can be
combined to make two-bedroom accommodations, with
full self-catering facilities in the living area and 2½ baths.
Guests may dine at elegant Dolphins Restaurant; at Hi
Tide, a casual beachside restaurant; at the Lo Tide deli;
or at any of a dozen or so excellent restaurants in the
Rodney Bay neighborhood. The Bay Gardens properties
are known for their friendly hospitality and exceptional
service; in fact, the hotel clientele is 75% repeat guests.
Add a beautiful beach to the equation, and this newest
member of the family is definitely a winner. **Pros:** idyllic
beachfront location; family friendly; excellent value. **Cons:**
popular place, so you need to book far in advance in sea-
son. ⊠ Reduit Beach, Rodney Bay, Gros Islet ⓓ Box 1892,
Gros Islet ☎ 758/457–8500 ⊕ www.baygardensbeachresort.
com ⇨ 36 rooms, 36 suites ⚙ In-room: safe, kitchen (some),
refrigerator, DVD, Internet. In-hotel: 3 restaurants, bars,
pool, gym, spa, beachfront, diving, water sports, children's
programs (ages 4–12), laundry service, Internet terminal,
Wi-Fi hotspot ⊟ AE, D, MC, V ⊠ EP.

¢–$ ⊞ **Bay Gardens Hotel.** *Hotel.* Independent travelers and
regional businesspeople swear by this cheerful, well-run
boutique hotel at Rodney Bay Village. In fact, it's often
fully booked. Never fear: Bay Gardens Inn, a 33-room sister
property, is next door, and the Bay Gardens Beach Resort is
minutes away. Modern, colorful, and surrounded by pretty
flower gardens, the hotel is a short walk from beautiful
Reduit Beach (shuttle transportation is also provided),
several popular restaurants, and shops. Some rooms sur-
round the serpentine pool and Jacuzzi and are close to the
restaurant and lobby; more secluded rooms near the back
of the property have easy access to a second pool that's

Cotton Bay Village

Cap Maison Resort & Spa

Sandals Halcyon Beach, lu-The Pierhouse Resta

Sandals Grande St. Lucian Spa & Beach Resort

smaller and quieter. The 16 "Croton" suites have full kitchens and interconnect to become two-bedroom suites. Spices restaurant offers modern Caribbean cuisine. **Pros:** excellent service; unusual value; "Croton" suites are a best bet. **Cons:** not beachfront; heavy focus on business travelers, so it's not exactly a vacation environment. ⊠ *Rodney Bay* ✑ *Box 1892, Castries* ☎ *758/452–8060* ⊕ *www.baygardenshotel. com* ↶ *59 rooms, 28 suites* ⚹ *In-room: safe, kitchen (some), refrigerator, Internet, Wi-Fi (some). In-hotel: restaurant, room service, bar, pools, laundry service, Internet terminal, Wi-Fi hotspot* ⊟ *AE, D, MC, V* ⏺⏺*EP.*

★ **Fodor's**Choice ▦ **Body Holiday at LeSPORT.** *All-Inclusive.* Even
$$$$ before you leave home, you can customize your own "body holiday" online—from robe size to tee time—at this adults-only resort in luxurious tropical surroundings. Indulge in aromatherapy, a dozen different massages, ayurvedic treatments, wraps, yoga, and personal-trainer services at the splendid Oasis spa; daily treatments are included in the rates. Otherwise, enjoy the beach, scuba diving, golf (green fees are free at St. Lucia Golf Club, next door), and other sports. Rooms have marble floors and king-size four-poster or twin beds. The food is excellent at Cariblue (the main dining room), the Club House casual buffet restaurant, the Deli, or the top-of-the-line Tao. Enjoy nightly entertainment at the beachside lounge. Special rates are offered for single guests. **Pros:** daily spa treatment included; excellent dining; unusual activities such as archery. **Cons:** unremarkable rooms; small bathrooms with skimpy towels; must climb steps to get to the spa. ⊠ *Cariblue Beach, Cap Estate, Gros Islet* ✑ *Box 437, Castries* ☎ *758/450–8551* ⊕ *www.thebody-holiday.com* ↶ *152 rooms, 2 suites* ⚹ *In-room: safe, refrigerator, no TV. In-hotel: 3 restaurants, bars, tennis courts, pools, gym, spa, beachfront, diving, water sports, Internet terminal, no kids under 18* ⊟ *AE, MC, V* ⏺⏺*AI.*

★ **Fodor's**Choice ▦ **Cap Maison.** *Vacation Rental.* This boutique
$$$$ villa community, built on a seaside bluff, has 22 units that can be configured as up to 49 rooms; junior suites; and oversize one-, two-, or three-bedroom villa suites. The Ocean View Grand Villa suites, for example, measure 3,000 square feet. The elegant Spanish Caribbean architecture features wooden jalousie doors and windows, terra-cotta roof tiles, large private balconies, and large roof terraces— nine of which have their own private plunge pool. A large infinity pool at the edge of the bluff and a smaller pool are available to everyone. Truly luxurious service includes no formal check-in required, an unpacking service upon

request, an honor bar, and a personal butler for any little needs and requests that may come up—including arranging a romantic dinner, prepared and served in your suite by one of the resort's chefs. French Caribbean cuisine at the resort's cliff-top restaurant, Cliff at Cap, is another option. For extra pampering, there's a full-service spa and a calming zen garden. The resort is on a seaside cliff, so getting down to Smugglers Cove beach, a secluded crescent of sand, requires hiking down (and back up) 62 steps. The resort also has a 46-foot, 15-passenger powerboat to take guests on day trips to Soufrière or nearby Martinique or on honeymoon cruises. **Pros:** golf and tennis privileges nearby; private and elegant; those rooftop plunge pools. **Cons:** a/c in bedrooms only; beach access (62 steps) is strenuous. ⊠ *Smugglers Cove, Cap Estate, Gros Islet* ⬚ *Box 2188, Gros Islet* ☎ *758/457–8678* ⊕ *www.capmaison.com* ⇆ *10 rooms, 39 suites in 22 villas* ⚐ *In-room: safe, kitchen (some), refrigerator, DVD, Internet. In-hotel: restaurant, room service, bars, pool, gym, spa, beachfront, water sports, laundry facilities, laundry service, Internet terminal, Wi-Fi hotspot* ⊟ *AE, MC, V* ⊙⧟ *EP.*

★ **Fodor's**Choice ▧ **Coco Palm.** *Hotel.* This stylish boutique hotel
$–$$ in Rodney Bay Village also includes Coco Kreole, a cozy guesthouse at the edge of the property and right in the middle of the Rodney Bay Village action. Coco Palm guest rooms—including six swim-up rooms adjacent to the pool and a dozen spacious suites—are beautifully decorated in French Caribbean plantation style but with every modern convenience. Cordless phones, CD and DVD players, free Wi-Fi and Internet access, flat-screen TVs (in suites), and ultramodern baths with walk-in showers and claw-foot tubs (in suites) are amenities you'd expect at much pricier resorts. The 20 Coco Kreole rooms are smaller and wrap around what is more like a comfortable living room than a hotel lobby. The excellent Ti Bananne restaurant and bar overlook Coco Palm's pool and bandstand, and all the action of Rodney Bay Village and beautiful Reduit Beach is within walking distance. **Pros:** excellent value; fabulous swim-up rooms; fantastic dining. **Cons:** not directly on the beach; nightly entertainment can get noisy. ⊠ *Reduit Beach Ave., Rodney Bay* ⊠ *Box GM605, Rodney Bay* ☎ *758/456–2800* ⊕ *www.coco-resorts.com* ⇆ *80 rooms, 12 suites* ⚐ *In-room: safe, refrigerator, DVD, Wi-Fi. In-hotel: restaurant, bars, pools, laundry service, Internet terminal, Wi-Fi hotspot* ⊟ *AE, D, MC, V* ⊙⧟ *EP.*

★ Fodor'sChoice ☷ **Cotton Bay Village.** *Vacation Rental.* Wedged
$$$$ between a quiet ocean beach and the St. Lucia Golf Club,
☾ luxurious, individually designed and decorated colonial-
style town houses and chateau-style villas surround a free-
form lagoon pool. Units have spacious sitting rooms, dining
terraces, fully equipped kitchens, and up to four bedrooms.
All are beautifully furnished in eclectic style—painted
French furniture, modern metal designs, and traditional
plantation mahogany. Accommodations also include dedicated service from a personal butler, who carries out special
requests and the little chores associated with independent
living. Guests may patronize the Heaven Spa, two bars,
a deli, coffee shop, and two restaurants—the Beach Club
14'61" (its latitude and longitude) and Piano Piano, a fine-
dining restaurant—or arrange for a private chef to prepare
a meal in your villa. Cotton Bay beach is more than a mile
long and is so secluded it's virtually private. Take lessons
in windsurfing or kite boarding, arrange a horseback trek
along the beach, enjoy golf next door, or charter a yacht
for a day. You're living like royalty here, so you might as
well go whole hog. Of course, green fees at the next-door
golf club are free. **Pros:** truly luxurious accommodation;
privacy; family-friendly. **Cons:** a/c in bedrooms only; bathrooms have showers only; a rental car is advised if you
plan to leave the property. ⊠ *Cotton Bay, Cap Estate, Gros
Islet* ☎ *758/456–5700* ⊕ *www.cottonbayvillage.com* ⤳ *206
suites in 74 villas* ⚭ *In-room: safe, kitchen, DVD, Wi-Fi.
In-hotel: 2 restaurants, room service, bars, pool, gym, spa,
beachfront, water sports, children's programs (ages 2–16),
laundry facilities, Wi-Fi hotspot* ☐ *AE, MC, V* ⦿ *EP.*

$$ ☷ **Ginger Lily.** *Hotel.* A small, modern hotel with its own
restaurant and a swimming pool, the Ginger Lily is across
the street from Reduit Beach and smack in the middle of
Rodney Bay Village. It's so comfortable, so well located,
and such a good deal that wedding parties and family
reunions sometimes book the entire hotel. All rooms have
a queen-size bed and a sofa bed in the sitting area. A pair
of executive suites have separate bedrooms and full kitch-
ens. Ground-floor rooms have a terrace; upper-level rooms
have a balcony. This is a good place to hang your hat if
you don't need or want the amenities of a big resort, yet
everything you might need or want—the beach, dining
options, shopping, nightlife—is virtually at the front door.
For anything else—such as diving, horseback riding, or
tours—management will gladly make arrangements for
you. **Pros:** friendly service; good value; excellent location.

Cons: few on-site activities. ⊠ *Rodney Bay, Gros Islet* ⊕ *Box CP6013, Rodney Bay Village* ☎ *758/458–0300* ⊕ *www.gingerlilyhotel.com* ⇨ *9 rooms, 2 suites* ⚭ *In-room: safe, kitchen (some), Wi-Fi. In-hotel: restaurant, room service, bar, pool, Wi-Fi hotspot* ⊟ *AE, MC, V* ⊺⊙⊺ *EP.*

$$–$$$ ⊺ **Harmony Suites.** *Hotel.* Harmony Suites guests (adults only) are scuba divers, boaters, or others who don't need luxury but appreciate comfort and just like being on the waterfront. Of the 30 large, one-bedroom suites cloistered around the swimming pool, the 8 waterfront suites with a whopping 700 square feet each, as well as a private sun-deck, are the best choice. The Edge restaurant, where chef Bobo Bergstrom creates his self-described "Eurobbean" fusion cuisine, is on-site and is one of the best restaurants in Rodney Bay. There's also a dive center, and Reduit Beach is just across the road. **Pros:** marina location; excellent on-site restaurant; waterfront suites. **Cons:** rooms are fairly basic. ⊠ *Rodney Bay, Gros Islet* ⊕ *Box 155, Castries* ☎ *758/452–8756* ⊕ *www.harmonysuites.com* ⇨ *30 suites* ⚭ *In-room: refrigerator. In-hotel: restaurant, bar, pool, diving, laundry service, Internet terminal, no kids under 13* ⊟ *AE, MC, V* ⊺⊙⊺ *EP.*

★ **Fodor's** Choice ⊺ **The Landings.** *Resort.* On 19 acres along the
$$$$ Pigeon Point Causeway at the northern edge of Rodney Bay,
☙ the Landings is so-called because the property surrounds a private, 80-slip yacht harbor where residents can dock their own yachts literally at their doorstep. About half of the 231 waterfront residences are in the rental pool; units range in size from 900 to 2,300 square feet (half with plunge pools). Each unit has a beautifully appointed living room, dining room, and kitchen, as well as one, two, or three bedrooms with en suite baths and an enormous balcony or terrace. The atmosphere is particularly conducive to yachting and boating; nevertheless, landlubbers will love the 7,000-square-foot RockResorts Spa, socializing at the lobby bar in the Grand Pavilion, and soaking up the sun at the beach club or at one of the pools. You can prepare your own meals, grab a snack at the gourmet deli, have a light meal on the pier at the open-air Yacht Haven restaurant, or enjoy the latest cuisine concepts in the Palms, a fine-dining restaurant. Guests are also entitled to preferred tee times at the nearby St. Lucia Golf Club. The pampering begins, in fact, with the personalized greeting upon arrival at the airport. **Pros:** spacious, beautifully appointed units; perfect place for yachties to come ashore; personal chef service. **Con:** $30 per day activities fee in addition

Sandals Regency St. Lucia Golf Resort & Spa

to the room rate. ⊠ *Pigeon Island Causeway, Gros Islet* ☎ *758/458–7300* ⊕ *www.landings.rockresorts.com* ⇨ *80 units* ⬡ *In-room: safe, kitchen, DVD, Internet. In-hotel: 2 restaurants, room service, bars, tennis courts, pools, gym, spa, beachfront, water sports, children's program (ages 4–12), laundry service, Internet terminal, Wi-Fi hotspot* ⊟ *AE, D, MC, V* ⊚ *EP.*

$$$$ ⌧ **Morne Trulah.** *Private Villa.* On a clear day you can see as far as Martinique; otherwise, you merely get a long-range view of Pigeon Island, Rodney Bay, and the Caribbean Sea from this private villa, which was built on the site of an old French fort. The four bedrooms are of equal size, making this a good choice for couples traveling together (no one fights for the master suite), and each bedroom has its own bathroom, sitting area, and private patio. The pool and sundeck are in a pretty garden with a beautiful view, Bois d'Orange beach is within walking distance, and water sports are available at nearby Windjammer Landing Resort. You'll want to rent a jeep, though, to explore the island or to get to Rodney Bay to do errands, have dinner, or enjoy the nightlife. The cook and the maid work six days a week, from 8 AM to 4 PM. Managed and rented by Tropical Villas. **Pros:** four equal-size bedrooms; fully air-conditioned; family friendly. **Cons:** you'll need that jeep to get around. ⊠ *Bois d'Orange, Gros Islet* ☎ *758/450–8240 for Tropical Villas* ⊕ *www.tropicalvillas.net* ⇨ *4 bedrooms,*

4 baths ♿ DVD, *daily maid service, cook, pool, laundry
facilities* ⊟ AE, MC, V.

★ **Fodor'sChoice** ▦ **Royal St. Lucian.** *Resort.* This all-suites resort
$$$$ on St. Lucia's best beach caters to every whim. The recep-
♻ tion area has a vaulted atrium, marble walls, a fountain,
and a sweeping grand staircase. Just beyond, the free-form
pool has Japanese-style bridges, a waterfall, and a swim-up
bar. Guest suites are huge, with such amenities as a wide-
screen TV, DVD, and stereo. Massages, hydrotherapy,
and other treatments can be arranged at the Royal Spa.
Restaurants include the elegant Chic! and the sea-view
L'Epicure; lunch is served at the casual Beach Tent. Or you
can walk to a dozen or so Rodney Bay restaurants, nightclubs, and shopping areas. Tennis, water-sports facilities,
and the children's club are shared with the adjacent Rex St.
Lucian hotel. **Pros:** great beachfront; roomy accommodations; convenient to Rodney Bay Village. **Cons:** dated guest
rooms and baths. ⊠ *Reduit Beach, Rodney Bay, Gros Islet*
🖂 *Box 977, Castries* ☎ 758/452–9999 ⊕ *www.rexcarib-
bean.com* ⇱ *96 suites* ♿ *In-room: safe, refrigerator, Wi-Fi.
In-hotel: 3 restaurants, room service, bars, tennis courts,
pool, gym, spa, beachfront, diving, water sports, children's
programs (ages 4–12), laundry service, Internet terminal,
Wi-Fi hotspot* ⊟ *AE, MC, V* ⦿ *EP.*

★ **Fodor'sChoice** ▦ **Sandals Grande St. Lucian Spa & Beach Resort.**
$$$$ *All-Inclusive.* Grand, indeed! And busy, busy, busy. Couples
love this place—particularly young honeymooners and
those getting married here—the biggest and splashiest of
the three Sandals resorts on St. Lucia. In fact, several weddings take place each day. Perched on the narrow Pigeon
Island causeway at St. Lucia's northern tip, Sandals Grande
offers panoramic views of Rodney Bay on one side and
the Atlantic Ocean on the other. All rooms have king-size
beds; 24 lagoon-side rooms have swim-up verandahs. With
a plethora of land and water sports, a European-style full-
service spa, five excellent restaurants, and nightly entertainment, it's never dull. A complimentary shuttle connects
all three Sandals properties. **Pros:** excellent beach; lots of
activities; lovely spa; airport shuttle. **Cons:** the long ride to/
from Hewanorra is a turnoff; buffet meals are uninspired.
⊠ *Pigeon Island causeway, Gros Islet* 🖂 *Box 2247, Castries*
☎ 758/455–2000 ⊕ *www.sandals.com* ⇱ *271 rooms, 11
suites* ♿ *In-room: safe, refrigerator, Internet, Wi-Fi (some).
In-hotel: 5 restaurants, room service, bars, tennis courts,
pools, gym, spa, beachfront, diving, water sports, laundry*

service, Internet terminal, Wi-Fi hotspot, no kids under 18
⊟ AE, D, MC, V ⍍AI.

★ Fodor'sChoice ⊡ **Sandals Halcyon Beach St. Lucia.** *All-Inclusive.*
$$$$ This is the most intimate and low-key of the three Sandals
resorts on St. Lucia. Like the others, though, it's beachfront,
all-inclusive, for couples only, and loaded with amenities
and activities. And it's just 10 minutes north of downtown
Castries. Learn something new—perhaps sailing, windsurfing, or waterskiing—or just enjoy the sea and any of the
three pools. Take a break and play a game of croquet, table
tennis, or billiards. There are four restaurants: Bayside
serves three meals daily, inside or outside. Beach Bistro
serves grilled specials and snacks all day long. Mario's
specializes in northern Italian cuisine. And the Pier, which
is perched on a 150-foot pier on the waterfront, is the
place to go for seafood. Then, of course, there are the five
bars, which are always good places to meet and greet new
friends. Still looking for something to do? An hourly shuttle
connects the sister properties, so you can stay at one—but
play (and eat) at three. And low-rise architecture is entirely
friendly to the physically challenged. **Pros:** all the Sandals
amenities in a more intimate setting; lots of dining and
activity choices; exchange privileges (including golf) at two
other Sandals properties. **Cons:** it's Sandals, so it's a theme
property after all. ⊠ *Choc Bay, Castries* ⊠ *Box GM910,
Castries* ☎ *758/453–0222 or 800/223–6510* ⊕ *www.sandals.
com* ⇆ *169 rooms* ⌂ *In-room: safe, refrigerator (some),
Internet, Wi-Fi. In-hotel: 4 restaurants, room service, bars,
tennis courts, pools, gym, spa, beachfront, diving, water
sports, laundry service, Internet terminal, Wi-Fi hotspot,
no kids under 18* ⊟ *AE, D, DC, MC, V* ⍍*AI.*

★ Fodor'sChoice ⊡ **Sandals Regency St. Lucia Golf Resort & Spa.**
$$$$ *All-Inclusive.* One of three Sandals resorts on St. Lucia,
this is the second-largest and distinguishes itself with its
own 9-hole golf course (for guests only). Like the others,
it's for couples only and it's all-inclusive. The resort covers
200 acres on a hillside overlooking the sea at La Toc on
the southern shore of Castries Bay. Guest rooms are lav-
ishly decorated with rich mahogany furniture and king-size
four-poster beds. Many rooms have private plunge pools.
The main pool, with its waterfall and bridges, and a long
crescent beach are focal points for socializing and enjoying
water sports. Massages, scrubs, and wraps are available at
the full-service spa for an additional charge. Six restaurants
serve Asian, Continental, French, Mediterranean, Southwestern, or Caribbean cuisine. A dozen bars serve unlimited

3

liquid refreshments. An hourly shuttle connects all three Sandals properties. **Pros:** lots to do; picturesque location; on-site golf; airport shuttle. **Cons:** somewhat isolated location; expert golfers will prefer St. Lucia Golf Club in Cap Estate. ⊠ *La Toc Rd.* ✆ *Box 399, Castries* ☎ *758/452–3081* ⊕ *www.sandals.com* ⮑ *212 rooms, 116 suites* ♻ *In-room: safe, refrigerator (some), Internet, Wi-Fi (some). In-hotel: 6 restaurants, room service, bars, golf course, tennis courts, pools, gym, spa, beachfront, diving, water sports, laundry service, Internet terminal, Wi-Fi hotspot, no kids under 18* ▭ *AE, D, MC, V* ⊙ *AI.*

$$–$$$ ☒ **St. Lucian by Rex Resorts.** *Resort.* This 260-room resort on a
☽ long stretch of Reduit beachfront is surrounded by gardens. Deluxe rooms face the beach; superior rooms have a sea or garden view. Standard Papillon rooms have no TVs, and the bathrooms have showers only. If you don't have a room TV, there's one in the lounge if you want to catch up on the news or your favorite sports. Caribbean cuisine and international dishes are served at Mariners restaurant; Asian cuisine is served à la carte in the Oriental restaurant, and buffet-style meals are served in the Monarch restaurant. Admirals Lounge is the place to go for after-dinner drinks and nightly entertainment—steel bands and limbo dancing, for example. A covered walkway leads to the Royal St. Lucian, a sister resort, where guests can also dine, shop at its boutiques and vendors market, or visit the Royal Spa. **Pros:** great beach and lots of water sports; excellent Rodney Bay Village location; easy access to Royal sister hotel. **Cons:** basic Papillon rooms are pretty basic; the spa is not on-site. ⊠ *Reduit Beach, Rodney Bay, Gros Islet* ✆ *Box 512, Castries* ☎ *758/452–8351* ⊕ *www.rexresorts.com* ⮑ *260 rooms* ♻ *In-room: safe, refrigerator (some), no TV (some), Internet, Wi-Fi. In-hotel: 3 restaurants, room service, bars, tennis courts, pool, gym, beachfront, diving, water sports, children's program (ages 4–12), laundry service, Internet terminal, Wi-Fi hotspot* ▭ *AC, MC, V* ⊙ *EP.*

$$$–$$$$ ☒ **Tree Tops.** *Private Villa.* If you're looking for something rustic, unique, and inexpensive, yet comfortable, interesting, and well located, consider a tree house. A Canadian architect, who came to St. Lucia in the 1960s to "upgrade the architecture," designed Tree Tops, one of the oldest homes in Cap Estate. His masterpiece is this one-of-a-kind villa, with hardwood floors, cathedral ceilings, walls that slide to capture every breeze, and broad decks that connect one room to another. It's, well, very much like living in a tree house. A great room has a sitting area, dining and

games tables, and a desk. The kitchen is large and bright. The two bedrooms have ceiling fans and mosquito netting on the beds. A kidney-shape pool has lap lanes at one end and a sundeck for relaxing. Built on a hilltop, Tree Tops has expansive views. You can see spectacular sunsets to the west, the sea to the north and east, and as far away as Mt. Gimie to the south. Managed and rented by Tropical Villas. Pros: rather exotic; convenient to beach and golf course. **Cons:** no a/c, perhaps an issue in humid periods during October and early November. ⌧ *Saddleback, Cap Estate, Gros Islet* ☎ *758/450–8240 for Tropical Villas* ⊕ *www. tropicalvillas.net* ⇆ *2 bedrooms, 2 baths* ⌂ *No a/c, daily maid service, pool, laundry facilities* ⊟ *AE, MC, V.*

$$ ▨ **Villa Beach Cottages.** *Vacation Rental.* Tidy housekeeping cottages with gingerbread-laced facades are steps from the beach at this family-run establishment 3 mi (5 km north of the airport in Castries. The self-contained units have either one or two bedrooms and fully equipped kitchens and are decorated with handcrafted wooden furniture. A pair of cottages date back to World War II. Dismantled and moved here in 1958 from Beanfield Air Base in Vieux Fort, one of those cottages was subsequently occupied several times by one of St. Lucia's two Nobel Laureates, Sir Derek Walcott, during holiday visits. Now dubbed "Nobel Cottage," it is decorated with some of his watercolors. Another, called the "Honeymoon Cottage," is a duplex; the sitting/dining room and kitchen are on the ground floor, and a spiral staircase leads to the upstairs bedroom and bath. Units are cozy and fairly close together, but each has a large balcony (with a hammock) facing the water, guaranteeing glorious sunset viewing every evening. Coconuts, a small open-air restaurant, serves meals only on request. There's a mini-mart on-site for the convenience of guests, and a supermarket, bank, post office, and other shops are nearby. **Pros:** directly on the beach; beautiful sunsets; peaceful and quiet. **Cons:** close quarters. ⌧ *Choc Bay, Castries* ⌖ *Box 129, Castries* ☎ *758/450–2884* ⊕ *www.villabeachcottages. com* ⇆ *14 units* ⌂ *In-room: safe, kitchen, Internet. In-hotel: restaurant, pool, beachfront, water sports, laundry service* ⊟ *AE, D, MC, V* ⊚ *EP.*

$$$$ ▨ **Villa Tranquility.** *Private Villa.* Overlooking Anse Galet Bay, all the rooms in Villa Tranquility—and the terrace that runs the length of the home—have a view of the sea. The three bedrooms are air-conditioned, while ceiling fans and natural sea breezes cool all the other rooms. The villa has a large pool with a 45-foot lap lane and a big deck for

DID YOU KNOW?

Many people believe that Reduit Beach (pronounced red-wee) in Rodney Bay is the best beach in St. Lucia.

CLOSE UP

Bananas

More than 10,000 St. Lucian banana farmers produced 134,000 tons of the familiar fruit in the early 1990s, most of which was exported to Europe. By 2005, when the Caribbean nations had lost their preferential treatment in the European market, fewer than 2,000 banana farmers were producing about 30,000 tons. Nevertheless, you'll still see bananas growing throughout St. Lucia, especially in the rural areas around Babonneau in the northeast and south of Castries near Marigot Bay. As you pass by the banana fields, you'll notice that the fruit is wrapped in blue plastic. That's to protect it from birds and insects—because there's no market for an imperfect banana.

poolside dining. Three beaches are five minutes away by car. Villa guests also enjoy a complimentary membership (for two people) at the nearby St. Lucia Golf Club, where the only cost for golf will be $15 for cart rental. Besides daily maid service, the property has a gardener and pool boy; a chef can be provided upon request. A five-day minimum stay is required in winter, four-day minimum in the off-season. Managed and rented by Discover Villas of St. Lucia. **Pros:** a good choice for golfers, couples traveling together, or families with grown children. **Cons:** no a/c in the kitchen and living areas. ⊠ *Cap Estate, Gros Islet* ☎ *758/484–3066 for Discover Villas of St. Lucia* ⊕ *www.1stluciavillas.com* ⌖ *3 bedrooms, 3 baths* ⚠ *No a/c (some), safe, DVD, Wi-Fi, daily maid service, on-site security, pool, laundry facilities, no kids under 12, no-smoking* ⊟ *AE, MC, V.*

$$$–$$$$ ▦ **Windjammer Landing Villa Beach Resort.** *Resort.* Windjammer Landing's Mediterranean-style villas climb the hillside on one of St. Lucia's prettiest bays. As perfect for families as for a romantic getaway, the resort offers lots to do yet still affords everyone plenty of privacy. Villas can easily be closed off or opened up to become one-, two-, three-, or four-bedroom suites. Some have private plunge pools. The resort's reception area opens onto shops, restaurants, a children's playground, and two pools. Eat excellently prepared cuisine in the restaurants, make your own meals, or have dinner prepared and served in your villa. Shuttles whoosh you between villa and activity areas—including two hillside pools connected by a waterfall. **Pros:** lovely, spacious villas; beautiful sunset views; family-friendly, in-villa dining. **Cons:**

some units have living rooms with no a/c; you'll need to rent a car if you plan to leave the property, as it's far from the main road. ⊠ *Labrelotte Bay* ⌖ *Box 1504, Castries* ☎ *758/456–9000* ⊕ *www.windjammer-landing.com* ⤳ *330 rooms in 261 units* ⚭ *In-room: kitchen (some), refrigerator, DVD, Internet. In-hotel: 5 restaurants, room service, bars, tennis courts, pools, gym, spa, beachfront, diving, water sports, children's programs (ages 4–12), laundry service, Internet terminal, Wi-Fi hotspot* ⊟ *AE, MC, V* ⌑ *EP.*

GREATER CASTRIES

Hotel locations can be found on the Castries map.

$ ⊡ **Auberge Seraphine.** *Hotel.* This is a good choice for independent vacationers who don't require a beachfront location or a breadth of resort activities. Accommodations are spacious, cheerful, and bright, and all but six rooms have a water view. A broad, tiled sundeck, the center of activity, surrounds a small pool. Reserve ahead, as business travelers appreciate the Auberge's convenience to downtown Castries, the airport, and great eateries—including the inn's excellent restaurant, which offers fine Caribbean, French, and Continental cuisine in addition to a well-stocked wine cellar. **Pros:** nice pool; good restaurant. **Cons:** no beach; no resort activities. ⊠ *Vigie Cove, Castries* ⌖ *Box 390, Castries* ☎ *758/453–2073* ⊕ *www.aubergeseraphine.com* ⤳ *24 rooms* ⚭ *In-room: refrigerator (some), Wi-Fi. In-hotel: restaurant, room service, bar, pool, laundry service, Wi-Fi hotspot* ⊟ *AE, MC, V* ⌑ *EP.*

$$$$ ⊡ **Rendezvous.** *All-Inclusive.* Romance is alive and well at this easygoing, all-inclusive, couples resort (for male–female couples only), which stretches along the dreamy white sand of Malabar Beach opposite the George F. L. Charles Airport runway. The occasional distraction of prop aircraft taking off and landing is overshadowed by the beautiful gardens on what was once a coconut plantation. Accommodations are in cheerful gingerbread cottages, elegant oceanfront rooms with sunset-facing terraces, or cozy poolside suites. A host of activities and sports are all included. Buffet-style meals are served at the beachfront terrace restaurant, with fine dining by reservation at the air-conditioned Trysting Place. **Pros:** convenient to Castries and Vigie Airport; great beach; romance in the air. **Cons:** no room TVs; occasional flyover noise. ⊠ *Malabar Beach, Vigie* ⌖ *Box 190, Castries* ☎ *758/457–7900* ⊕ *www.theromanticholiday.com* ⤳ *21 rooms, 35 suites, 8 cottages* ⚭ *In-room: safe, refrigerator*

(some), no TV. In-hotel: 2 restaurants, bars, tennis courts, pools, gym, spa, beachfront, diving, bicycles, laundry service, Internet terminal, no kids under 18 ⊟ *AE, D, MC, V* ¶⊙¶ *AI.*

BETWEEN CASTRIES AND CANARIES

Hotel locations can be found on the St. Lucia map.

$$ ▣ **Inn on the Bay.** *B&B.* Renting just five rooms, Normand Viau and Louise Boucher, the owners of this delightful aerie on the southern hillside at the entrance of Marigot Bay, treat you as their personal guests (adults only). The million-dollar view of the bay, the sea, and the constant comings and goings of beautiful yachts is sensational from guest-room balconies and the pool. Cool sea breezes truly obviate the need for air-conditioning. You won't mind the absence of a TV here, either. Breakfast is prepared by Louise and served in their kitchen whenever you're ready. Walk down a hillside path, through thick jungle, to a small white-sand beach. And if you need a lift to the village, a short but very steep walk, Normand is happy to comply. **Pros:** the view; the value; the pleasant hosts; the personalized service. **Cons:** few, if any, amenities besides peace, quiet, and nature. ⊠ *Marigot Bay* ☎ *758/451–4260* ⊕ *www.saint-lucia.com* ⇆ *5 rooms* ⑇ *In-room: no a/c, no phone. In-hotel: pool, Internet terminal, no kids under 16* ⊟ *MC, V* ¶⊙¶ *BP.*

$$ ▣ **Mango Beach Inn.** *B&B.* When the Marigot Bay ferry deliv-
� ers you to the dock at Rainforest Hideaway restaurant, a small gate next to the bar opens to a stone staircase leading up to delightful Mango Beach Inn. Hosts John and Judith Verity, British transplants to St. Lucia, welcome guests to their inn, which is also their home. And with six grandchildren (though not in residence), they have the temperament and the toys to amuse little kids. A garden room, in fact, has an adjoining room set up with kids in mind. Guest rooms are comfortable but small, though the living/dining room, to which you're always invited, is huge and has large windows open to the view—beautiful day or night. Take a walk to the ridge before enjoying a delicious breakfast, then either lounge around the pool or at Marigot's picturesque beach, enjoy water sports, or poke around the shops at Marina Village. The little ferry will collect you for dinner at your choice of several restaurants, fancy or casual, around the bay. Or you can barbecue poolside, if you prefer. **Pros:** spectacular views of Marigot Bay; beach,

water sports, restaurants, and shopping nearby; attentive hosts; kid-friendly. **Cons:** tiny rooms, some bathrooms have showers only; negotiating the steps to the inn would be difficult for those with physical challenges. ⊠ *Marigot Bay* ☏ *758/451–4872* ⊕ *www.mangobeachmarigot.com* ⥿ *4 rooms ⟨⟩In-room: no a/c (some), no phone, refrigerator, no TV (some), Wi-Fi (some). In-hotel: pool, gym, Wi-Fi hotspot* ⊟ *MC, V* ⊚ *BP.*

★ **Fodor's Choice** ☒ **Marigot Bay Hotel.** *Hotel.* Five miles (8 km)
$$$ south of Castries, this chic, eco-friendly hotel (formerly called Discovery at Marigot Bay) climbs the hillside of what author James Michener called "the most beautiful bay in the Caribbean." Each unit in the hotel is exquisitely decorated with dark Balinese furniture accented by comfy earth-tone cushions, a four-poster bed with pillow-top mattress, and dark hardwood flooring. Oversize bathrooms have walk-in "drench" showers and double basins set in slate vanities. Each suite has a full kitchen equipped with modern Euro-designer appliances, a spacious living room with a sofa bed and dining area, a balcony or deck, and a washer and dryer; half the suites have private plunge pools. Guests enjoy fine dining at Boudreau or casual meals at the Hurricane Hole Bar. Mega-yachts tie up at the resort's dock, and a solar-powered ferry transports guests to the beach or to nearby bars and restaurants. **Pros:** stunning bay view; excellent service; oversize accommodations. **Cons:** you'll want a rental car to explore beyond Marigot Bay; beach is picturesque but tiny. ⊠ *Marigot Bay* ⊠ *Box MG7227, Marigot* ☏ *758/458–5300* ⊕ *www.marigotbay.com* ⥿ *67 rooms, 57 suites* ⟨⟩ *In-room: safe, kitchen (some), DVD, Internet, Wi-Fi. In-hotel: restaurant, room service, bars, pools, gym, spa, water sports, laundry facilities, Internet terminal, Wi-Fi hotspot* ⊟ *AE, MC, V* ⊚ *BP* ⊘ *Closed Sept.*

$$ ☒ **Marigot Beach Club & Dive Resort.** *Resort.* Divers love this place, and everyone loves the location facing the little palm-studded beach at Marigot Bay. Some accommodations are right on the beachfront; others are on the hillside with a sweeping view of the bay. All units have either a kitchen or kitchenette. Villa accommodations, suitable for families and large groups, have two, three, or five bedrooms; the largest has two kitchens. Scuba courses and dive trips are available from the on-site PADI dive center; special dive packages include accommodations, meals, daily two-tank boat dives, and all equipment. Doolittle's, the waterfront restaurant, is popular for guests who want to escape their kitchenettes, as well as nonguests and yachties who like

JADE POOL, Saint Lucia. Jade Mountain Club

Jalousie Plantation

the food and the live entertainment. The Marina Village, the wonderful restaurants and bars at Marigot Bay Hotel, Rainforest Hideaway, and Chateau Mygo are a one-minute ferry ride away. All guests get a ferry pass to come and go at will. **Pros:** great value for divers; beautiful views of Marigot Bay, good casual dining; easy access to Marina Village. **Cons:** beach is tiny (though picturesque). ⊠ *Marigot Bay* ☎ *758/451–4974* ⊕ *www.marigotdiveresort.com* ⌨ *24 rooms, 3 villas* ⚭ *In-room: safe, kitchen, Internet, Wi-Fi. In-hotel: restaurant, bar, pool, tennis court, gym, beachfront, diving, water sports, laundry service, Internet terminal* ▭ *MC, V* ⊙ *BP.*

SOUFRIÈRE AND VICINITY

Hotel locations can be found on the St. Lucia and Soufrière and Vicinity maps.

★ **Fodor's**Choice ☒ **Anse Chastanet Beach Hotel.** *Resort.* Anse Chas-
$$$$ tanet is magical, if you don't mind the bone-crushing dirt road between the town and the resort and the steep climb to most rooms. But there's a helipad so you can get to the airport by helicopter if you prefer; a water taxi offers yet another alternative way into town, or you can simply soak in the gorgeous isolation; shuttle service is available between the beach and the hillside rooms, 100 steps up. Spectacular rooms, some with stunning Piton vistas, peek through the thick rain forest that cascades down to the sea. Deluxe hillside rooms have a balcony, tile floors, madras fabrics, handmade wooden furniture, and impressive artwork. But you won't find any communication devices, technology, or interruption: it's delightfully peaceful. Diving, jungle biking through the estate's 600 acres, and ocean kayaking are premier activities; rejuvenate afterward at the Kai Belte Spa. **Pros:** great for divers; Room 14B with the tree growing through the bathroom; the Piton views. **Cons:** no pool; entrance road is difficult to negotiate; steep hillside certainly not conducive to strolling; some may miss in-room TVs, phones, and a/c. ⊠ *Anse Chastanet Rd., Soufrière* ⊡ *Box 7000, Soufrière* ☎ *758/459–7000* ⊕ *www.ansechas-tanet.com* ⌨ *49 rooms* ⚭ *In-room: no a/c, no phone, safe, refrigerator, no TV. In-hotel: 4 restaurants, room service, bars, tennis court, spa, beachfront, diving, water sports, bicycles, laundry service, Internet terminal, no kids under 10* ▭ *AE, MC, V* ⊙ *EP.*

$$$$ ☒ **Arc en Ciel.** *Private Villa.* Architect Lane Pettigrew has put his stamp on many fabulous homes and resorts throughout the Caribbean, and Arc en Ciel is another example. The exterior of the house incorporates Caribbean verandahs, jalousie shutters, and traditional wooden railings as well as hand-chipped stones reminiscent of the old French forts found on St. Lucia. Spectacularly situated on Beau Estate, just south of Petit Piton, this lovely villa accommodates up to 10 guests in its five air-conditioned bedrooms. Each bedroom, as well as the centrally located living/dining area, has its own TV, DVD, and stereo system. (TV reception ranges from bad to nonexistent; but there's a library of DVDs, or you can bring your own.) The master bedroom, which faces Petit Piton, has a glass wall in its en suite bathroom, so you can take advantage of the unparalleled view as you enjoy a shower or soak in the Jacuzzi. In fact, all bedrooms have Jacuzzis in their en suite bathrooms, as well as private patios or gardens. The sitting room opens onto a patio and dining gazebo, with a wonderful view as a backdrop. On the lower level, two of the bedrooms face an infinity-edge pool—which weaves its way around a series of patios and sundecks and through a stone cave with a waterfall. Anse des Pitons Beach, Jalousie Plantation resort, and Ladera are nearby; the Drive-in Volcano, Diamond Botanical Gardens, and the town of Soufrière are just a short drive away. The resident staff is available seven days a week. Managed by Tropical Villas. **Pros:** spectacular Pitons view; easily accommodates up to 10 guests; perfect for a big family or group. **Cons:** no TV reception, but there is a DVD library; expensive. ⊠ *Beau Estate, Soufrière* ☎ *758/450–8240 for Tropical Villas* ⊕ *www.tropicalvillas.net* ⤳ *5 bedrooms, 5 baths* ⚇ *No a/c (some), safe, dishwasher, DVD, on-site security, fully staffed, pools, laundry facilities* ⊟ *AE, MC, V.*

$$$–$$$$ ▦ **Bananaquit House.** *Private Villa.* Named for the little black-and-yellow birds that frequent alfresco breakfast tables, Bananaquit House is located in a garden setting along the dirt road between Soufrière and Anse Chastanet resort. The view of the sea and the Pitons is unparalleled, and Anse Chastanet and Anse Mamin beaches are five minutes away. The five bedrooms can sleep 11 people comfortably; the house is equipped with two cribs and two high chairs. The large sitting/dining area has a small library of books, games, and puzzles, as well as a stereo system and a TV with a DVD player. Because of the mountains, TV reception is virtually nonexistent in this area. You enter the living area through a pool terrace, with a fenced-in swimming pool—making it safe for families with small kids. The caretaker, who will provide security at no charge if you wish, has a dog that he will remove from the property upon request. Managed by Tropical Villas. **Pros:** family-friendly; great views; cozy and charming yet big enough for a large family or group. **Cons:** little or no TV reception; no a/c, although bedrooms have fans. ⊠ *Anse Chastanet Rd., Soufrière* ☎ *758/450–8240 for Tropical Villas* ⊕ *www.tropicalvillas.net* ⇩ *5 bedrooms, 3 baths* ♿ *No a/c, safe, DVD, daily maid service, on-site security, pool, laundry facilities* ⊟ *AE, MC, V.*

$$–$$$ ⌧ **Fond Doux Holiday Plantation.** *Resort.* Ever wish you could stay in a cottage in the rain forest—with all (or at least most) of the conveniences of home? Here at Fond Doux, one of Soufrière's most active agricultural plantations, 10 historic homes salvaged from all around the island and meticulously disassembled have been rebuilt and refurbished on the estate. Now they are private, beautifully furnished, one- and two-bedroom cottages surrounded by dense tropical foliage and marked trails that meander through the estate. All of the cottages are also down a short circular path that ends up at Fond Doux's two restaurants, a three-level pool, the spa, and the cocoa fermentary. It's a totally different type of vacation experience that allows you to soak up the environment, engage local culture, and feel part of history. **Pros:** beautifully refurbished historic cottages; exotic and eco-friendly; striking location on an 18th-century plantation. **Cons:** a rental car is advised, as beach and local sites are a few miles away; not all cottages have a full kitchen where you can cook meals. ⊠ *Soufrière* ⛫ *Box 250, Soufrière* ☎ *758/459–7545* ⊕ *www.fonddoux-estate.com* ⇩ *10 cottages* ♿ *In-room: no a/c, safe, kitchen (some), refrigerator, no TV. In-hotel: 2 restaurants, bar, pools, spa, laundry service, Internet terminal, Wi-Fi hotspot* ⊟ *MC, V* ⊠⊡ *EP.*

$–$$ ⌧ **Hummingbird Beach Resort.** *Inn.* Unpretentious and welcoming, this delightful little inn on Soufrière Harbour has simply furnished rooms—a traditional motif emphasized by four-poster beds and African wood sculptures—in small seaside cabins. Most rooms have modern baths; two rooms share a bath. A two-bedroom country cottage—with a sitting room, kitchenette, and spectacular Piton view—is suitable for a family or two couples vacationing together. The Hummingbird's Lifeline Restaurant is a favorite of locals as well as vacationers spending a day or more in Soufrière. **Pros:** local island hospitality; small and quiet; good food; batik studio on-site. **Cons:** few resort amenities—but that's part of the charm. ⊠ *Anse Chastanet Rd., Soufrière* ⛫ *Box 280, Soufrière* ☎ *758/459–7232* ⊕ *www.istlucia.co.uk* ⇩ *9*

rooms, 7 with bath; 1 suite; 1 cottage ⚙ In-room: no a/c
(some), no phone (some), Wi-Fi. In-hotel: restaurant, bars,
pool, beachfront, diving, laundry service, Wi-Fi hotspot
🖃 AE, D, MC, V ⚏ CP.

★ **Fodor's**Choice ⊞ **Jade Mountain Club.** Resort. This premium-class
$$$$ and premium-priced hotel is a five-level behemoth looming
out of the side of a mountain. The interior ("jungle") is
a mass of concrete bridges, each accessing a huge private
suite (called sanctuaries here) that exudes style, luxury,
privacy, and comfort. The suites have a truly open-space
plan—1,450 to 1,950 square feet of space with a missing
fourth wall open to an incredible Piton view, an enormous
infinity-edge plunge pool right in the sitting room, and literally en suite bathrooms. Guests have a private restaurant,
bar, and sky-top terrace at their disposal and can also use
facilities at adjacent sister property Anse Chastanet. Given
the amenities of the sanctuaries, though, it's no wonder
that room service is so popular here. Jade Mountain Club
is techno-free in terms of communication from the rooms
to the outside world. **Pros:** amazing accommodations;
huge in-room pools; incredible Piton views. **Cons:** sky-
high rates; lack of in-room communication and a/c; not
appropriate for anyone with disabilities. ⊠ Anse Chastanet,
Soufrière ⌖ Box 7000, Soufrière ☎ 758/459–4000 ⊕ www.
jademountainstlucia.com ⇆ 28 suites ⚙ In-room: no a/c,
no phone, refrigerator, no TV. In-hotel: restaurant, room
service, bar, gym, spa, beachfront, diving, water sports,
bicycles, laundry service, Internet terminal, no kids under
15 🖃 AE, MC, V ⚏ EP.

★ **Fodor's**Choice ⊞ **Jalousie Plantation.** Resort. Located on the
$$$$ most dramatic 192 acres in St. Lucia, this resort flows
☾ down Val des Pitons—the steep valley smack between the
Pitons—on the remains of an 18th-century sugar plantation
2 mi (3 km) south of Soufrière. The location is so stunning
that it almost takes your breath away. Clusters of private
villas have spacious bedrooms with walk-in closets, separate
sitting rooms with custom-made white furnishings, huge
bathrooms with claw-foot tubs and showers big enough
for a crowd, and a Piton-view deck with an oversize plunge
pool. Luxury suites include a personal butler who tends to
any request, including unpacking, making reservations, and
calling the shuttle to take you to the lobby, a restaurant or
bar, or the beach. The Cane Bar, which specializes in rum
drinks and tasty treats, and the adjoining Late Night Bar
are right out of Miami's South Beach in terms of decor—
very cool. Meals range from breakfast on the Verandah to

barbecues and buffets at the Bayside Grill to fine dining in the Great Room. Swimming and snorkeling at the beach are magical because of the incomparable Piton views on either side and the abundant sea life underwater. Dive, windsurf, or sail; play tennis, squash, or pitch-and-putt golf. Take a nature walk, climb Gros Piton (with a guide), or chill by the pool. The spa offers outdoor massage, aromatherapy, and beauty treatments; there are also fitness classes and weight-training sessions. Scuba diving is complimentary (one certified beach dive daily or one beginner dive per stay). And weddings are complimentary, too, with stays of seven or more nights—now that's a deal. Meal and AI plans are available and recommended. (Following a $100 million renovation project expected to be completed by early 2011, Jalousie Plantation will be renamed Tides Sugar Beach.) **Pros:** incomparable scenery; wonderful spa; lots of water sports; children under five stay free. **Cons:** fairly isolated so a meal plan makes sense; cottages are surrounded by thick foliage, so bring mosquito spray. ✉ *Val des Pitons, Soufrière ⌖ Box 251, Soufrière ☎ 800/544–2883 or 758/459–7666 ☎ 758/459–7667 ⊕ www.jalousieplantation. com ⇌ 12 rooms, 100 villas ♿ In-room: safe, refrigerator, Internet. In-hotel: 3 restaurants, room service, bars, golf course, tennis courts, pool, gym, spa, beachfront, diving, water sports, children's programs (ages 5–12), Internet terminal ⊟ AE, MC, V ⊚ EP.*

$$–$$$ ☷ **La Haut Plantation.** *Inn.* It's all about the view—the Pitons, ⌚ of course—and the appeal of staying in an intimate and affordable family-run inn that happens to have that view. Nestled into what was a mountaintop cocoa and coconut estate 100 years ago, just north of the town of Soufrière, the main six-room guesthouse was once the cocoa house, where cocoa beans were fermented and dried; an adjacent cottage had been the copra house, where the coconuts were processed. Each room has a private balcony with a "to-die-for" view, king beds draped with rather romantic mosquito netting, and shutters or French doors that open to the breeze. A two-bedroom unit is ideal for families or two couples. The two-story cottage has a huge upstairs balcony, where you can gaze at the Pitons, the rain forest, or the sunset; it's perfect for honeymooners. Halfway down the mountainside, the owner's mansion has six additional guest rooms, an infinity pool, and that picture-postcard Piton view. When they're not taking a dip in one of the pools or the free shuttle to Anse Chastanet Beach, guests are encouraged to roam the 52 acres of gardens and

A private in-suite plunge pool at Ladera Resort

grounds, where they're likely to come across goats, cows, birds, and a couple of donkeys—a real treat for kids. La Haut's restaurant employs local seafood, fruits and vegetables, and herbs and spices in its excellent creole cuisine and international dishes. Anyone who plays the piano is invited to tickle the ivories on the old upright. **Pros:** lovely for weddings and honeymoons but also for families with kids; stunning Piton views; excellent restaurant; excellent value. **Cons:** very quiet, especially at night, unless that's the point; bathrooms have showers only; vehicle recommended. ⊠ *Soufrière* ⌂ *Box 304, Soufrière* ☎ *758/459–7008* ⊕ *www. lahaut.com* ⇝ *13 rooms* ⚿ *In-room: no a/c (some), safe, refrigerator, no TV (some), Internet. In-hotel: restaurant, room service, bar, pools, gym, laundry service, Internet terminal, Wi-Fi hotspot* ▭ *MC, V* ⊚ *BP.*

★ **Fodor's**Choice ▨ **Ladera.** *Hotel.* One of the most sophisticated
$$$$ small inns in the Caribbean, the elegantly rustic Ladera is perched 1,100 feet above the sea. With a local approach to furnishings, food, and staff, each tree house–style suite or villa in this ecohotel is uniquely decorated with colonial antiques and local craftsmanship. Each unit has an open fourth wall with a dazzling view of the Pitons as a backdrop for the private plunge pool. The Ti Kai Posé Spa (Creole for "Little House of Rest") offers relaxing and therapeutic massages, beauty services, and restorative bathing pools. Dasheene, the open-air restaurant, has a stunning view of the Pitons. The hotel provides shuttle service to Soufrière

3

and its private, fully staffed beach at Anse Jambette, a 20-minute boat ride from the Soufrière dock. The minimum stay in the winter season is three nights. **Pros:** breathtaking Pitons vista; in-room pools; excellent cuisine. **Cons:** the hotel's single pool is not very big; open fourth walls and steep drops make this inappropriate for children (and also means no a/c); a rental car is advised. ⊠ *Val de Pitons, Soufrière* ⊕ *Box 225, Soufrière* ☎ *758/459 6600* ⊕ *www. ladera-stlucia.com* ⊅ *23 suites, 9 villas* ⚅ *In-room: no a/c, no phone, refrigerator, DVD, no TV, Wi-Fi. In-hotel: restaurant, bars, pool, gym, spa, Internet terminal, Wi-Fi hotspot, no kids under 10 (except during the Christmas and Easter holidays)* ▭ *AE, D, MC, V* ◯ *BP.*

$$$-$$$$ ⊠ **Stonefield Estate Villa Resort & Spa.** *Resort.* One 18th-century plantation house and several gingerbread-style cottages dot this 26-acre property. All accommodations have oversize, handcrafted furniture and one or two bathrooms; some also have garden showers, and each has its own secluded plunge pool. Villas have one, two, or three bedrooms, and the largest can accommodate three families or up to 10 guests. Living-dining rooms open onto verandahs with double hammocks and panoramic views, perfectly romantic at sunset. Although there are no room phones, guests are given a cell phone to use during their stay. The Mango Tree Restaurant serves meals with a view. A complimentary shuttle goes to Soufrière or to the beach at Anse des Pitons. The minimum stay in the winter season is three nights. **Pros:** very private; picturesque pool; great sunset views from villa decks; lovely wedding venue. **Cons:** a rental car is recommended; you have to drive to restaurants. ⊠ *1 mi (1½ km) south of Soufrière* ⊕ *Box 228, Soufrière* ☎ *758/459–5648 or 758/459–7037* ⊕ *www.stonefieldvillas.com* ⊅ *17 villas* ⚅ *In-room: no a/c (some), safe, kitchen (some), refrigerator, no TV. In-hotel: restaurant, room service, bar, pool, gym, spa, diving, laundry service, Internet terminal, Wi-Fi hotspot, no kids under 5* ▭ *MC, V* ◯ *BP.*

$$$-$$$$ ⊠ **St. Remy Plantation.** *Private Villa.* If you prefer ambience to amenities, then spending your vacation in an historic plantation estate near a colonial town may have more appeal than a modern beachfront resort. St. Remy Plantation is a restored, 150-year-old estate house, with wooden floors, traditional furniture, and a verandah that wraps around three sides of the house. High in the hills just outside the town of Soufrière, the house is surrounded by beautiful gardens that are visited by countless species of birds. Don't expect to get any TV reception, but the house's sitting/din-

ing room has an entertainment center with a video library. There are two double bedrooms, a bathroom, and a shower room. A separate guest cottage with two single beds is available upon request. The pool has a sundeck; Anse Chastanet Beach is nearby. Each St. Remy Plantation guest is treated to a complimentary visit to Diamond Mineral Baths. The housekeeper and cook are available daily until 5 PM but will stay to cook and serve dinner upon request (and at additional cost). **Pros:** perfect spot for a honeymoon; great for bird-watchers and nature lovers. **Cons:** no a/c, although hillside location catches the breeze. ⊠ *Soufrière* ⊕ *Box 1020, Castries* ☎ *758/452–4759* ⊕ *www/villastremy. com* ⤳ *2 bedrooms, 2 baths* ⚏ *DVD, pool, cook, daily maid service, fully staffed, on-site security, laundry facilities, no kids under 12* ⊟ *AE, MC, V* ⍟ *BP.*

★ Fodor'sChoice ⊞ **Ti Kaye Village.** *Resort.* There is a special-ness

$$$–$$$$ to this aerie overlooking Anse Cochon Beach and down a 1-mi-long (1½-km-long) dirt road off the main highway. Gingerbread-style cottages all face the ocean and are surrounded by lush greenery and are furnished with hand-crafted furniture. Each room has a private garden shower, a large balcony with double hammock, and wooden louvers in doors and windows to catch every breeze; some have private plunge pools. Or you can maneuver the 166-step wooden stairway down the cliff to the beach—which is one of the best snorkeling sites in St. Lucia. Kai Manje (Creole for "house of eating") serves fabulous food on a breezy terrace—which is a good thing, since the location is so remote. Lunch is available at the Ti Manje beach bar. The icing on the cake: The Kai Koko spa offers divine treatments using locally formulated products. **Pros:** perfect for a honeymoon or private getaway; garden showers are fabulous; excellent restaurant. **Cons:** far from anywhere; all those steps to the beach; not a good choice for anyone with physical challenges. ⊠ *Anse Cochon* ⊕ *Box GM669, Castries* ☎ *758/456–8101* ⊕ *www.tikaye.com* ⤳ *33 rooms* ⚏ *In-room: safe, refrigerator, no TV, Wi-Fi. In-hotel: 2 restaurants, bars, pool, gym, spa, beachfront, diving, water sports, laundry service, Internet terminal, Wi-Fi hotspot, no kids under 12* ⊟ *AE, D, MC, V* ⍟ *BP.*

VIEUX FORT

Hotel location can be found on the St. Lucia map.

$$$$ ⊞ **Coconut Bay Beach Resort & Spa.** *All-Inclusive.* The only ☾ resort in Vieux Fort, Coconut Bay is a sprawling seaside

retreat minutes from St. Lucia's Hewanorra International Airport. The ocean views are beautiful, and the beach has lovely white sand; but the resort faces the Atlantic Ocean, so swimming in the sea is not advised. Instead, you'll find three swimming pools and a water park with a lazy river, waterslides, and swim up bar. The resort is divided into two sections: Harmony is for adults only and, on the opposite side of the property, Splash is the tropical playground for families with kids. The Frégate Island and Maria Islands are just offshore, and St. Lucia's Pitons and other natural attractions in Soufrière are 30 minutes by car. Otherwise, you'll have to be content with the activities in and around the resort—four restaurants, a full-service spa, and plenty of space to relax and socialize. **Pros:** great for families; perfect for windsurfers; friendly and sociable atmosphere. **Cons:** bathrooms have showers only; rough surf precludes ocean swimming; close to the airport but far from everything else. ⊠ *Vieux Fort* ⊠ *Box 246, Vieux Fort* ☎ *758/459–6000* ⊕ *www.cbayresort.com* ⇦ *254 rooms* ⚘ *In-room: safe, Wi-Fi. In-hotel: 4 restaurants, bars, tennis courts, pools, gym, spa, beachfront, water sports, children's programs (ages 3–12), Internet terminal, Wi-Fi hotspot* ▭ *AE, MC, V* †⚬† *AI.*

BEACHES

Beaches are all public, but many along the northwest coast, particularly north of Castries, are flanked by hotels. A few secluded stretches of beach on the west coast south of Marigot Bay are accessible primarily by boat and are popular swimming and snorkeling stops on catamaran or powerboat sightseeing trips. Don't swim along the windward (east) coast, as the Atlantic Ocean is too rough—but the views are spectacular. Beaches on St. Lucia are quite beautiful, but none has really soft white sand; given the island's volcanic origins, this shouldn't be surprising, but anyone looking for powdery soft beaches may be slightly disappointed.

Anse Chastanet. In front of the resort of the same name, just north of the city of Soufrière, this palm-studded dark-sand beach has a backdrop of green hills, brightly painted fishing skiffs bobbing at anchor, and the island's best reefs for snorkeling and diving. The resort's gazebos are nestled among the palms; its dive shop, restaurant, and bar are on the beach and open to the public. ⊠ *Anse Chastanet Rd., Soufrière.*

★ **Anse Cochon.** This remote dark-sand beach is reached only by boat or via Ti Kaye Village's 1-mi-long (1½–km-long) access road. The water and adjacent reef are superb for swimming, diving, and snorkeling. Moorings are free, and boaters can enjoy lunch or dinner at Ti Kaye's beach bar. ⊠ *3 mi (5 km) south of Marigot Bay. Anse Cochon.*

Anse des Pitons (*Jalousie Beach*). Between the Pitons on Jalousie Bay, the white sand on this crescent beach was imported over a decade ago and spread over the natural black sand. Accessible from Jalousie Plantation resort or by boat, the beach offers good snorkeling, diving, and breathtaking scenery. ⊠ *Jalousie Bay, 1 mi (1½ km) south of Soufrière.*

Anse des Sables. This long, white-sand beach at the southern tip of the island is washed by Atlantic surf and is the place to go windsurfing or kite surfing. Refreshments are available at the Reef. ⊠ *Vieux Fort.*

Marigot Beach (*Labas Beach*). Calm waters rippled only by passing yachts lap a sliver of sand studded with palm trees on the north side of Marigot Bay. The beach is accessible by a ferry that operates continually from one side of the bay to the other, and you can find refreshments at several nearby restaurants. ⊠ *Marigot Bay.*

Pigeon Point. At this small beach within Pigeon Island National Park, on the northwestern tip of St. Lucia, a restaurant serves snacks and drinks, but this is also a perfect spot for picnicking. ⊠ *Pigeon Island.*

★ **Fodor's Choice Reduit Beach.** This long stretch of golden sand frames Rodney Bay and is within walking distance of many small hotels and restaurants in Rodney Bay Village. The Rex St. Lucian Hotel, which faces the beach, has a watersports center, where you can rent sports equipment and beach chairs and take windsurfing or waterskiing lessons. Many feel that Reduit (pronounced red-*wee*) is the island's finest beach. ⊠ *Rodney Bay.*

Vigie Beach. This 2-mi (3-km) strand runs parallel to the George F. L. Charles Airport runway in Castries and continues on to become Malabar Beach, the beachfront in front of the Rendezvous resort. ⊠ *Castries, across the street from the airport.*

SPORTS AND ACTIVITIES

BIKING

Although the terrain is pretty rugged, two tour operators have put together fascinating bicycle and combination bicycle-hiking tours that appeal to novice riders as well as those who enjoy a good workout. Prices range $60–$100 per person.

★ **Bike St. Lucia** (⊠ *Anse Chastanet, Soufrière* ☎ *758/451–2453* ⊕ *www.bikestlucia.com*) takes small groups of bikers on Jungle Biking tours along trails that meander through the remnants of an 18th-century plantation near Soufrière. Stops are made to explore the French colonial ruins, study the beautiful tropical plants and fruit trees, enjoy a picnic lunch, and take a dip in a river swimming hole or a swim at the beach. If you're staying in the north, you can arrange a tour that includes transportation to the Soufrière area.

Palm Services Bike Tours (⊠ *Castries* ☎ *758/458–0908* ⊕ *www. adventuretoursstlucia.com*) is suitable for all fitness levels. Jeep or bus transportation is provided across the central mountains to Dennery, on the east coast. After a 3-mi (5-km) ride through the countryside, bikes are exchanged for shoe leather. The short hike into the rain forest ends with a picnic and a refreshing swim next to a sparkling water-fall—then the return leg to Dennery. All gear is supplied.

BOATING AND SAILING

Rodney Bay and Marigot Bay are centers for bareboat and crewed yacht charters. Their marinas offer safe anchorage, shower facilities, restaurants, groceries, and maintenance for yachts sailing the waters of the eastern Caribbean. Charter prices range from $1,750 to $10,000 per week, depending on the season and the type and size of vessel, plus $250 extra per day if you want a skipper and cook.

Bateau Mygo (⊠ *Marigot Bay* ☎ *758/451–4772* ⊕ *www. bateaumygo.com*) specializes in customized, crewed char-ters on its 40- to 44-foot yachts for either a couple of days or a week.

Destination St. Lucia (DSL) Ltd. (⊠ *Rodney Bay Marina, Gros Islet* ☎ *758/452–8531* ⊕ *www.dsl-yachting.com*) offers bareboat yacht charters; vessels range in length from 38 to 51 feet.

The **Moorings Yacht Charters** (✉ *Marigot Bay* ☎ *758/451–4357 or 800/535–7289* ⊕ *www.moorings.com*) rents bareboat and crewed yachts ranging from Beneteau 39s to Morgan 60s.

CRICKET

Is it a passion or an obsession? In either case, the country nearly shuts down when an important local or international match takes place. International and test series cricket matches are played at the Beausejour Cricket Ground in Gros Islet and at the impressive National Stadium in Vieux Fort. Contact the tourist board for details on schedules and tickets.

St. Lucia is particularly noted for having a great women's cricket team. In 1986, Verna Felicien founded the first St. Lucia women's team. In 1998 St. Lucia—with Felicien as captain—won the Caribbean Women's Cricket Championships and retained the title for five years. During that time, 10 St. Lucians—including Captain Felicien—also played on the West Indies Women's team. In 2005 Felicien represented St. Lucia in the World Cup tournament, which was held in South Africa.

DIVING AND SNORKELING

★ Fodor's Choice **Anse Chastanet,** near the Pitons on the southwest coast, is the best beach-entry dive site. The underwater reef drops from 20 feet to nearly 140 feet in a stunning coral wall.

A 165-foot freighter, *Lesleen M,* was deliberately sunk in 60 feet of water near **Anse Cochon** to create an artificial reef; divers can explore the ship in its entirety and view huge gorgonians, black coral trees, gigantic barrel sponges, lace corals, schooling fish, angelfish, sea horses, spotted eels, stingrays, nurse sharks, and sea turtles.

Anse La Raye, midway up the west coast, is one of St. Lucia's finest wall and drift dives and a great place for snorkeling.

At the base of **Petit Piton** a spectacular wall drops to 200 feet. You can view an impressive collection of huge barrel sponges and black coral trees; strong currents ensure good visibility.

At the **Pinnacles,** four coral-encrusted stone piers rise to within 10 feet of the surface.

Depending on the season and the particular trip, prices range from about $40 to $60 for a one-tank dive, $175–$260 for a 6-dive package over three days, and $265–$450 for a 10-dive package over five days. Dive shops provide instruction for all levels (beginner, intermediate, and advanced). For beginners, a resort course (pool training), followed by one open-water dive, runs $75–$105. Snorkelers are generally welcome on dive trips and usually pay $25–$50, which includes equipment and sometimes lunch and transportation.

Buddies (✉ *Rodney Bay Marina, Rodney Bay* ☎ 758/452–9086) offers wall, wreck, reef, and deep dives; resort courses and open-water certification with advanced and specialty courses are taught by PADI-certified instructors.

Dive Fair Helen (✉ *Vigie Marina, Castries* ☎ 758/451–7716, 888/855–2206 *in U.S. and Canada* ⊕ *www.divefairhelen. com*) is a PADI center that offers half- and full-day excursions to wreck, wall, and marine reserve areas, as well as night dives.

Scuba St. Lucia (✉ *Anse Chastanet Resort, Anse Chastanet Rd., Soufrière* ☎ 758/459–7755 ⊕ *www.scubastlucia.com*) is a PADI five-star training facility. Daily beach and boat dives and resort and certification courses are offered; underwater photography and snorkeling equipment are available. Day trips from the north of the island include round-trip speedboat transportation.

FISHING

Among the deep-sea creatures you can find in St. Lucia's waters are dolphin (also called dorado or mahimahi), barracuda, mackerel, wahoo, kingfish, sailfish, and white and blue marlin. Sportfishing is generally done on a catch-and-release basis, but the captain may permit you to take a fish back to your hotel to be prepared for your dinner. Neither spearfishing nor collecting live fish in coastal waters is permitted. Half- and full-day deep-sea fishing excursions can be arranged at either Vigie Marina or Rodney Bay Marina. A half day of fishing on a scheduled trip runs about $75–$80 per person. Beginners are welcome.

Captain Mike's (✉ *Vigie Marina, Castries* ☎ 758/452–1216 *or* 758/452–7044 ⊕ *www.captmikes.com*) has a fleet of Bertram powerboats (31 to 38 feet) that accommodate as many as eight passengers; tackle and cold drinks are supplied.

A large brain coral off the coast of St. Lucia

Hackshaw's Boat Charters (✉ *Vigie Marina, Castries* ☎ *758/453–0553 or 758/452–3909* ⊕ *www.hackshaws.com*), in business since 1953, runs charters on boats ranging from the 31-foot *Blue Boy* or *Miss T.* to the 50-foot, custom-built *Lady Hack*.

Mako Watersports (✉ *Rodney Bay Marina, Rodney Bay* ☎ *758/452–0412*) takes fishing enthusiasts out on the well-equipped six-passenger *Annie Baby*.

GOLF

Although St. Lucia has only one 18-hole championship course at this writing, two more are on the drawing board and/or under construction. One will be in Praslin, on the east coast, as part of a new resort development; the other will be near the existing course in Cap Estate. **Sandals Regency Golf Resort and Spa** has a 9-hole course for its guests. **Jalousie Plantation** has a par-3 Executive course.

St. Lucia Golf and Country Club (✉ *Cap Estate* ☎ *758/452–8523* ⊕ *www.stluciagolf.com*), the island's only public course, is at the northern tip and offers panoramic views of both the Atlantic and the Caribbean. It's an 18-hole championship course (6,836 yards, par 71). The clubhouse has a fine-dining restaurant called the Cap Grill that serves breakfast, lunch, and dinner; the Sports Bar is a convivial meeting place any time of day. You can rent clubs and shoes and arrange lessons at the pro shop and perfect your swing at the 350-yard driving range. Depending on the season, green fees range from $90 for 9 holes to $140 for 18 holes; carts are required and included in the green fee; club and shoe rentals are available. Reservations are essential. Complimentary transportation from your hotel or cruise ship is provided for parties of three or more people. The St. Lucia Golf Open, a two-day tournament held in March, is open to amateurs; it's a handicap event, and prizes are awarded.

GUIDED TOURS

Taxi drivers are well informed and can give you a full tour—and often an excellent one, thanks to government-sponsored training programs. From the Castries area, full-day island tours cost $140 for up to four people; sightseeing trips to Soufrière, $120. If you plan your own day, expect to pay the driver $20 per hour plus tip.

★ **Jungle Tours** (⊠ *Cas en Bas, Gros Islet* ☎ *758/450–0434*) specializes in rain-forest hiking tours for all levels of ability. You're required only to bring hiking shoes or sneakers and have a willingness to get wet and have fun. Prices range from $80 to $90 and include lunch, fees, and transportation via open Land Rover truck.

St. Lucia Helicopters (⊠ *Pointe Seraphine, Castries* ☎ *758/453–6950* ⊕ *www.stluciahelicopters.com*) offers a bird's-eye view of the island. A 10-minute North Island tour ($85 per person) leaves from Pointe Seraphine, in Castries, continues up the west coast to Pigeon Island, then flies along the rugged Atlantic coastline before returning inland over Castries. The 20-minute South Island tour ($145 per person) starts at Pointe Seraphine and follows the western coastline, circling picturesque Marigot Bay, Soufrière, and the majestic Pitons before returning inland over the volcanic hot springs and tropical rain forest. A complete island tour combines the two and lasts 30 minutes ($175 per person).

St. Lucia Heritage Tours (⊠ *Pointe Seraphine, Castries* ☎ *758/451–6058* ⊕ *www.heritagetoursstlucia.org*) has put together an "authentic St. Lucia experience," specializing in the local culture and traditions. Groups are small, and some of the off-the-beaten-track sites visited are a 19th-century plantation house surrounded by nature trails, a 20-foot waterfall hidden away on private property, and a living museum presenting Creole practices and traditions. Plan on paying $75 per person for a full-day tour.

Sunlink Tours (✉ *Reduit Beach Ave., Rodney Bay* ☎ *758/452–8232 or 800/786–5465* ⊕ *www.sunlinktours.com*) offers dozens of land, sea, and combination sightseeing tours, as well as shopping tours, plantation, and rain-forest adventures via jeep safari, deep-sea fishing excursions, and day trips to other islands. Prices range from $20 for a half-day shopping tour to $120 for a full-day land-and-sea jeep safari to Soufrière.

HIKING

The island is laced with trails, but you shouldn't attempt the more challenging ones on your own.

Seasoned hikers may aspire to climb the Pitons, the two volcanic cones rising 2,461 feet and 2,619 feet, respectively, from the ocean floor just south of Soufrière. Hiking is recommended only on Gros Piton, which offers a steep but safe trail to the top. The first half of the hike is moderately difficult; reaching the summit is challenging and should be attempted only by those who are physically fit. The view from the top is spectacular. Tourists are permitted to hike Petit Piton, but the second half of the hike requires a good deal of rock climbing, and you'll need to provide your own safety equipment. Hiking the Pitons requires the permission of the St. Lucia Forest and Lands Department and a knowledgeable guide ($25) from the **Pitons Tour Guide Association** (☎ *758/459–9748*).

The **St. Lucia Forest and Lands Department** (☎ *758/450–2231 or 758/450–2078*) manages trails throughout the rain forest and provides guides who explain the plants and trees you'll encounter and keep you on the right track for a small fee.

The **St. Lucia National Trust** (☎ *758/452–5005* ⊕ *www.slunatrust.org*) maintains two trails: one is at Anse La Liberté, near Canaries on the Caribbean coast; the other is on the Atlantic coast, from Mandélé Point to the Frégate Island Nature Reserve. Full-day excursions with lunch cost about $50–$85 per person and can be arranged through hotels or tour operators.

HORSEBACK RIDING

Creole horses, a breed indigenous to South America and popular on the island, are fairly small, fast, sturdy, and even-tempered animals suitable for beginners. Established stables can accommodate all skill levels and offer countryside trail rides, beach rides with picnic lunches, plantation tours, carriage rides, and lengthy treks. Prices run about $45 for one hour, $60 for two hours, and $75 for a three-hour beach ride and barbecue. Transportation is usually provided between the stables and nearby hotels. Local people sometimes appear on beaches with their steeds and offer 30-minute rides for $10–$15; ride at your own risk.

International Riding Stables (⊠ *Beauséjour Estate, Gros Islet* ☎ *758/452–8139 or 758/450–8665*) offers English- and Western-style riding. The beach-picnic ride includes time for a swim—with or without your horse.

Trim's National Riding Stable (⊠ *Cas-en-Bas, Gros Islet* ☎ *758/ 452–8273* ⊕ *www.trimsnationalridingacademy.com*), the island's oldest riding stable, offers four sessions per day, plus beach tours, trail rides, and carriage tours to Pigeon Island.

SEA EXCURSIONS

★ **Fodor's**Choice A day sail or sea cruise from Rodney Bay or Vigie Cove to Soufrière and the Pitons is a wonderful way to see St. Lucia and a great way to get to the island's distinctive natural sites. Prices for a full-day sailing excursion to Soufrière run about $100–$110 per person and include a land tour to the Sulphur Springs and the Botanical Gardens, lunch, a stop for swimming and snorkeling, and a visit to pretty Marigot Bay. Two-hour sunset cruises along the northwest coast cost about $60 per person.

The 140-foot tall ship **Brig Unicorn** (⊠ *Vigie Marina, Castries* ☎ *758/452–8644*), used in the filming of the TV miniseries *Roots* and more recently the movie *Pirates of the Caribbean,* is a 140-foot replica of a 19th-century sailing ship. Day trips along the coast are fun for the whole family. Several nights each week a sunset cruise, with drinks and a live steel band, sails to Pigeon Point and back.

Customized sightseeing or whale-watching trips can be arranged for small groups (four to six people) through **Captain Mike's** (⊠ *Vigie Marina, Castries* ☎ *758/452–0216 or 758/452–7044* ⊕ *www.captmikes.com*).

On **Endless Summer** (⊠ *Rodney Bay* ☎ *758/450–8651* ⊕ *www. stluciaboattours.com*), a 56-foot "party" catamaran, you can take a day trip to Soufrière or a half-day swimming and snorkeling trip. For romantics, there's a weekly sunset cruise, with dinner and entertainment.

L'Express des Iles (⊠ *La Place Carenage, Castries* ☎ *758/452–2211*) offers an interesting day trip to the French island of Martinique. A hydrofoil departs daily for the 20-mi (32-km) voyage ($116 round-trip). As you approach Martinique, try to be among the first to disembark. There's usually only one immigration-customs agent on duty, and it can take an hour to clear if you're at the end of the line.

Mystic Man Tours (⊠ *Bay St., Soufrière* ☎ *758/459–7783* ⊕ *www.mysticmantours.com*) operates whale- and dolphin-watching tours, which are great family excursions.

For a boat trip to Pigeon Island, the **Rodney Bay Ferry** (⊠ *Rodney Bay Marina, Rodney Bay* ☎ *758/452–8816*) departs the ferry slip adjacent to the Lime restaurant twice daily for $50 round-trip, which includes the entrance fee to Pigeon Island and lunch; snorkel equipment can be rented for $12.

TENNIS AND SQUASH

People staying at small inns without on-site tennis courts or those who wish to play squash can access private facilities for a small hourly fee; reservations are required.

St. Lucia Racquet Club (⊠ *Cap Estate* ☎ *758/450–0106*) is the best private tennis facility on the island, with seven flood-lighted, hard-surface tennis courts and a squash court, pro shop, restaurant, and bar. It is also the site of the St. Lucia Open each December.

St. Lucia Yacht Club (⊠ *Reduit Beach, Rodney Bay* ☎ *758/452–8350*) has two squash courts, and you can rent racquets.

WINDSURFING AND KITE BOARDING

Windsurfers and kite boarders congregate at Anse de Sables Beach in Vieux Fort, at the southeastern tip of St. Lucia, to take advantage of the blue-water and high-wind conditions that the Atlantic Ocean provides.

The **Reef Kite and Surf Centre** (⊠ *Anse de Sables, Vieux Fort* ☎ *758/454–3418*) rents equipment and offers lessons from certified instructors in both windsurfing and kite boarding. A three-hour beginning windsurfing course costs $90, plus

Des Cartiers Rainforest

$45 to rent equipment for a half day. For kite boarding, the three-hour starter course costs $125, including equipment. Kite boarding is particularly strenuous, so participants must be excellent swimmers and in good physical health.

NIGHTLIFE AND THE ARTS

THE ARTS

★ **Fodor's** Choice In early May, the weeklong **St. Lucia Jazz Festival** (⊕ *stluciajazz.org*) is one of the premier events of its kind in the Caribbean. International jazz greats perform at outdoor venues on Pigeon Island and at various hotels, restaurants, and nightspots throughout the island; free concerts are also held at Derek Walcott Square in downtown Castries.

THEATER
The small, open-air **Derek Walcott Center Theatre** (⊠ *Cap Estate, Gros Islet* ☎ *758/450–0551, 758/450–0450 for the Great House*), next to the Great House restaurant in Cap Estate, seats 200 people for monthly productions of music, dance, and drama, as well as Sunday brunch programs. The Trinidad Theatre Workshop also presents an annual performance here. For schedule and ticket information, contact the **Great House** restaurant.

Cocoa Tea

The homemade chocolate balls or sticks that vendors sell in the market are formed from locally grown and processed cocoa beans. The chocolate is used locally to make cocoa tea—a beverage that actually originated in Soufrière but has since become a popular drink wherever cocoa is grown throughout the Caribbean. The chocolate is grated and steeped in boiling water, along with a bay leaf and cinnamon stick. Sugar is added, along with a little milk or cream, and some vanilla. Some people add nutmeg, as well, and some cornstarch to make it thicker and more filling. Cocoa tea began as a breakfast treat but is now enjoyed with a slice of bread as a snack or even as a dessert. Be sure to bring some chocolate sticks or balls home with you. One sniff and you won't be able to resist buying a packet ($2–$4).

NIGHTLIFE

Most resort hotels have entertainment—island music, calypso singers, and steel bands, as well as disco, karaoke, and talent shows—every night in high season and a couple of nights per week in the off-season. Otherwise, there is nightlife in both Rodney Bay and Marigot Bay. The many restaurants and bars there attract a crowd nearly every night.

BARS

J. J.'s Paradise (✉ Marigot Bay ☎ 758/451–0476) has limbo and fire-eating shows Tuesday through Friday and karaoke on Saturday night.

Jambe de Bois (✉ Pigeon Island, Rodney Bay ☎ 758/450–8166) is a cozy Old English–style pub with live jazz on Sunday and violin on Thursday.

DANCE CLUBS

Rodney Bay has the most bars and clubs. Most dance clubs with live bands have a cover charge of $10–$12 (EC$25–EC$30), and the music usually starts at 11 PM.

At **Delirius** (✉ Rodney Bay ☎ 758/451–3354), visitors and St. Lucians alike "lime" over cocktails at the horseshoe-shape bar and at tables in the garden; the atmosphere is casual, the decor is contemporary, and the music (live bands or DJ) is from the 1960s, '70s, and '80s.

Doolittle's (⊠ *Marigot Bay* ☎ *758/451–4974*) has live bands and dance music—calypso, soul, salsa, steel band, reggae, and limbo—that changes nightly.

The Lime on the Bay (⊠ *Rodney Bay* ☎ *758/452–0761*) is a particular favorite of St. Lucians; upstairs above the restaurant of the same name, it's air conditioned and intimate, with live music, a DJ, or karaoke every night until the last patron leaves.

STREET PARTIES

☾ For a taste of St. Lucian village life, head for the **Anse La**
★ **Raye "Seafood Friday "** (⊠ *Anse La Raye*), a street festival held every Friday night. Beginning at 6:30 PM, the main street in this tiny fishing village—about halfway between Castries and Soufrière—is closed to vehicles, and the residents prepare what they know best: fish cakes, grilled or stewed fish, hot bakes (biscuits), roasted corn, boiled crayfish, even grilled-before-your-eyes lobster. Prices range from a few cents for a fish cake or bake to $10 or $15 for a whole lobster, depending on its size. Walk around, eat, chat with the local people, and listen to live music until the wee hours of the morning.

★ **Fodor's Choice** A Friday-night ritual for locals and visitors alike is to head for the **Gros Islet Jump-Up** (⊠ *Gros Islet*), the island's largest street party. Huge speakers are set up on the village's main street and blast out Caribbean music all night long. Sometimes there are live bands. When you take a break from dancing, you can buy barbecued fish or chicken, rotis, beer, and soda from villagers who set up cookers right along the roadside. It's the ultimate "lime" experience.

SHOPPING

The island's best-known products are artwork and wood carvings, clothing and household articles made from batik and silk-screened fabrics that are designed and produced in island workshops, straw mats, and clay pottery. You can also take home straw hats and baskets and locally grown cocoa, coffee, and spices.

AREAS AND MALLS

★ Along the harbor in Castries, the rambling structures with bright-orange roofs house several markets that are open from 6 AM to 5 PM Monday through Saturday. Saturday morning is the busiest and most colorful time to shop. For more than a century, farmers' wives have gathered at the **Castries Market** to sell produce—which, alas, you can't import to the United States. But you can bring back spices (such as cocoa, turmeric, cloves, bay leaves, ginger, peppercorns, cinnamon sticks, nutmeg, mace, and vanilla essence), as well as bottled hot pepper sauces—all of which cost a fraction of what you'd pay back home.

The **craft market,** adjacent to the produce market, has aisles and aisles of baskets and other handmade straw work, rustic brooms made from palm fronds, wood carvings and leather work, clay pottery, and souvenirs—all at affordable prices.

The **Vendor's Arcade,** across the street from the craft market, is a maze of stalls and booths where you can find handicrafts among the T-shirts and costume jewelry.

Gablewoods Mall, on the Gros Islet Highway in Choc Bay, a couple of miles north of downtown Castries, has about 35 shops that sell groceries, wines and spirits, jewelry, clothing, crafts, books and overseas newspapers, music, souvenirs, household goods, and snacks.

Along with 54 boutiques, restaurants, and other businesses that sell services and supplies, a large supermarket is the focal point of each **J.Q.'s Shopping Mall**; one is at Rodney Bay and another is at Vieux Fort.

The duty-free shopping areas are at **Pointe Seraphine,** an attractive Spanish-motif complex on Castries Harbour with more than 20 shops, and **La Place Carenage,** an inviting three-story complex on the opposite side of the harbor. You can also find duty-free items in a few small shops at the arcade at the Rex St. Lucian hotel in Rodney Bay and, of course, in the departure lounge at Hewanorra International Airport. You must present your passport and airline ticket to purchase items at the duty-free price.

Marigot Marina Village on Marigot Bay has shops and services for boaters and landlubbers alike, including a bank, grocery store, business center, art gallery, an assortment of boutiques, and a French bakery and café.

Vieux Fort Plaza, near Hewanorra International Airport in Vieux Fort, is the main shopping center in the southern part of St. Lucia. You'll find a bank, supermarket, bookstore, toy shop, and several clothing stores there.

SPECIALTY ITEMS

ART

Art & Antiques (⊠ *Pointe Seraphine, Castries* ☎ *758/451– 4150*) is a museum-type shop opened by artist Llewellyn Xavier and his wife, where you'll find fine art, antique maps and prints, sterling silver and crystal, rich linens, objets d'art, and mere collectibles.

Artsibit Gallery (⊠ *Brazil and Mongiraud Sts., Castries* ☎ *758/452–7865*) exhibits and sells moderately priced pieces by St. Lucian painters and sculptors.

Caribbean Art Gallery (⊠ *Rodney Bay Yacht Marina, Rodney Bay* ☎ *758/452–8071*) sells original artwork by local artists, along with antique maps and prints and hand-painted silk.

World-renowned St. Lucian artist **Llewellyn Xavier** (⊠ *Mount du Cap, Cap Estate* ☎ *758/450–9155* ⊕ *www.llewellynxavier.com*) creates modern art, ranging from vigorous oil abstracts that take up half a wall, to small objects made from beaten silver and gold. Much of his work has an environmental theme and is created from recycled materials. Xavier's work is on permanent exhibit at major museums in New York and Washington, D.C. Others are sold in gift shops throughout the island. Call to arrange a visit to his studio.

Modern Art Gallery (⊠ *Gros Islet Hwy., Bois d'Orange* ☎ *758/ 452–9079*) is a home studio, open by appointment only, where you can buy contemporary and avant-garde Caribbean art.

BOOKS AND MAGAZINES

Sunshine Bookshop (⊠ *Gablewoods Mall, Castries* ☎ *758/452– 3222*) has novels and titles of regional interest, including books by Caribbean authors—among them the works of the St. Lucian Nobel laureate Derek Walcott. You can also find current newspapers and magazines.

Valmont Books (⊠ *Jeremie and Laborie Sts., Castries* ☎ *758/ 452–3817*) has West Indian literature and picture books, as well as stationery.

CLOTHES AND TEXTILES

★ **Bagshaw Studios** (✉ *La Toc Rd., La Toc Bay, Castries* ☎ *758/451–9249*) sells clothing and table linens in colorful tropical patterns using Stanley Bagshaw's original designs. The fabrics are silk-screened by hand in the adjacent workroom. You can also find Bagshaw boutiques at Pointe Seraphine, La Place Carenage, and Rodney Bay, as well as a selection of items in gift shops at Hewanorra Airport. Visit the workshop to see how the designs are turned into colorful silk-screen fabrics, which are then fashioned into clothing and household articles. It's open weekdays 8:30–5, Saturday 8:30–4, and Sunday 10–1. Weekend hours may be extended if a cruise ship is in port.

Batik Studio (✉ *Hummingbird Beach Resort, on bay front, north of wharf, Soufrière* ☎ *758/459–7232*) has superb batik sarongs, scarves, and wall panels designed and created on-site by Joan Alexander-Stowe.

At **Caribelle Batik** (✉ *La Toc Rd., Morne Fortune, Castries* ☎ *758/452–3785*), craftspeople demonstrate the art of batik and silk-screen printing. Meanwhile, seamstresses create clothing and wall hangings, which you can purchase in the shop. The studio is in an old Victorian mansion, high atop Morne Fortune, overlooking Castries. There's a terrace where you can have a cool drink and a garden full of tropical orchids and lilies. Caribelle Batik creations are featured in many gift shops throughout St. Lucia.

Sea Island Cotton Shop (✉ *Gablewoods Mall, Choc Bay* ☎ *758/451–6946* ✉ *J. Q.'s Shopping Mall, Rodney Bay* ☎ *758/458–4220*) sells quality T-shirts, Caribelle Batik clothing and other resort wear, and colorful souvenirs.

GIFTS AND SOUVENIRS

Caribbean Perfumes (✉ *Jacques Waterfront Dining, Vigie Marina, Castries* ☎ *758/453–7249*) blends a half dozen lovely scents for women and two aftershaves for men from exotic flowers, fruits, tropical woods, and spices. Fragrances are all made in St. Lucia, reasonably priced, and available at the perfumery (in the garden adjacent to the restaurant) and at many hotel gift shops.

Noah's Arkade (✉ *Jeremie St., Castries* ☎ *758/452–2523* ✉ *Pointe Seraphine, Castries* ☎ *758/452–7488*) has hammocks, wood carvings, straw mats, T-shirts, books, and other regional goods.

HANDICRAFTS

On the southwest coast, halfway between Soufrière and Vieux Fort, you can find locally made clay and straw pieces at the **Choiseul Arts & Crafts Centre** (✉ *La Fargue* ☎ *758/454–3226*). Many of St. Lucia's artisans come from this area.

Eudovic Art Studio (✉ *Morne Fortune, Castries* ☎ *758/452–2747*) is a workshop and studio where you can buy trays, masks, and abstract figures sculpted by Vincent Joseph Eudovic from local mahogany, red cedar, and eucalyptus wood.

At **Zaka** (✉ *Malgretoute, Soufrière* ☎ *758/457–1504* ⊕ *www. zaka-art.com*), you may get a chance to talk with artist and craftsman Simon Gajhadhar, who fashions totems and masks from driftwood and other environmentally friendly sources of wood—taking advantage of all the natural nibs and knots that distinguish each piece. Once the "face" is carved, it is painted in vivid colors to highlight the exaggerated features and provide expression. Each piece is unique.

Travel Smart Barbados and St. Lucia

WORD OF MOUTH

"Best thing about Barbados is the transportation system . . . which makes getting anywhere SO easy and very inexpensive. I love Barbados."

—KayO416

GETTING HERE & AROUND

Barbados and St. Lucia are two popular resort destinations in the eastern Caribbean's southern arc. St. Lucia is situated between Martinique to the north and St. Vincent to the south. Barbados is about 100 mi (160 km) farther east of the rest of the Windward Islands. They are about 20 or 30 minutes apart by air and are now connected by a superfast ferry service.

▮ AIR TRAVEL

BARBADOS
American Airlines and JetBlue offer nonstop flights between Barbados and New York or Miami. Delta offers connecting flights to Barbados via Atlanta, and Caribbean Airlines offers service from Fort Lauderdale, Miami, and New York via Port of Spain, Trinidad. US Airways offers nonstop service from Philadelphia. Barbados is also well connected to other Caribbean islands via LIAT. Mustique Airways, SVG Air, and Trans Island Air (TIA) link Barbados with St. Vincent and the Grenadines.

Airline Contacts **American Airlines** (☎ 246/428–4170). **Caribbean Airlines** (☎ 246/428–1950 or 800/744–2225). **Delta** (☎ 800/221–1212). **JetBlue** (☎ 877/596–2413 ⊕ www.jetblue. com). **LIAT** (☎ 246/428–0986 or 888/844–5428). **Mustique Airways** (☎ 246/428–1638). **SVG Air** (☎ 784/457–5124). **Trans Island Air** (☎ 246/418–1654). **US Airways** (☎ 800/622–1015).

AIRPORTS AND TRANSFERS
Grantley Adams International Airport (BGI) is a stunning, modern facility located in Christ Church Parish, on the south coast. The airport is about 15 minutes from hotels situated along the south or east coast, 45 minutes from the west coast, and about 30 minutes from Bridgetown. If your hotel does not offer airport transfers, you can take a taxi (actually a shared van service) to your resort. Helicopter transfers are also available.

Airport Contacts **Grantley Adams International Airport** (BGI ☎ 246/428–7101).

ST. LUCIA
American Airlines flies nonstop between Hewanorra and Miami and between Hewanorra and New York (JFK); American also offers connecting service from New York and other major U.S. cities through San Juan via American Eagle to George F. L. Charles Airport in Castries. Delta flies to Hewanorra from Atlanta. JetBlue flies to Hewanorra from New York (JFK). US Airways flies to Hewanorra from Philadelphia and Charlotte.

Air Caraïbes flies between George F. L. Charles Airport and Guadeloupe and Martinique; LIAT flies into George F. L. Charles Airport from several neighboring islands.

Airline Contacts **Air Caraïbes** (☎ 758/453–0357 ⊕ www.aircaraibes.com). **American Airlines/ American Eagle** (☎ 758/452–1820,

758/454–6777, or 800/744–0006
⊕ www.aa.com). **Delta** (☎ 800/221–
1212 ⊕ www.delta.com). **JetBlue**
(☎ 877/596–2413 ⊕ www.jetblue.
com). **LIAT** (☎ 758/452–3056 or
888/844–5428 ⊕ www.liat.com). **US
Airways** (☎ 758/454–8186 ⊕ www.
usairways.com).

AIRPORTS AND TRANSFERS

St. Lucia has two airports. Hewanorra International Airport (UVF)
accommodates large jet aircraft
and is at the southeastern tip of
the island in Vieux Fort. George
F. L. Charles Airport (SLU), which
is also referred to as Vigie Airport,
is at Vigie Point in Castries, which
is in the northwestern part of the
island, and accommodates only
small prop aircraft due to its location and runway limitations.

Some large resorts—particularly
the all-inclusive ones—and package tour operators provide round-
trip airport transfers. That's a
significant amenity if you're landing at Hewanorra, as the one-way
taxi fare for the 60- to 90-minute
ride (depending on whether you're
headed to Soufrière or Castries) is
expensive—$55 to $75 for up to
four passengers. Taxis are always
available at the airports.

If you land at George F. L. Charles
Airport, it's a short drive to resorts
in the north, about 20 minutes to
Marigot Bay, but more than an
hour to Soufrière.

Some people opt for a helicopter
transfer between Hewanorra and
either Castries or Soufrière, a quick
7- to 10-minute ride with a beautiful view at a one-way cost of $145
per passenger. Helicopters operate

in daylight hours only and carry up
to six passengers.

**Airport Contacts George F. L.
Charles Airport** (SLU ☎ 758/452–
1156). **Hewanorra International
Airport** (UVF ☎ 758/454–6355).
St. Lucia Helicopters (✉ Pointe
Seraphine, Castries ☎ 758/453–6950
⊕ www.stluciahelicopters.com).

▌ BOAT AND FERRY TRAVEL

BARBADOS

Half the annual visitors to Barbados are cruise passengers.
Bridgetown's Deep Water Harbour
is on the northwest side of Carlisle
Bay, and up to eight cruise ships
can dock at the cruise-ship terminal. Downtown Bridgetown is a
0.5-mi (1-km) walk from the pier;
a taxi costs about $3 each way.

BEDY Oceanline provides daily
regional fast ferry service between
Barbados and St. Lucia and
between Barbados and St. Vincent.
The voyage between Barbados and
St. Lucia takes 3½ hours each way
and costs $140 round-trip or $110
one-way; between Barbados and
St. Vincent, the trip takes three
hours each way at a cost of $120
round-trip or $90 one-way. Travel-
ers wishing to continue on to Grenada or Trinidad can connect in
St. Vincent.

**Ferry Contacts BEDY Informa-
tionOceanline** (☎ 473/440–2339
⊕ www.bedytravel.com).

ST. LUCIA

Cruise ships from major lines call at Castries and sometimes at Soufrière. At Port Castries, ships tie up at berths right in town and are convenient to duty-free shops, the market, and transportation for sightseeing excursions. When cruise ships are in port, a water taxi shuttles back and forth between Pointe Seraphine on the north side of the harbor and Place Carenage on the south side of the harbor for $1 per person each way. In Soufrière, ships anchor offshore, and passengers are transferred ashore by tenders.

BEDY Oceanline provides daily regional fast ferry service between St. Lucia and Barbados or St. Vincent. The high-speed catamaran voyage between St. Lucia and Barbados takes 3½ hours each way and costs $140 round-trip or $110 one-way; between St. Lucia and St. Vincent, travel time is approximately two hours each way at a cost of $90 round-trip or $60 one-way. (Travelers can continue on to Grenada or Trinidad from St. Vincent.)

Visitors combining a visit to St. Lucia with a visit to Martinique, Dominica, or Guadeloupe may opt for the L'Express des Iles fast ferry, a modern, high-speed catamaran that calls in Castries four days a week. The trip between St. Lucia and Fort de France, Martinique, takes 1½ hours; Roseau, Dominica, 3½ hours; and Point a Pitre, Guadeloupe, 5½ hours.

For visitors arriving at Rodney Bay on their own or chartered yachts, Rodney Bay Marina is an official port of entry for customs and immigration purposes. A ferry travels between the marina and the shopping complex daily on the hour, from 9 to 4, for $4 per person round-trip.

Ferry Contacts BEDY Ocean line (☎ 473/440–2339 ⊕ www. bedytravel.com). **L'Express des Iles** (☎ 758/456–5022 ⊕ www.express-des-iles.com). **Rodney Bay Ferry** (☎ 758/452–8816).

▌BUS TRAVEL

BARBADOS

Bus service is efficient, inexpensive, and plentiful. Blue buses with a yellow stripe are public, yellow buses with a blue stripe are private, and private "Zed-R" vans (so called for their ZR license plate designation) are white with a maroon stripe. All buses travel frequently along Highway 1 (St. James Road) and Highway 7 (South Coast Main Road), as well as inland routes. The fare is Bds$1.50 (75¢) for any one destination; exact change in either local or U.S. currency is appreciated. Buses pass along main roads about every 20 minutes. Stops are marked by small signs on roadside poles that say TO CITY or OUT OF CITY, meaning the direction relative to Bridgetown. Flag down the bus with your hand, even if you're standing at the stop. Bridgetown terminals are at Fairchild Street for buses to the south and east and at Lower Green for buses to Speightstown via the west coast.

ST. LUCIA

Privately owned and operated minivans constitute St. Lucia's bus system, an inexpensive and efficient means of transportation used primarily by local people. Minivan routes cover the entire island and run from early morning until approximately 10 PM. You may find this method of getting around most useful for short distances—between Castries and the Rodney Bay area, for example; longer hauls can be uncomfortable. The fare between Castries and Gablewoods Mall is EC$1.25; Castries and Rodney Bay, EC$2; Castries and Gros Islet, EC$2.25; Castries and Vieux Fort (a trip that takes more than two hours), EC$7; Castries and Soufrière (a bone-crushing journey that takes even longer), EC$10. Minivans follow designated routes (signs are displayed on the front window); ask at your hotel for the appropriate route number for your destination. Wait at a marked bus stop or hail a passing minivan from the roadside. In Castries, buses depart from the corner of Micoud and Bridge streets, behind the markets.

In addition to the driver, each minivan usually has a conductor, a young man whose job it is to collect fares, open the door, and generally take charge of the passenger area. If you're sure of where you're going, simply knock twice on the metal window frame to signal that you want to get off at the next stop. Otherwise, just let the conductor or driver know where you're going, and he'll stop at the appropriate place.

▮ CAR TRAVEL

BARBADOS

Barbados has good roads, but traffic can be busy, particularly around Bridgetown. Small signs tacked to trees and poles at intersections point the way to most attractions, and local people are helpful if you get lost.

Drive on the left, British style. Be mindful of pedestrians and, in the countryside, occasional livestock walking in the road. When someone flashes headlights at you at an intersection, it means "after you." Be especially careful negotiating roundabouts (traffic circles). The speed limit, in keeping with the pace of life and the narrow roads, is 30 MPH (50 KPH) in the country, 20 MPH (30 KPH) in town. Bridgetown actually has rush hours: 7–9 and 4–6. Park only in approved parking areas; downtown parking costs Bds75¢ to Bds$1 per hour.

To rent a car in Barbados, you must have a valid driver's license and major credit card. Most agencies require renters to be between 21 and 70 or 75 years of age. Those over the maximum age may need a certified doctor's note indicating a continuing ability to drive safely. A local driver's permit, which costs $5, is obtained through the rental agency. More than 75 agencies rent cars, jeeps, or minimokes (small, open-sided vehicles), and rates are expensive—about $55 per day for a minimoke to $85 or more per day for a four-wheel-drive vehicle (or $400–$500 or more per week) in high season, depending on the vehicle and whether it has air-conditioning. Most firms also offer discounted three-day rates, and many require at least a two-day rental in high season. The rental generally includes insurance, pickup and delivery service, maps, 24-hour emergency service, and unlimited mileage.

Car-Rental Contacts Coconut Car Rentals (✉ Bay St., Bridgetown, St. Michael ☎ 246/437–0297 ⊕ www.coconutcars.com). **Courtesy Rent-A-Car** (✉ Grantley Adams International Airport, Christ Church ☎ 246/431–4160 ⊕ www.courtesyrentacar.com). **Drive-a-Matic Car Rental** (✉ Lower Carlton, St. James ☎ 246/422–3000 ⊕ www.carhire.tv).

ST. LUCIA

To rent a car you must be at least 25 years old and provide a valid driver's license and a credit card. If you don't have an international driver's license, you must buy a temporary St. Lucian driving permit at car-rental firms, the immigration office at either airport, or the Gros Islet police station. The permit costs $20 (EC$54) and is valid for three months. Car-rental rates are usually quoted in U.S. dollars and range $50–$80 per day or $300–$425 per week, depending on the car. Car-rental agencies generally include free pickup at your hotel and unlimited mileage.

St. Lucia has about 500 mi (800 km) of roads, but only about half (281 mi [450 km]) are paved. All towns and villages are connected to major routes. The highways on both coasts are winding and mountainous—particularly on parts of the West Coast Road. Driving in

St. Lucia is on the left, British style. Observe speed limits, particularly the 30-MPH (50-KPH) limit within Castries. Respect no-parking zones; police issue tickets, and penalties start at about $15 (EC$40). And wear your seat belts—it's the law!

Car-Rental Contacts Avis (✉ Vide Bouteille, Castries ☎ 758/452–2700 ✉ Vieux Fort ☎ 758/454–6325 ✉ Vigie ☎ 758/452–2046 ⊕ www.avisstlucia.com). **Cool Breeze Jeep/Car Rental** (✉ Soufrière ☎ 758/459–7729). **Courtesy Car Rental** (✉ Bois d'Orange, Gros Islet ☎ 758/452–8140 ⊕ www.courtesycarrentals.com). **Hertz** (✉ Castries ☎ 758/452–0679 ✉ Vieux Fort ☎ 758/454–9636 ✉ Vigie ☎ 758/451–7351 ⊕ www.hertzcaribbean.com).

❙ TAXI TRAVEL

BARBADOS

Taxis operate 24 hours a day. They aren't metered but charge according to fixed rates set by the government. They carry up to three passengers, and the fare may be shared. Sample one-way fares from Bridgetown are: $17 to Holetown, $23 to Speightstown, $15 to St. Lawrence Gap, and $30 to Bathsheba. Drivers are courteous and knowledgeable; most will narrate a tour at an hourly rate of about $25 for up to three people. Be sure to settle the price before you start off and agree on whether it's quoted in U.S. or Barbados dollars.

ST. LUCIA

Taxis are always available at the airports, the harbor, and in front of major hotels. They're unmetered, although nearly all drivers belong to a taxi cooperative and adhere to standard fares. Sample fares for up to four passengers are as follows: Castries to Rodney Bay, $20; Rodney Bay to Cap Estate, $10; Castries to Cap Estate, $25; Castries to Marigot Bay, $30; Castries to Anse-La-Raye, $40; Castries to Soufrière, $80. Always ask the driver to quote the price *before you get in*, and be sure that you both understand whether it's quoted in EC or U.S. dollars. Drivers are generally careful, knowledgeable, and courteous.

ESSENTIALS

▮ ACCOMMODATIONS

In Barbados, visitors may choose an appropriate vacation retreat from among hundreds of choices: full-service resorts, large hotels, boutique hotels, small inns, serviced apartments, or private villas. The island offers something to suit every taste and every pocketbook. The fashionable west coast, north of Bridgetown, is known for its very luxurious (and pricey) resorts and villas. Christ Church Parish on the south coast is the location of many hotels and resorts, both large and small, which are less secluded and more reasonably priced. Generally speaking, British visitors and those seeking a more quiet retreat tend to prefer the west coast; Americans tend to congregate on the action-packed south coast. On the remote east and southeast coasts, a few small inns are, what you might call, off the beaten track.

St. Lucia prides itself in being the most romantic Caribbean island, and many of its all-inclusive resorts cater to that market. The island also has its eyes on return visitors—lovers and others who may have spent a honeymoon or romantic vacation here and who now want a reprise in one of the luxury resorts or who may be interested in investing in a vacation property. Luxury villa communities and condo complexes have sprouted up all over the northern tip of St. Lucia and in Marigot Bay—and it looks like there's no end in sight. New developments are underway on the east coast—virtually untouched until now by the tourist market—and the southern coast will probably be next. In the meantime, visitors to the island have a huge array of wonderful all-inclusive resorts, luxury hotels, boutique inns, and small apartments from which to choose in the areas north and south of Castries and in and around Soufrière.

Most hotels and other lodgings require you to give your credit-card details before they will confirm your reservation. If you don't feel comfortable e-mailing this information, ask if you can fax it (some places even prefer faxes). However you book, get confirmation in writing and have a copy of it handy when you check in.

Be sure you understand the hotel's cancellation policy. Some places allow you to cancel without any kind of penalty—even if you prepaid to secure a discounted rate—if you cancel at least 24 hours in advance. Others require you to cancel a week in advance or penalize you the cost of one night. Small inns and B&Bs are most likely to require you to cancel far in advance. Most hotels allow children under a certain age to stay in their parents' room at no extra charge, but others charge for them as extra adults; find out the cutoff age for discounts.

▮ TIP → **Assume that hotels operate on the European Plan (EP, no meals)** unless we specify that they use the Breakfast Plan (**BP**, with full breakfast), Continental Plan (**CP**, Continental breakfast), Full American Plan (**FAP**, all meals), or Modified American Plan (**MAP**, breakfast and dinner), or are all-inclusive (**AI**, all meals and most activities).

▌ COMMUNICATIONS

INTERNET

BARBADOS

Most hotels and resorts provide Internet terminals—either free or for a small fee—for their guests. You'll also find Internet cafés in and around Bridgetown, in Holetown and Speightstown on the west coast, and at St. Lawrence Gap on the south coast. Rates range from $2 for 15 minutes to $8 or $9 per hour.

Information **Bean-n-Bagel Internet Cafe** (✉ *St. Lawrence Gap, Dover, Christ Church* ☎ 246/420–4604 ✉ *West Coast Mall, Holetown, St. James* ☎ 246/432–1103 ✉ *The Wharf, Bridgetown, St. Michael* ☎ 246/436–7778). **Connect Internet Cafe** (✉ *Shop 9, 27 Broad St., Bridgetown, St. Michael* ☎ 246/228–8648). **Global Links** (✉ *Main Rd., Worthing, Christ Church* ☎ 246/436–4456).

ST. LUCIA

Many hotels and resorts in St. Lucia offer free or inexpensive Internet access to their guests. Internet cafés can be found in and around Rodney Bay Marina. LIME (Cable & Wireless) maintains a public Internet kiosk at Pointe Seraphine, in Castries, that accepts major credit cards or cash.

Internet Cafés **CIBS Cafe** (✉ *Chisel and St. Louis Sts., Castries* ☎ 758/458–2195). **Cyber Connections** (✉ *Rodney Bay Marina, Gros Islet* ☎ 758/450–9309). **Destination St. Lucia (DSL) Ltd.** (✉ *Rodney Bay Marina, Gros Islet* ☎ 758/452–8531).

PHONES

BARBADOS

The area code for Barbados is 246.

Local calls are free from private phones; some hotels charge a small fee. For directory assistance, dial 411. Calls from pay phones cost Bds25¢ for five minutes. Prepaid phone cards, which can be used throughout Barbados and other Caribbean islands, are sold at shops, attractions, transportation centers, and other convenient outlets.

Direct-dialing to the United States, Canada, and other countries is efficient and reasonable, but always check with your hotel to see if a surcharge is added. Some toll-free numbers cannot be accessed in Barbados. To charge your overseas call on a major credit card or U.S. calling card without incurring a surcharge, dial 800/225–5872 (800/ CALL-USA) from any phone.

Depending on your carrier, you may find that you can use your cell phone in Barbados to call home, though roaming charges can be expensive. Renting a cell phone if you're planning an extended stay or expect to make a lot of local calls may be a less-expensive alternative. A cell phone can be rented for as little as $5 a day (minimum one-week rental); prepaid cards are available at several locations throughout the island and in varying denominations.

ST. LUCIA

The area code for St. Lucia is 758. You can make direct-dial overseas and interisland calls from St. Lucia, and the connections are excellent. You can charge an overseas call to a major credit card with no surcharge. From public phones and many hotels, dial 811 and charge the call to your credit card to avoid expensive rates or hotel surcharges. Phone cards can be purchased at many retail outlets and used from any touch-tone telephone (including pay phones) in St. Lucia. You can dial local calls throughout St. Lucia directly from your hotel room by connecting to an outside line and dialing the seven-digit number. Some hotels charge a small fee (usually about EC50¢) for local calls. Pay phones accept EC25¢ and EC$1 coins. Phone cards can be used for local calls, as well as for international calls.

Cell phones may be rented from LIME (formerly Cable & Wireless) offices in Castries, Gablewoods Mall, Rodney Bay Marina, and Vieux Fort; or you can purchase a local SIM card for $20 (which includes an $8 call credit) at Digicel offices in those same areas. The cards can be topped up at hundreds of business locations around the island.

Information **AT&T** (☎ 800/872–2881). **Digicel** (☎ 758/456–3400 or 758/456–3444). **LIME** (Cable & Wireless ☎ 758/453–9000).

▮ EATING OUT

Barbados prides itself on its many wonderful restaurants, many of which can compete with top-notch dining experiences anywhere in the world. On the west coast, excellent restaurants are concentrated in St. James Parish along Highway 1, particularly in and around Holetown. In fact, 1st Street and 2nd Street in Holetown are lined with restaurants that offer a variety of cuisines and prices that range from inexpensive to plan ahead! On the south coast, St. Lawrence Gap is the mother lode of Barbados restaurants, with about 20 possible choices lining both sides of the street (or "gap").

The bulk of St. Lucia's restaurants—both casual and classy—are concentrated in Rodney Bay Village, although some excellent dining establishments are in the Vigie area of Castries and in pretty Marigot Bay. In Soufrière, the best dining is in small hotels and inns, which always welcome nonguests for both lunch and dinner.

MEALS AND MEALTIMES

Resort breakfasts are frequently lavish buffets that offer tropical fruits and fruit juices, cereal, fresh rolls and pastries, hot dishes (such as codfish, corned-beef hash, and potatoes), and prepared-to-order eggs, pancakes, and French toast. Lunch could be a sit-down meal at a beachfront café or a picnic at a secluded cove. But dinner is the highlight, often combining the expertise of internationally trained chefs with local know-how and ingredients.

Of course, you'll want to take advantage of the weekend evening street parties in both Barbados (Oistins) and St. Lucia (Gros Islet and Anse La Raye), where you can buy and try local food barbecued right before your eyes and accompanied by music and conviviality—a wonderful experience for the whole family.

Expect breakfast to be served from 7:30 AM to 10 AM; lunch from noon to 2 PM or so; and dinner from 7 PM to about 10 PM. Some restaurants have specific mealtimes; others serve continuously all day long.

Unless otherwise noted, the restaurants listed in this guide are open daily for lunch and dinner.

PAYING

Major credit cards (American Express, Diners Club, Discover, MasterCard, and Visa) are accepted in most Caribbean restaurants. We note in reviews when credit cards are not accepted. Price charts for restaurants are included in each destination chapter's Planner.

RESERVATIONS AND DRESS

It's always a good idea to make a reservation if you can. In some small or pricey restaurants, it's required. We mention specifically only when reservations are essential (there's no other way you'll ever get a table) or when they are not accepted. For very popular restaurants, book as far ahead as you can (often 30 days), and reconfirm as soon as you arrive. (Large parties should always call ahead to check the reservations policy.) We mention dress only for the very few restaurants where men are required

to wear a jacket or a jacket and tie. Shorts and T-shirts at dinner and beach attire anytime are universally frowned upon in restaurants throughout the Caribbean.

WINES, BEER, AND SPIRITS

Mount Gay and Malibu in Barbados and Bounty in St. Lucia are the local rum brands. Their distilleries are open to the public for tours, tastings, and duty-free shopping.

Both islands also have their own breweries—Banks in Barbados and Piton in St. Lucia. They're both light, refreshing beers—perfect for hot summer afternoons at the beach.

Those who prefer a nonalcoholic drink will love the fresh fruit punch, lime squash, or Ting—a carbonated grapefruit drink from Jamaica that's often available in Barbados and St. Lucia. For something unusual and purely local, try mauby, a strong, dark, rather bitter beverage made from the bark of a tree; ginger beer; sea moss, a reputed aphrodisiac made from a combination of seaweed, sweetener, milk, and spices; and coconut water, the liquid inside a green "jelly coconut" often sold on the street by a "jellyman" who, for 25¢ or 50¢, will nip off the top of the coconut with his sharp machete.

| ELECTRICITY

Electric current on Barbados is 110 volts–50 cycles, U.S. standard. Hotels generally have plug adapters and transformers available for guests who bring appliances to Barbados from countries that operate on 220-volt current.

The electric current on St. Lucia is 220 volts, 50 cycles with a square, three-pin plug (U.K. standard). A few large hotels have 110-volt outlets for electric razors only. To use most North American appliances, you'll need a transformer to convert voltage and a plug adapter; dual-voltage computers or appliances will still need a plug adapter. Hotels will sometimes lend you a plug adapter for use during your stay.

▌ EMERGENCIES

BARBADOS

Emergency Services **Ambulance** (☎ 511). **Fire** (☎ 311). **Police** (☎ 211 emergencies, 242/430–7100 non-emergencies).

Hospitals **Bayview Hospital** (✉ St. Paul's Ave., Bayville, St. Michael ☎ 246/436–5446). **Queen Elizabeth Hospital** (✉ Martindales Rd., Bridgetown, St. Michael ☎ 246/436–6450).

Scuba-Diving Emergencies **Coast Guard Defence Force (24-hour hyperbaric chamber)** (✉ St. Ann's Fort, Garrison, St. Michael ☎ 246/427–8819 emergencies, 246/436–6185 nonemergencies). **Divers' Alert Network** (☎ 246/684–8111 or 246/684–2948).

EMBASSIES

United States **Embassy of the United States** (✉ Broad St., Bridgetown, St. Michael ☎ 246/436–4950).

WORD OF MOUTH

Was the service stellar or not up to snuff? Did the food give you shivers of delight or leave you cold? Did the prices and portions make you happy or sad? Rate restaurants and write your own reviews in Travel Ratings or start a discussion about your favorite places in Travel Talk on www.fodors.com. Your comments might even appear in our books. Yes, you, too, can be a correspondent!

ST. LUCIA

Victoria Hospital, St. Lucia's main hospital, is on the southwest side of Castries Harbour heading toward La Toc. Regional medical facilities are at Dennery Hospital on the island's east coast, St. Jude's Hospital near Hewanorra International Airport, and Soufrière Hospital in the southwest.

Ambulance and Fire **Ambulance and fire emergencies** (☎ 911).

Hospitals **Dennery Hospital** (✉ Main Rd., Dennery ☎ 758/453–3310). **St. Jude's Hospital** (✉ Airport Rd., Vieux Fort ☎ 758/454–6041). **Soufrière Hospital** (✉ W. Quinlan St., Soufrière ☎ 758/459–7258). **Victoria Hospital** (✉ Hospital Rd., Castries ☎ 758/452–2421).

General Emergency Contacts **Police** (☎ 999). **Marine police** (☎ 758/453–0770 or 758/452–2595). **Sea-Air Rescue** (☎ 758/452–2894, 758/452–1182, or 758/453–6664).

▌ HEALTH

Dengue fever is one of the common viral diseases transmitted to humans by the bite of mosquitoes, and the Caribbean—including the islands of Barbados and St. Lucia—is one of the regions of the world that is considered a "risk area" by the CDC. No vaccine is available to prevent dengue fever, but travelers are advised to protect against mosquito bites by using insect repellent and protective clothing when in swampy or forested areas.

HIV is also a growing problem throughout the Caribbean, and visitors to the region should take appropriate precautions to prevent contracting the virus.

Tap water in both Barbados and St. Lucia is generally safe to drink, although bottled water is always available if you prefer.

The major health risk in the Caribbean is sunburn or sunstroke. Protect your skin, wear a hat, and use sunscreen.

Swimming on the windward (Atlantic Ocean) side of either island is not recommended—even for experienced swimmers. Tricky currents, powerful waves, strong undertows, and rocky bottoms can be extremely dangerous—and lifeguards are nonexistent.

Watch out for black, spiny sea urchins that live on the rocky sea floor in both shallow and deep waters. Stepping on one is guaranteed to be painful for quite some time, as the urchin releases its spikes into the offending body. To remove a spike simply pull it out and apply an antiseptic. To remove an embedded spike, first apply some warm oil (preferably olive oil) to soften and dilate the skin, then remove the spike with a sterile needle.

The worst insect problem may well be the tiny "no-see-ums" (sand flies) that appear after a rain, near swampy ground, and at the beach around sunset.

On the west coast of Barbados in particular, beware of the manchineel tree, which grows near the beach and has fruit that looks like little green apples—but is poisonous—and bark and leaves that can burn the skin if you touch them; even the droplets of water that might reach your skin if you seek protection under the tree during a shower can burn you.

Do not fly within 24 hours of scuba diving.

MEDICAL INSURANCE AND ASSISTANCE

Consider buying trip insurance with medical-only coverage. Neither Medicare nor some private insurers cover medical expenses anywhere outside the United States. Medical-only policies typically reimburse you for medical care (excluding that related to pre-existing conditions) and hospitalization abroad, and provide for evacuation. You still have to pay the bills and await reimbursement from the insurer, though.

Another option is to sign up with a medical-evacuation assistance company. A membership in one of these companies gets you doctor referrals, emergency evacuation or repatriation, 24-hour hotlines for medical consultation, and other assistance. International SOS Assistance Emergency and AirMed International provide evacuation services and medical referrals. MedjetAssist offers medical evacuation.

Medical Assistance Companies
AirMed International (⊕ www.airmed.com). **International SOS Assistance Emergency** (⊕ www.intsos.com). **MedjetAssist** (⊕ www.medjetassist.com).

Medical-Only Insurers
International Medical Group (☎ 800/628-4664 ⊕ www.imglobal.com). **International SOS** (⊕ www.internationalsos.com). **Wallach & Company** (☎ 800/237-6615 or 540/687-3166 ⊕ www.wallach.com).

▌ HOURS OF OPERATION

BARBADOS
Banks are open Monday through Thursday 8–3, Friday 8–5 (some branches in supermarkets are open Saturday morning 9–noon). At the airport, the Barbados National Bank is open from 8 AM until the last plane leaves or arrives, seven days a week (including holidays). The General Post Office in Bridgetown is open weekdays 7:30–5; the Sherbourne Conference Center branch is open weekdays 8:15–4:30 during conferences; and branches in each parish are open weekdays 8–3:15. Most stores in Bridgetown are open weekdays from 8:30 or 9 to 4:30 or 5, Saturday from 8:30 to 1 or 2. Stores in shopping malls outside Bridgetown may stay open

later. Some supermarkets are open daily 8–6 or later.

ST. LUCIA
Banks are open Monday through Thursday 8–2, Friday 8–5; a few branches in Rodney Bay are also open Saturday 9–noon. Post offices are open weekdays 8:30–4:30. Most stores are open weekdays 8:30–4:30, Saturday 8–12:30; Gablewoods Mall shops are open Monday through Saturday 9–7; J. Q.'s Shopping Mall shops are open weekdays 9–7 and Saturday 9–8; Pointe Seraphine shops are open weekdays 9–5, Saturday 9–2. Some hotel gift shops may be open on Sunday.

▌ MAIL

BARBADOS
An airmail letter from Barbados to the United States or Canada costs Bds$1.15 per half ounce; an airmail postcard, Bds45¢. Letters to the United Kingdom cost Bds$1.40; postcards, Bds70¢. Letters to Australia and New Zealand cost Bds$2.75; postcards, Bds$1.75. When sending mail to Barbados, be sure to include the parish name in the address.

ST. LUCIA
The General Post Office is on Bridge Street in Castries and is open weekdays 8:30–4:30; all towns and villages have branches. Postage for airmail letters to the United States, Canada, and the United Kingdom is EC95¢ per ½ ounce; postcards are EC65¢. Airmail letters to Australia and New Zealand cost EC$1.35; postcards, EC70¢. Airmail can take two or three weeks to

be delivered—even longer to Australia and New Zealand.

MONEY

BARBADOS

The Barbados dollar is pegged to the U.S. dollar at the rate of Bdo$1.90 to $1. U.S. paper currency, major credit cards, and traveler's checks are all accepted island-wide. Be sure you know which currency is being quoted when making a purchase. Major credit cards are also readily accepted throughout Barbados.

Barbados National Bank has a branch at Grantley Adams International Airport that's open every day from 8 AM until the last plane lands or departs. ATMs are available 24 hours a day at bank branches, transportation centers, shopping centers, gas stations, and other convenient spots throughout the island.

ST. LUCIA

The official currency is the Eastern Caribbean dollar (EC$). It's linked to the U.S. dollar at EC$2.67, but, simply for convenience, stores and hotels often exchange at EC$2.50 or EC$2.60. U.S. paper currency is readily accepted, but you'll receive change in EC dollars—so use your smallest-denomination U.S. bill when making a purchase. Major credit cards and traveler's checks are widely accepted, as well. ATMs are available 24 hours a day at bank branches, transportation centers, and shopping malls, where you can use major credit cards to obtain cash (in local currency only). Major banks on the island include the Bank of Nova Scotia, FirstCaribbean International Bank, and the Royal Bank of Canada.

Prices quoted in this chapter are in U.S. dollars unless otherwise indicated.

PASSPORTS AND VISAS

All visitors to both Barbados and St. Lucia must have a valid passport and a return or ongoing ticket. A birth certificate and photo ID are *not* sufficient proof of citizenship.

U.S. Passport Information U.S. Department of State (☎ 877/487–2778 ⊕ travel.state.gov).

SAFETY

Although crime isn't a significant problem in either Barbados or St. Lucia, take the same precautions you would at home—lock your door, secure your valuables, and don't carry too much money or flaunt expensive jewelry on the street.

TAXES

BARBADOS

A departure tax or $12.50, which used to be collected in cash at the airport when departing Barbados, is now automatically added into the price of your airfare.

A 7.5% government tax is added to all hotel bills. A 10% service charge is often added to hotel bills and restaurant checks in lieu of a tip. At your discretion, tip beyond the service charge to recognize extraordinary service.

A 15% V.A.T. is imposed on restaurant meals, admissions to attractions, and merchandise sales (other than duty-free). Prices are often tax inclusive; if not, the V.A.T. will be added to your bill.

ST. LUCIA

The departure tax of $26 (EC$68), which used to be collected in cash at the airport when departing St. Lucia, is now incorporated into the price of your airfare. A government tax of 8% is added to all hotel and restaurant bills. There's no sales tax on goods purchased in shops. Most restaurants add a service charge of 10% to restaurant bills in lieu of tipping.

▌ TIME

Barbados and St. Lucia are both in the Atlantic Standard Time zone, which is one hour later than Eastern Standard Time and four hours earlier than GMT. As is true throughout the Caribbean, neither island observes daylight saving time, so Atlantic Standard is the same time as Eastern Daylight Time during that period (March through October).

▌ TIPPING

BARBADOS

If no service charge is added to your bill, tip waiters 10%–15% and maids $2 per room per day. Tip bellhops and airport porters $1 per bag. Taxi drivers and tour guides appreciate a 10% tip.

ST. LUCIA

Most restaurants add a 10% service charge to your bill in lieu of a tip; if one has not been added, a 10%–15% tip is appropriate for good service. Tip porters and bellhops $1 per bag and hotel maids $1 or $2 per night, although many of the all-inclusive resorts have a no-tipping policy. Taxi drivers and tour guides also appreciate a 10%–12% tip.

▌ TRIP INSURANCE

Comprehensive trip insurance is valuable if you're booking a very expensive or complicated trip (particularly to an isolated region) or if you're booking far in advance. Comprehensive policies typically cover trip-cancellation and interruption, letting you cancel or cut your trip short because of illness, or, in some cases, acts of terrorism in your destination. Such policies might also cover evacuation and medical care. (For trips abroad you should have at least medical-only coverage. *See Medical Insurance and Assistance under Health*.). Some also cover you for trip delays because of bad weather or mechanical problems as well as for lost or delayed luggage.

Another type of coverage to consider is financial default—that is, when your trip is disrupted because a tour operator, airline, or cruise line goes out of business. Generally you must buy this when you book your trip or shortly thereafter, and it's available to you only if your operator isn't on a list of excluded companies.

Always read the fine print of your policy to make sure that you're covered for the risks that most concern you. Compare several policies to be sure you're getting the best price and range of coverage available.

Insurance Comparison Sites
Insure My Trip.com (☎ 800/487–4722 ⊕ www.insuremytrip.com). **Square Mouth.com** (☎ 800/240–0369 or 727/490–5803 ⊕ www.squaremouth.com).

Comprehensive Travel Insurers
Access America (☎ 866/729–6021 ⊕ www.accessamerica.com). **AIG Travel Guard** (☎ 800/826–4919 ⊕ www.travelguard.com). **CSA Travel Protection** (☎ 800/873–9855 ⊕ www.csatravelprotection.com). **HTH Worldwide** (☎ 610/254–8700 ⊕ www.hthworldwide.com). **Travelex Insurance** (☎ 888/228–9792 ⊕ www.travelex-insurance.com). **Travel Insured International** (☎ 800/243–3174 ⊕ www.travelinsured.com).

▍ VISITOR INFORMATION

BARBADOS
Before You Leave **Barbados Tourism Authority** (☎ 212/986–6516 in New York City; 305/442–7471 in Coral Gables, FL; 213/380–2198 in Los Angeles; 800/221–9831 ⊕ www.visitbarbados.org).

In Barbados **Barbados Hotel & Tourism Association** (✉ 4th Ave., Belleville, St. Michael ☎ 246/426–5041 ⊕ www.bhta.org). **Barbados Tourism Authority** (✉ Harbour Rd., Bridgetown, St. Michael ☎ 246/427–2623 ✉ Grantley Adams International Airport, Christ Church

☎ 246/428–5570 ✉ Cruise-ship terminal, Bridgetown, St. Michael ☎ 246/426–1718 ⊕ www.visitbarbados.org).

ST. LUCIA
Before You Leave **St. Lucia Tourist Board** (☎ 212/867–2950 in New York, 800/456–3904 ⊕ www.stlucia.org).

In St. Lucia **St. Lucia Tourist Board** (✉ Sureline Bldg., Vide Bouteille, Box 221, Castries ☎ 758/452–4094 or 758/452–5968 ✉ Jeremie St., Castries ☎ 758/452–2479 ✉ Pointe Seraphine, Castries ☎ 758/452–7577 ✉ Bay St., Soufrière ☎ 758/459–7419 ✉ George F.L. Charles Airport, Vigie, Castries ☎ 758/452–2596 ✉ Hewanorra International Airport, Vieux Fort ☎ 758/454–6644 ⊕ www.stlucia.org).

▍ WEDDINGS

BARBADOS
Barbados makes weddings relatively simple for nonresidents, as there are no minimum residency requirements. Most resorts, therefore, offer wedding packages and have on-site wedding coordinators to help you secure a marriage license and plan a personalized ceremony and reception. Alternatively, you may wish to have your wedding at a scenic historic site or botanical garden, on the grounds of a restored greathouse, or at sunset on a quiet beach.

To obtain a marriage license, which often can be completed in less than a half hour, both partners must apply in person to the Ministry of Home Affairs (located in the General Post Office building, Cheapside, Bridgetown, ☎ 246/228–8950, and open 8:15–4:30 weekdays) by presenting valid passports. If either party was previously married and widowed, you need to present a certified copy of the marriage certificate and a death certificate for the deceased spouse; if either party is divorced, you need a certified copy of the official divorce decree. Nonresidents of Barbados must pay a fee of $75 (Bds$150) plus a stamp fee of $12.50 (Bds$25). Finally, you must make arrangements for an authorized marriage officer (a magistrate or minister) to perform the ceremony.

ST. LUCIA

St. Lucia may be *the* most popular island in all of the Caribbean for weddings and honeymoons. Nearly all of St. Lucia's resort hotels and most of the small inns offer attractive wedding-honeymoon packages, as well as coordinators to handle the legalities and help plan a memorable event. Several resorts, including the three Sandals resorts on St. Lucia, offer complimentary weddings to couples booking a minimum-stay honeymoon. The most striking setting, though, is probably between the Pitons at Ladera or Jalousie Plantation resorts.

You can marry on the same day that you arrive in St. Lucia if you apply for a "special" marriage license, pay the $200 special marriage license fee, and have all the necessary documents. You must present valid passports, birth certificates, a divorce decree if either party is divorced, an appropriate death certificate if either party is widowed, and a notarized parental consent if either party is under the age of 18. Most couples opt for the standard marriage license, which costs $125 and requires three days of residence on the island prior to the wedding ceremony. In either case, special or standard, you can expect additional registrar and certificate fees amounting to about $40. Resort wedding coordinators will help you put together the correct paperwork and, if you wish, will arrange photographer, flowers, musicians, a church or other locations for the ceremony, and food and beverage for a reception.

INDEX

A

Accommodations,
216–217
Accra Beach, 101
Accra Beach Hotel &
Spa 🏨, 65, 67
Air Travel, 210–211
Airports, 14, 210–211
All Seasons Resort-
Europa 🏨, 83
Allamanda Beach Hotel
🏨, 67
Almond Beach Club &
Spa 🏨, 83–84
Almond Beach Village
🏨, 84
Almond Casuarina
Beach Resort 🏨,
67–68
Almond Morgan Bay
Beach Resort 🏨,
162
Almond Smugglers Cove
🏨, 162–163
Andromeda Botanic
Gardens, 40, 80–81
Angry Annie's ✕, 59
Animal Flower
Cave, 45
Anse Chastanet, 189,
194
Anse Chastanet Beach
Hotel 🏨, 181
Anse Cochon, 192, 194
Anse des Pitons, 192
Anse des Sables, 192
Anse La Raye "Seafood
Friday", 194, 203
Antiques, shopping for,
117, 205
Apartment rentals, 65
Apsara ✕, 157–158
Aquariums
Barbados, 43
Arc en Ciel 🏨, 181–182
Art, shopping for,
117–118, 205
Atlantic Rally for
Cruisers, 130
ATMs, 223

Auberge Seraphine 🏨,
177
Azzuro at Old Trees Bay
🏨, 84–85

B

Bagshaw Studios, 207
Baguet Shop ✕, 157
Bananaquit House 🏨,
182–183
Bananas, 176
Banks Brewery Visitor
Centre, 40
Barbados, 26–120
beaches, 12, 14,
100–104
Bridgetown, 31–34, 50
Central Barbados,
39–40, 42–45
East Coast, 57–58,
79–83, 102–103
exploring, 32–34, 36–40,
42–48
festivals and seasonal
events, 31, 99
history, 26
hotels, 28–29, 63–79,
82–89, 92–98, 100
Northern Barbados,
45–48
price categories, 30
restaurants, 29–30,
49–63
South Coast, 65, 67–73,
76–79, 101–102
Southern Barbados,
34, 36–39, 50–51,
53–56
timing the visit, 30–31
West Coast, 59–63,
83–89, 92–98, 100,
103–104
Barbados Beach Club
🏨, 68
Barbados Condorde
Experience, 34, 36
Barbados Jazz
Festival, 31
Barbados Military
Cemetary, 36

Barbados Museum,
36–37
Barbados Sea Turtle
Project, 98
Barbados Tourism
Authority, 65
Barbados Wildlife
Reserve, 46
Barclays Park, 40,
102–103
Barre de l'Isle Forest
Reserve, 137
Barrow, Errol, 33
Bars
Barbados, 114–115
St. Lucia, 202
Bathsheba/Cattlewash,
103
Baxter's Road, 113
Bay Gardens Beach
Resort 🏨, 163
Bay Gardens Hotel 🏨,
163, 166
Beaches
Barbados, 12, 14,
100–104
St. Lucia, 14, 189, 192
Bellini's Restaurant ✕,
50–51
Bike St. Lucia, 193
Biking
St. Lucia, 193
Black spiny sea urchins,
112
Boat travel, 211–212
Boating & sailing
Barbados, 12, 110–111
St. Lucia, 19, 193–194
Body Holiday at
LeSPORT 🏨, 166
Bonita Beach Bar &
Restaurant 🏨, 57
Book & magazines,
shopping for, 205
Bottom Bay Beach, 101
Boudreau ✕, 155–156
Bougainvillea Beach
Resort 🏨, 68–69
Bounty Rum Distillery,
137–138
Breweries, 40

Bridgetown, Barbados, *30–34*
Brighton Beach, *103*
Brown Sugar ✕, *51, 53*
Bus travel, *212–213*
Business hours, *222*
Buzz ✕, *149–150*

C

Café Luna ✕, *53*
Café Sol ✕, *53–54*
Cap Grill ✕, *150–151*
Cap Maison ☷,
  166–167
Car rentals
Barbados, 213
St. Lucia, 131, 214
Car travel, *14, 213–214*
Careenage, The, *32*
Carlisle Bay Beach,
  101
Carnival, *128, 130*
Castries, St. Lucia,
  and environs, *132–*
  133, 136, 154–155,
  177–178
Castries Market, *133,*
  204
Casuarina Beachm,
  101
Cathedral of the Immac-
  ulate Conception,
  133, 136
Caves, *16, 43, 45*
Cell phones, *217–218*
Cemeteries, *36*
Chalky Mount, *42*
Champers ✕, *54*
Charthouse ✕, *152*
Chateau Mygo ✕, *156*
Cherry Tree Hill, *48*
Children, attractions
Barbados, 34, 36–37,
  38, 43, 45, 46, 47, 61,
  110–111, 113, 115,
  120
St. Lucia, 131, 139, 141,
  142–143, 192, 199,
  203
Children, dining
Barbados, 51, 53, 54,
  57, 62
St. Lucia, 152, 156, 157

Children, lodging
Barbados, 67–68, 69,
  70–71, 77–78, 79, 84,
  87, 92–93, 95, 96, 97
St. Lucia, 162–163, 168,
  169–170, 171, 173,
  176–177, 178–179,
  184–186, 188–189
Churches
Barbados, 34
St. Lucia, 133, 136
Cliff, The ☷, *59*
Cliffside Restaurant
  ☷, *57*
Climate, *20*
Clothes & textiles, shop-
  ping for, *118, 207*
Coal Pot, The ✕, *154*
Cobblers Cove Hotel
  ☷, *85*
Coco Palm ☷, *167*
Cocoa Tea, *202*
Coconut Bay Beach
  Resort & Spa ☷,
  188–189
Coconut Court Beach
  Hotel ☷, *69*
Codrington Theological
  College, *42*
Colleges and universi-
  ties, *42*
Colony Club Hotel ☷,
  85–86
Communications,
  217–218
Condominium rentals,
  63–65, 160
Coral Reef Club ☷, *86*
Cotton Bay Village ☷,
  168
Country Club at Sandy
  Lane, *107–108*
Craft Market, *204*
Crane, The ☷, *69–70*
Crane Beach, *101–102*
Credit cards, *5, 219*
Creole, *148*
Creole Heritage Month,
  130
Cricket, *106, 194*
Crop Over, *31*
Crystal Cove Hotel ☷,
  86–87

Crystal Springs ☷, *87*
Cuban Monument, *40*

D

Dance clubs
Barbados, 115
St. Lucia, 202–203
Daphne's ✕, *59–60*
Dasheene Restaurant &
  Bar ✕, *18, 158*
David's Place ✕, *54*
Derek Walcott Square,
  136
Diamond Botanical Gar-
  dens & Waterfall, *16,*
  142–143
Dining, *218–219*. ⇨
  Also Restaurants
Discovery Bay ☷,
  87–88
Distilleries, *17, 43–44,*
  46, 137–138
Divi Heritage Beach
  Resort ☷, *88*
Divi Southwinds Beach
  Resort ☷, *70–71*
Diving & snorkeling
Barbados, 12, 104–106
St. Lucia, 19, 194–195
Doolittle's ✕, *156*
Duty-free shopping,
  118–119

E

Earthworks Pottery
  (shop), *119*
Edge, The ✕, *151–152*
Edmund Forest Reserve,
  142
Electricity, *13, 15,*
  219–220
Emancipation Statue, *37*
Embassies, *220*
Emergencies, *220*

F

Fairmont Royal Pavilion
  ☷, *88–89*
Farley Hill, *46–47*
Ferry travel, *211–212*
Festivals
Barbados, 31, 99
St. Lucia, 128, 130, 201,
  203

Fish Pot, The ✕, 60–61
Fisherman's Pub ✕, 61
Fishing
 Barbados, 14, 106–107
 St. Lucia, 195–196
Flower Forest, 17, 42
Folkestone Marine Park
 & Visitor Centre, 43
Fond Doux Estate,
 142–143
Fond Doux Holiday
 Plantation 🏠, 183
Fort Charlotte, 138
Frégate Island Nature
 Reserve, 147

G
Gardens
 Barbados, 17, 33–34, 40,
 42, 44
 St. Lucia, 141–142,
 147–147
George Washington
 House, 37
Gift shops, 207
Ginger Lily 🏠, 168–169
Golf
 Barbados, 12, 18,
 107–108
 St. Lucia, 196–197
Gospelfest, 31
Government House, 138
Great House, The 🏠,
 152
Green Parrot ✕, 155
Gros Islet Jump-Up,
 19, 203
Guides
 Barbados, 108
 St. Lucia, 197–198
Gun Hill Signal
 Station, 43

H
Handicrafts, shopping
 for, 119–120, 208
Harmony Suites 🏠, 169
Harrison's Cave, 16, 43
Harry Bayley Observa-
 tory, 37–38
Health issues, 221–222
High Constantia Cottage
 🏠, 89

Hiking
 Barbados, 109–110
 St. Lucia, 198
Hilton Barbados 🏠, 71
Holetown. 42
Holetown Festival,
 31, 42
Horse racing, 110
Horseback riding, 199
Hospitals, 220
Hotel PommMarine 🏠,
 71–72
Hotels, 6
 Barbados, 28–29, 63–79,
 82–89, 92–98, 100
 price categories, 13, 128
 St. Lucia, 126–127, 159–
 174, 176–189
House, The 🏠, 89, 92
Hummingbird Beach
 Resort 🏠, 183–184

I
Inn on the Bay 🏠, 178
Insurance, 221–222,
 224–225
Internet, 217
Itineraries, 21

J
Jacaranda 🏠, 92
Jacques Waterfront
 Dining 🏠, 155
Jade Mountain Club
 🏠, 184
Jalousie Plantation 🏠,
 184–185
Josef's Restaurant ✕,
 55
Jungle tours, 197
Just Breezing Water
 Sports, 111

K
Kadooment Day, 31
Kiteboarding, 200–201
Kwéyòl, 148

L
La Haut Plantation 🏠,
 185–186
La Place Carenage, 136

La Soufrière Drive-In
 Volcano, 143
Ladera 🏠, 186–187
Landings, The 🏠,
 169–170
Language, 148
L'Azure at The Crane
 ✕, 55
Le Pavillon Royal
 Museum, 138
Lewis, Sir W. Arthur,
 147
Lexy Piano Bar, 114–115
Lifeline Restaurant at
 the Hummingbird
 ✕, 158
Lighthouses
 Barbados, 38
Lime, The ✕, 152
Little Arches Hotel 🏠,
 72
Little Good Harbour 🏠,
 92–93
Lodging, 216–217.
 ⇨ *Also Hotels*
 apartment rentals, 65
 condo rentals, 63–65,
 160
 villa rentals, 63–65,
 160–161
Lone Star ✕, 61
Lone Star Hotel 🏠, 93

M
Mail, 222–223
Malibu Beach Club &
 Visitor Centre, 43
Mamiku Gardens,
 147–148
Manchineel trees, 100
Mango Bay 🏠, 93–94
Mango Beach Inn 🏠,
 178–179
Maria Islands Nature
 Reserve, 148–149
Marigot Bay, 17,
 138–139
Marigot Bay Hotel 🏠,
 179
Marigot Beach, 192
Marigot Beach Club &
 Dive Resort 🏠, 179,
 181

Massage, *100*
Meal plans, *216–217*
Mews, The ✕, *61–62*
Miami Beach, *102*
Money matters, *13*, *15*, *223*
Morgan Lewis Sugar Mill, *47*
Morne Coubaril, *143*
Morne Trulah ☷, *170–171*
Mount Gay Rum Visitors Centre, *43–44*, *46*
Mullins Beach, *90–91*, *103*
Museums
Barbados, *16*, *36–37*, *38*, *40*, *43*, *44–45*
St. Lucia, *138*, *142–143*

N
Naniki Restaurant ✕, *57*
National Heroes Square, *32*
Nature preserves
Barbados, *17*, *42*, *45*, *46*
St. Lucia, *21*, *137*, *139*, *142*, *147*, *148–149*
New Edgewater Hotel ☷, *79*, *82*
Nidhe Israel Synagogue, *33*
Nightlife
Barbados, *112–116*
St. Lucia, *201–203*
Nobel Laureates, *147*

O
Oistins Fish Fry, *18*, *113*
Olives Bar & Bistro ✕, *62*
OPA! ✕, *55*
Orchid World, *44*

P
Parks
Barbados, *33–34*, *43*
St. Lucia, *131*
Parliament Buildings, *33*
Passports, *223*
Paynes Bay Beach, *104*
Peach & Quiet ☷, *72–73*

Pelican Craft Centre, *120*
Pigeon Island National Park, *131*
Pigeon Point, *192*
Pisces ✕, *55–56*
Pitons, The, *17*, *143*, *146*
Plantation Restaurant and Garden Theater, *115–116*
Plantations, *16*, *38*, *142–143*
Plas Kassav Bread Bakery, *137*
Pointe Seraphine, *136*
Port St. Charles ☷, *94–95*
Price categories
Barbados, *13*
dining, *13*, *15*, *30*, *128*
lodging, *13*, *15*, *30*, *128*
St. Lucia, *15*, *128*

Q
Queen's Park, *33–34*

R
Ragamuffins ✕, *62*
Ragged Point, *38*
Rain Forest Sky Rides, *139*
Rainforest Hideaway ✕, *156–156*
Reduit Beach, *130*, *192*
Reggae Lounge, *115*
Rendezvous ☷, *177–178*
Restaurants, *6*
Barbados, *29–30*, *49–63*
price categories, *30*, *128*
St. Lucia, *127*, *149–159*
Rodney Bay, *131–132*
Round House ✕, *58*
Round House Inn ☷, *82*
Rowley's Café/Baguet Shop ☷, *157*
Royal St. Lucian ☷, *171*
Royal Westmoreland Golf Club, *108*
Royal Westmoreland Villas ☷, *95*
Rum, *17*, *43–44*, *46*, *137–138*

S
Safety, *30*, *128*, *223*
Sailing. ⇨ See Boating and sailing
St. James Apartment Hotel ☷, *96–97*
St. Lawrence Gap, *114*
St. Lucia, *122–208*
beaches, *189*, *192*
East coast, *146–149*
exploring, *124*, *126*, *131–133*, *136–143*, *146–149*
festivals and seasonal events, *128*, *130*, *201*, *203*
Greater Castries, *132–133*, *136*, *154–155*, *177–178*
history, *122–123*
hotels, *126–127*, *159–174*, *176–189*
North of Vigie to Pointe du Cap, *131–132*, *149–154*, *162–163*, *166–177*
price categories, *128*
restaurants, *127*, *149–159*
Soufriére and the South, *141–143*, *146*, *157–159*, *181–188*
timing the visit, *128*, *130*
St. Lucia Billfishing Tournament, *130*
St. Lucia Golf Open, *128*
St. Lucia Jazz Festival, *128*, *201*
St. Lucian by Rex Resorts ☷, *173*
St. Michael's Cathedral, *34*
St. Nicholas Abbey, *47–48*
St. Omar, Dunstan, *133*
St. Remy Plantation ☷, *187–188*
Sandals Grande St. Lucian Spa & Beach Resort ☷, *171–172*
Sandals Halcyon St. Lucia ☷, *172*

Sandals Regency St. Lucia Resort & Spa 🖼, *172–173*

Sandpiper, The 🖼, *95–96*

Sandy Bay Beach Club 🖼, *73*

Sandy Beach, *102*

Sandy Lane Hotel & Golf Club 🖼, *96*

Savannah, The 🖼, *73, 76*

Scarlet ✕, *62*

Scuba diving
Barbados, *104–106*
St. Lucia, *194–195*

Sea-U Guest House 🖼, *82–83*

Sea excursions
Barbados, *110–111*
St. Lucia, *199–200*

Shopping
areas & malls, *116–117, 204–205*
department stores, *117*
duty-free, *118–119, 136*
Barbados, *116–120*
St. Lucia, *203–208*

Silver Point 🖼, *76*

Silver Sands Hotel 🖼, *76–77*

Silver Sands-Silver Rock Beach, *102*

Sir Frank Hutson Sugar Museum, *44–45*

Snake man, *139*

Snorkeling
Barbados, *12, 104–106*
St. Lucia, *194–195*

Sobers, Sir Garfield, *106*

Soufrière, St. Lucia, *141–143, 146, 157–159, 181–188*

South Beach Resort 🖼, *77*

South Point Light, *38*

Southern Palms Beach Club 🖼, *77–78*

Souvenirs, shopping for, *207*

Sports & the outdoors
Barbados, *12, 104–112*
St. Lucia, *193–201*

Squash, *200*

Still, The 🖼, *158, 159*

Stonefield Estate Villa Resort 🖼, *187*

Street parties, *203*

Sugar, *44–45, 46, 47, 49*

Sunbury Plantation House & Museum, *16, 38*

Surfing, *111–112*

Sweet Potatoes ✕, *56*

Sweetfield Manor 🖼, *78*

Symbols, *6*

Synagogues, *33*

T

Tamarind Cove Hotel 🖼, *97*

Tao ✕, *152–153*

Taxes & service charges, *223–224*

Taxis, *14, 214–215*

Telephones, *217–218*

Tennis, *200*

Theater
Barbados, *115–116*
St. Lucia, *201*

Theme nights, *115–116*

Ti Bananne ✕, *153–154*

Ti Kaye Village 🖼, *188*

Tides, The ✕, *62–63*

Time zones, *224*

Tipping, *13, 15, 224*

Tours
Barbados, *43–44, 45, 108*
St. Lucia, *137–138, 147, 197–198*

Tram ride, *139*

Treasure Beach 🖼, *97–98*

Tree Tops 🖼, *173–174*

Trip insurance, *224–225*

Turtle Beach Resort 🖼, *78–79*

Turtle Nest 🖼, *98, 100*

Turtles, *98*

Tyrol Cot Heritage Village, *38–39, 120*

V

Vendor's Arcade, *136, 204*

Vieux Fort, *146–149, 188–189*

Vigie Beach, *192*

Villa Beach Cottages 🖼, *174*

Villa rentals, *63–65, 160–161*

Villa Tranquility 🖼, *174, 176*

Visas, *223*

Visitor Information, *225*

Volcano, *143*

W

Walcott, Sir Derek, *136, 147*

Waterfalls, *16, 141–142*

Waterfront Cafe ✕, *50*

Weather, *20*

Weddings
Barbados, *22–23, 225–226*
St. Lucia, *22–23, 226*

Welchman Hall Gully, *45*

Windjammer Landing Villa Beach Resort 🖼, *176–177*

Windsurfing
Barbados, *112*
St. Lucia, *200–201*

Wispers on the Bay, *50*

Z

Zen at The Crane ✕, *56*

Zip-line rides, *139*

Photo Credits:

1, Gavin Hellier/age fotostock. 2-3, Barbados Tourism Authority. 7, Barbados Tourism Authority. Chapter 1 Experience Barbados and St. Lucia: 8-9, Benjamin Howell/iStockphoto. 10 (top), Saint Lucia Tourism Board. 10 (bottom), Barbados Tourism Authority. 11 (left), Barbados Tourism Authority/Mike Toy. 11 (right), Saint Lucia Tourism Board. 16 (left), Barbados Tourism Authority/Jim Smith. 16 (right), Saint Lucia Tourism Board. 17 (top left), Barbados Tourism Authority/Jim Smith. 17 (bottom left), ben.ramirez/Flickr. 17(right), Saint Lucia Tourism Board. 18(left), Sandy Lane Hotel. 18 (right), Kristine Dear. 19 (top left), Barbados Tourism Authority/Harold Davis. 19 (bottom left), Ladera. 19 (right), Saint Lucia Tourism Board. 20, Barbados Tourism Authority/Jim Smith. 21, melissa bouyounan/Shutterstock. 23, Barbados Tourism Authority/Craig Lenihan. 24, Mrs. Joan Devaux/ Diamond Botanical Gardens and Waterfall, Soufriere, St. Lucia. Chapter 2 Barbados : 25, John Miller / age fotostock. 31, Barbados Tourism Authority/Andrew Hulsmeier copyright 2008. 36, Barbados Concorde Experience. 39, Walter Bibikow / age fotostock. 44, Shirley Kilpatrick / Alamy. 48, St. Nicholas Abbey. 51, Brown Sugar Restaurant. 60, Julie Webster. 66, Ingolf Pompe / age fotostock. 74 (top), Coral Reef Club. 74 (bottom), Sweetfield Manor. 75 (top), Addison Cumberbatch/Willie Alleyne Photography. 75 (bottom left), Hilton Barbados. 75 (bottom right), Sandy Lane Hotel. 80-81, PetePhipp/Travelshots / age fotostock. 90-91, Barbados Tourism Authority/Mike Toy. 94, graham tomlin/Shutterstock. 99, World Pictures / age fotostock. 104, Barbados Tourism Authority/Ronnie Carrington. 109, MAT/Shutterstock. 113, Roy Riley / Alamy. 118, david sanger photography / Alamy. Chapter 3 St. Lucia: 121, Colin Sinclair / age fotostock. 129, Helene Rogers / age fotostock. 134-135, Ian Cumming / age fotostock. 140, Ian Cumming / age fotostock. 144-145, Hauke Dressler / age fotostock. 153, The Edge Restaurant, St Lucia West Indies. 154, Coal Pot. 159, Ladera. 164 (top), Cotton Bay Village. 164 (bottom), leonardo.com. 165 (top), Sandals Resorts. 165 (bottom), Sandals Resorts. 170, Sandals Resorts. 175, Ian Cumming / age fotostock. 180 (top), Saint Lucia Tourism Board. 180 (bottom), Christian Horan. 186, Ladera. 190-191, Ian Cumming / age fotostock. 196, Stephen Frink Collection / Alamy. 201, M. Timothy O'Keefe / Alamy. 206, Gavin Hellier / age fotostock.

NOTES

NOTES

NOTES

ABOUT OUR WRITER

Jane E. Zarem characterizes herself as a globe-trotting writer, intrepid researcher, fastidious editor, and curious soul with a positive outlook, mature view, and big-picture perspective. Notwithstanding the sheer enthusiasm for her work, she loves the chance to kick back in the Caribbean each year on her updating missions to Barbados, St. Lucia, and several other islands for *Fodor's Caribbean.*

Jane's love affair with the Caribbean began several decades ago, when she joined a 10-day Windjammer cruise that called on islands that, at the time, she never knew existed: Tortola, Virgin Gorda, Nevis, St. Kitts, St. Maarten, Saba, St. Barth's. Tourism hadn't yet hit those island paradises, and most claimed more goats than people. Times have changed.

She has since made more than 75 trips to the Caribbean and has visited Barbados and St. Lucia—two of her favorite islands—more than a dozen times each. She has stared at the awesome east coast of Barbados and swum between the Pitons in St. Lucia. She has visited historic great houses and wandered through St. Lucia's Diamond Botanical Gardens. She has explored shops and markets in both Bridgetown and Castries, off-roaded along the northern tip of Barbados, and sailed along the west coast of St. Lucia. She's also met wonderful people on both islands, who have welcomed her back with a big hug and a broad smile on each subsequent visit.

Jane has been a freelance travel writer for more than 25 years. Her very first travel-writing assignment involved updating the Connecticut chapter of Fodor's *New England* in the late 1970s. Since then, she has worked on many Fodor's guides, contributed travel articles to various newspapers and magazines, written travel and other business-related newsletters, and contributed numerous articles and research reports to trade magazines and other organizations. Most significantly, she has been a contributor to *Fodor's Caribbean* since 1994, writing and updating the Grenada and St. Vincent and the Grenadines chapters, along with Barbados and St. Lucia.

Acknowledgments

Writing this second edition of *In Focus Barbados and St. Lucia* was a natural assignment for her and, she will tell you, "a labor of love." She could not have accomplished it, though, without the assistance of the good people at the Barbados Tourism Authority and the St. Lucia Tourist Board, who have coordinated her trips to the respective islands over the many years that she has focused on these wonderful destinations.